Praise for *One Good Deed*

"Engaging, funny, wise, and winning, *One Good Deed* is a measure of humanity and of McHugh's own striving towards it."

—Susan Orlean, author of *Rin Tin Tin* and
The Orchid Thief

"*One Good Deed* is original, sweet-natured and often funny . . . Erin McHugh makes us ordinary mortals feel like real heels."

—Meg Wolitzer, author of *The Uncoupling*
and *The Ten-Year Nap*

"I loved this book. It's charming and high-spirited and then it sneaks up from behind and breaks/mends your heart!"

—Susan Cheever, writer, teacher, and author of
Louisa May Alcott: A Personal Biography

"Erin McHugh spent one year performing one good deed a day and recording her experiences. The result, this lovely, heartfelt book, shows humanity at its very best. Sometimes her good deeds are small and go unnoticed; other times, they're quite important, and will bring a sting of tears to the reader's eyes. Perhaps McHugh will start a trend. We could certainly do with more people like her in the world."

—Kaylie Jones, author of *Lies My Mother
Never Told Me: A Memoir*

"In Erin McHugh's inspiring book—so gently, so directly written from her gentle, direct heart—she tells us at one point to make someone feel visible. I felt more visible myself as I read it, for she sees quite clearly what we all need—to be shown that showing kindness to others is showing kindness to ourselves."

—Kevin Sessums, author of *Mississippi Sissy*

ONE
GOOD
DEED

365 DAYS OF TRYING TO BE
JUST A LITTLE BIT BETTER

Erin McHugh

ABRAMS IMAGE
NEW YORK

Editor: David Cashion
Designer: Kris Tobiassen
Production Manager: Ankur Ghosh

Library of Congress Cataloging-in-Publication Data

McHugh, Erin.
    One good deed : 365 days of trying to be just a little bit better /
Erin McHugh.
        p. cm.
    ISBN: 978-1-4197-0417-8 (alk. paper)
    1. McHugh, Erin.   2. Conduct of Life.   3. Charity.   4. Kindness.
    I. Title.
    BJ1589.M34 2012
    158.1—dc23

                        2012008317

Printed and bound in the United States
10 9 8 7 6 5 4 3 2

THE ART OF BOOKS SINCE 1949

115 West 18th Street
New York, NY 10011
www.abramsbooks.com

FOR MY PARENTS

James Francis McHugh
Dorothy Kavanaugh McHugh

INTRODUCTION

It's not like the concept of *One Good Deed* needs a lot of explaining—it's an easy one to grasp: consciously try to do one small thing for someone else every single day. When I talk about it with people, I can very nearly hear the wheels turning. *Interesting idea*, they're thinking. *Possibly even fun. Could I actually do it?* And of course everyone asks me the same question: What gave me the idea to do—and then to write—*One Good Deed*? Where did this idea come from—and why now?

Good questions. The answer is simply that I was just feeling . . . a little off. For many years, I'd done a lot of volunteer and activism work, and I loved it. It made me feel happy and proud, in the simplest ways. I'm the kind of person who loves to be part of a gang, too—a team, a work family, a committee. I like being a cog in the wheel and seeing change occur.

But when I was fifty-two years old, I decided I wanted to write seriously—I had been an advertising copywriter for almost two decades, but now I really wanted to fulfill my longtime dream of writing books. I got myself a job as a bookseller during the day, and at night, I came home and wrote. So I was proud in a different way, but now my volunteering life all but disappeared. I even bowed out of chairing my college reunions, which I had been doing for thirty years. I was too busy.

But I missed helping out, in whatever guise. It started bothering me; first just a tiny bit, now and again, way in the back of my mind. Then it grew to something unnameable, a malaise, like a low-level temperature the doctor can do nothing about. And then this other thing happened. A sort of crazy thing.

We got a saint in our family.

No, *really*.

His name is André Bessette, and he is my aunt Tessie's great-great-uncle. She's my aunt by marriage, so technically André is not a relation, but she remembers him from her childhood and has been telling me stories about him forever. And now news had come that he was to be canonized. I mean, who has a saint in their family? *Who?* Even if you're not religious, stories of Brother André's life are incredible; some, myself included, would say miraculous. When I prayed over the years, I would pray through Brother André. It was easy: he was a real person to me—just a man who did extraordinary things.

So, between the no volunteering and the Brother André news, I started to think: I could be doing a little better than this. A little more each day. A little kinder, a little more helpful, a little more thoughtful. I wondered if I tried to do something nice for someone else each day, if it would change the way I was feeling. And that's when I thought of *One Good Deed*.

I wanted to give it a try, write it all down and see if it would inspire me; I decided to keep a blog and see if I could inspire others to join in on the deed-doing. Mostly, I wondered whether I could actually do it, and whether it would make me feel changed.

From the start I found I had to get myself in training. I tend to look at the sidewalk when I walk—a bad habit. You miss a lot that way. It means I'm looking inward, thinking about my day, my problems, whatever, while literally missing what's right in front of me. I tried actually changing my outlook by making a concerted effort to notice what was going on around me—and trying to be more observant helped my good-deeding enormously. Opportunities are often right there. Having to watch over myself, having to really pay attention to each day, was sort of like being on a diet, but in a not unpleasant way. Before long, I found I started thinking about the day's good deed as I showered, got dressed for work, and started the day. I kept a calendar, so I wouldn't forget to bring my Christmas tree to the mulchfest, attend a local fair, participate in a winter-coat drive coming up. But most of the time? I was just winging it.

Sure, there was occasional foot-dragging or a day spent prone in front of the TV, but in the main I was *on it*. I made a point to talk to people and snap them out of their bored reverie: cashiers, commuters, garbagemen. Most appreciated it—all seemed surprised. But I found interacting with more people who crossed my path brought more chances to make a little bit of a difference. Most times, we both left our brief encounter feeling a little bit better.

Then there were days when something someone else did was far more interesting and poignant than anything I could muster (a favorite is my friend Erika's subway hero of April 7), or I wanted to share a long-ago memory or piece of advice. You'll find those stories here, too. I worried as I kept my diary that my deeds would be repetitive, because life is repetitive. But when the year ended and I read over my adventures, I found that even if the good deed seemed familiar, the players, and the story, changed every time.

If you expect a story rife with big changes and magic bullets, this is not the book for you. As a friend said to me after following the *One Good Deed* blog for a few months, "It's all about critical mass." And she was right. My hope was always to do a little bit better, feel a little prouder, clock the world surrounding me a little—and to take as many people along for the ride as possible. I hoped that *One Good Deed* might inspire, that together our critical mass could make a difference.

Did my year make any difference at all? Well, read on, friend.

Then you tell me.

Erin McHugh
New York
February 2012

It's never too late to do the little things.

Today is my birthday.

Yesterday was—and always will be to me, though they have long ago passed on—my parents' anniversary. I was their first anniversary present. The last week in July was always a big deal in our house.

An only child, I inherited a lovely home in a tiny village on Buzzards Bay, near Cape Cod. And though I've lived in Manhattan more than thirty years, my hometown is where I am today, hanging out on the beach with my family and visiting the cemetery where my folks are buried.

I am not here nearly enough, but I do try to tend to the graveyard when I can. As time has gone on, the plot has become inevitably fuller: an uncle from each side of my family, their two widowed wives here with us still. As in life, it turned out that everyone wanted to be together.

The grave is always graced with pebbles and shells from family visitors, and like today I try hard, often with a cousin's help, to have flowers and such that I think everyone would like: pansies in the spring, if I manage it, pink geraniums and alyssum in the summer, a wreath at Christmas.

Of course, I'm far from perfect, as you'll see all too often during this year of good deeds. I did have to steal some little pumpkins back from the grave one Thanksgiving morning when my cornucopia centerpiece looked a little sparse. Thanks, guys.

Always keep building.

This afternoon I paid five dollars for a free concert.

I grew up in New Bedford, Massachusetts—"Moby-Dick's hometown!" I like to tell people. And today is a special day. It is Melville's birthday celebration at the New Bedford Whaling Museum, and being a lover of New Bedford's most famous novel, I am all atwitter. And I love that he and I share a birthday week, with a mere 133 years between us. I'm running a little late, so I rush down to the city's historic district to hear a woodwind quartet play classical music and sea shanties in his name. As I turn a corner onto a cobblestone street that looks much the same as when the whaling industry made this the richest town in mid-nineteenth-century America, I hear the haunting strains of a familiar nautical tune. I start to cry.

"Lucem Diffundo" was New Bedford's proud motto back when it was a wealthy city: "We light the world." In the 1850s, no one dreamed that soon electricity would make oil lamps defunct and that New Bedford would falter; it has never recovered. It seems every effort at revival has been thwarted, despite the most valiant efforts (many, I can say proudly, by members of my family who reside here still); the economy has hit hard here, shuttering a thriving downtown and closing mill after mill. Perhaps most important of all, years of overfishing have shrunk the country's largest commercial fleet to a shadow of what I remember as a kid.

And yet. In the last two decades, what was a musty little museum to which we were shunted off on rainy days back in the 1960s has become a world-class showplace and educational center on all matters whaling.

I've been a member of the New Bedford Whaling Museum—as my parents were before me—since I became a grown-up, and I visit nearly every time I'm in town. It reminds me of where I came from, and what a place and a people can become again.

The concert is free, but I drop five dollars in the donation box in the lobby. A city is built brick by brick.

JULY 31

Share a memory.

I borrowed my aunt's car this weekend. She's eighty-seven, currently medicated, and not allowed to drive anyway. Still, she's not entirely happy about the lending.

Of course, along with borrowing the car comes running some errands, Auntie riding shotgun, and today was one of those days. First the bank, then a lengthy visit to the Stop & Shop ("They move things around every week!"), and filling the three-quarters-full gas tank, "Just in case." (In case what—I go to Florida for the afternoon?)

I knew she wanted to spend some time at the beach over the weekend, too—something she's always loved—so we agreed to go after our chores. I bought sandwiches, we spent a perfect seashore hour or so, and then I suggested getting some ice cream on the way home. She demurred. "Why?" I prodded, knowing her predilections. "You love ice cream." She relented, and off to the adorable milk can–shaped local haunt we went.

A simple scoop of vanilla was her initial choice, but I pushed once more. "How about frozen pudding? That was always Dad's favorite." (Dad being my father, her favorite brother.) Her eyes lit up. "Oh! I haven't had that in years." So, frozen pudding it was, and, cones in hand, we put the convertible top down and licked our way home in happy silence.

I can't say why going out for ice cream is so special—childhood, summer, long days, no school, who knows? But I do know this: a trip to get ice cream—for it always is a trip, no matter how close—is like nothing else. My theory is that it's not only about the ice cream; it's about all the other times you've been to get ice cream, every one of them, rolled into one huge, happy ice cream memory.

Patronize budding entrepreneurs.

The sign read "C & L Café." Dining was alfresco. In point of fact, it was a lemonade stand.

I screeched to the side of the road.

I have long made it a custom, nay, a mission, to stop at every lemonade stand I come across. For someone who takes a lot of anti-ulcer medicine, this acid-fraught hobby might not be a great idea, but it's forever rewarding.

I love a lemonade stand. Of course, like many kids, I had several of my own, and additionally I ran a high-volume (for a nine-year-old) candy retail operation under a tree outside my house during the summer. The important thing was that it was the first money I ever made. I love that as time marches on kids still have lemonade stands, and every cup that's sold still means the same thing to someone. It's a kid's first attempt at business, with a money box and a little padlock key, a place to learn confidence and practice social skills. Not that they're aware of any of that, which is the swell part.

It's where kids find out—for good or bad—that money is power, perhaps learn how to form a partnership, come to understand what it's like to earn. Plus, they're so damn funny. I also bought four cookies and tipped fifty cents. Total cost was $2.50. "*You,*" said Charlie, "are our best customer!"

There is no downside to stopping at lemonade stands. Ever. They are nothing but win, for everyone.

Do the right thing, even if it's a small thing.

Here's the good deed you always hope someone would do for you.

Today I was riding up an escalator, and this situation was smack in front of me: a hapless woman with toilet paper stuck to one of her sneakers. So when we both got to the top, I tapped the lady in question on the shoulder and notified her of the problem. I mean, it wasn't like her prom dress was stuck in her underpants or anything, but still.

She thanked me, did the toe-to-heel thing to remove the offending culprit, and then—*ick!*—picked it up off the floor. (Thoughtful, I know, but still. . . .)

Speaking frankly, though? I have to admit the removal of the errant TP did little to improve her sartorial presentation.

Stand up for your friends.

Today I did a secret good deed.

Someone I know and have worked with—let's call her Miss Scarlet—is interviewing for a job next week with a man I know: we'll call him Colonel Mustard. Scarlet knows I know the Colonel, but the Colonel doesn't know I'm acquainted with Miss Scarlet.

With me so far?

So I tossed off an e-mail to Colonel Mustard, ostensibly about something else, closing with a complimentary nod to Miss Scarlet. Guess I'd better tell her.

And then we shall see what we shall see.

AUGUST 4

Share the wealth.

Great news today! I got an offer from my publisher for the *One Good Deed* book. Proof positive that good deeds do not go unpunished!

I gave a big *"Woot!"* in the bookstore where I work when I found out, and yelled "Cheeseburgers all around," since everybody is dying to try the burger joint next door. OK, maybe I didn't yell it *that* loud, but loud enough that I certainly got a couple of takers. I took some orders, then ran over before the lunch line got too long.

It was a pretty exciting day for me, no doubt, but my coworkers—who are all booksellers themselves—were incredibly generous in showing their excitement. Burger takers or not.

So I lugged the lunch back to the break room, and we toasted with cheeseburgers. Can't believe my good fortune: I sold the book, and I have such nice people surrounding me day after day, selling what we love. Eventually, they'll be selling this book, too. And round and round we go.

Find a way to add a bright spot.

I don't get to see my old friend as much as I'd like—or as much as I used to. Life changes, naturally, and her case is the case of many: parents getting elderly and needing more attention and care.

My pal is an extraordinary daughter and always has been. She lives with her mother in a beautiful home, takes her on vacations, makes sure she has a new car every few years, and, well, I could go on and on. They are great, great friends and very lucky to have each other.

On this night the pal and I belatedly celebrated my birthday and went out to dinner. It was a real treat for me, as these excursions have gotten more rare with her mom getting older and having recently suffered a bout of ill health. She does not bounce back the way she used to.

I was thrilled to be spending the evening with my buddy, and I know she's always got her mother's welfare somewhere in the back of her mind. So before I headed to the restaurant, I stepped out into my garden and cut a little zinnia bouquet and took it to dinner with me.

"Tell your mom these are from me," I said, "so her evening shouldn't be a total loss." The report the next day was that they were the first thing she saw in the morning.

Make it unique.

My birthday, as you all know, was just last week, and though I had lots of festivities surrounding the day, on July 29 I had to shut myself up at home and work. I felt extremely sorry for myself.

However, I did get loads of calls, cards, and e-mails and well over a hundred shout-outs on Facebook. I was prepared to shrug them off, but when I saw the long, long list of happy greetings and well wishes, I was oddly touched.

So today, when I saw an old childhood friend's birthday come up on Facebook, I jotted her a little more than just a Happy Birthday:

"Hey, Marie: I remember misbehaving so badly in the back of your station wagon on the way to the amusement park one birthday that your mother actually *did* turn the car around! And yes, of course she relented, but it was a scary few minutes!"

Who wouldn't want a message like that, I figured. Who doesn't like to be remembered in a special way?

Remember the living.

OK, let's get this out of the way: I'm gay.

Lesbians are a funny group in lots of ways, one of which is that we are oddly tribal. It is not at all unusual for ex-lovers to remain very friendly, in many cases almost familial.

Such is the case with my last, most serious ex. Her father has been ill, though only in the past few weeks, and she has been down south with him much of this time. This afternoon he passed away, with her and some friends at his side.

I knew her dad, though not well. He was a gentleman, and a delight, and oh, did he adore his daughter. She loved him right back. I am a little at a loss for how to help her through this, the odd territory that is someone you once shared a life with. I can't afford to fly down for the funeral, and she won't be back home for several days, so there is a helpless limbo to fill.

In the time following a death, it's extremely hard crossing back and forth from remembering the person who has died and the people left behind who are now the ones hurting. The notes and flowers and casseroles you receive all blend into one after a while, but two things stood out for me when my parents passed away: flowers, and also a mass card, both sent just for me, because now I was the one left at home, and sick, at least at heart.

So today, I'm going to start making a basket. Not flowers, not muffins, just things she likes that I can give her when she returns to a life not quite what it used to be, to let her know I've been thinking about her while she's been gone.

Hospitality doesn't always have a door and a roof, just a heart.

I rent out my house in Massachusetts often, but this week I've lent it, gratis, to an old friend. She recently gave me a gift that meant the world to me: a book idea, which turned into a contract, which turned into—well, we'll soon see, as it will be published this week.

I knew she had been looking for a place to rent for a week this summer, and a house she particularly loved had become too expensive over the years. I was thrilled to be able to offer mine. Every year it's a financial struggle for me to hold on to this house, and she knows it. So we fought about it for a while: she wanted to pay; I wanted to gift it to her in return for being so thoughtful. She's been my friend for almost thirty years—she understood it was important to just graciously accept the gift.

So, I called to see how the guests were doing. A friend had arrived for a couple of days, the kids were playing cards, there were drinks on the porch, a day was planned at the beach tomorrow.

I've been working two jobs, six days a week, and it's been ninety-plus degrees here in New York for two weeks. Why am I so happy? Because she and I have been friends forever, and we just gave each other two of the most precious things around: a great idea, and a place by the sea.

Now this part's really corny, but it's true. When she and I get together, we're so happy to realize that we're still buddies all these years later that almost the first thing we say every single time is, "Aren't we lucky?" Life moves along, and we all know it's hard to keep in touch, no matter how good our intentions.

So I smiled like an idiot when I got a text at work today that read:

"Your house is fantastic. Aren't we lucky?"

AUGUST 9

Buy your friends' art, even if you're not sure that's what it is.

So now my French *amie* has asked me to go hear some music with her. Her accent is quite strong, and sometimes I miss a word here or there. Or a phrase. Maybe an entire idea. But I was pretty sure she had said "mudairn museec een the Veelage" when she called me on the phone, so off we went.

I met her outside the bookstore, she in her Brigitte Bardot sunglasses, ready for the subway. Eighty-one she is, and I could hardly keep up. I had no idea where we were going exactly, so I was thrilled when I learned we were off to the old home of the Village Gate, one of New York's most famous jazz joints, hosting, in its heyday, such luminaries as John Coltrane, Billie Holiday, Dizzy Gillespie, and countless others.

The pianist friend we had come to hear played pieces by avant-garde composers like Philip Glass and John Cage, which may not have been our first choice—he is renowned for playing more traditional classical works—but it was fabulous and served to remind me that I live in New York City, a fact that's really easy to forget. Every minute of every single day, something fantastic is happening here, and you have to be on the lookout for it, constantly. New York is—well, there's no other place like it; but it can take a lot of work to appreciate it.

So my friend did two good deeds, turning me on to a friend's talent and reminding me to pay attention. And I paid it forward a little by buying one of the pianist's CDs, which he kindly signed for me after the show. It was a little like we say in the book industry: "Books are sold one copy at a time." Just like lives are made: minute by minute.

AUGUST 10

Support your library system.

I'm a bookseller. I've spent my entire adult life working somewhere in the publishing business. I do not like giving away books—I prefer to hoard them.

Oh, sure, I like *sharing* a book—if I know for sure I'm going to get it back. And I like telling people about good books, assuming they can go buy their own. But that's not always the case. The fact is that although not everyone can afford to buy books, everyone can afford to read. That is, if we can manage to keep our libraries open.

Lots of libraries have an annual book sale, but my particular little branch of the New York Public Library has gone one step further: it has its own used bookstore. It's as well organized as any good shop, with the addition of some old jazz music playing and a little candy dish at the cash register. Also, the prices are generally fifty cents to two dollars. Recently one of the ladies in charge told me they had given ten thousand dollars—*ten thousand dollars amassed from books that cost mere pocket change!*—to a needier library branch for some new computers.

So fairly often, today included, I pack up a gigantic bag or two of books I no longer need and drop them off at the library shop. I get my friends to do it. Hell, I tell customers at the store where I work to take their old books there.

And to tell you the truth, my apartment is a little bit of loaves and fishes when it comes to books. There always seem to be piles everywhere, no matter how often I give a bagful away. Plus, every time I tote a bunch of books to the shop, I become a little bit better of a sharer, and a little less a hoarder.

(But yes, it still hurts just a little.)

Make someone feel visible.

This is sort of embarrassing.

I work in a big store. A huge store, really, and there are a ton of people working there at any given time. Let's say there are about 150 employees, and on busy days, half of them are working. Here's what I'm getting at: I don't know everyone's name. This seems impolite and makes me feel like my mother would be disappointed in me.

People come and go in retail, of course, and after all, we work in different sections of the store and don't interact at all during the day except when we hang up our coats or dive into our lunches at opposite ends of a long table. But still, this doesn't seem right. Today I'm going to learn someone's name, and I'm going to keep learning names, and use them. Because I hate it when someone doesn't know *my* name.

It really isn't that hard—we wear name tags. Now, to put it into practice.

"Good morning, Andrea. How was your weekend?"

A friend is a friend is a friend.

Another death: my friend M.'s dad has just died. It wasn't unexpected, but there were many tough decisions about care along the way. As a friend of mine once said, "Unfortunately, there's no other way out of this life." Still, it never gets easier, something we all realize as our lives march along.

I decided to call M. immediately, though the news was very fresh and his feelings would be very raw. He and his partner live right around the corner, and I knew they'd be leaving soon for the funeral, which is far away. In this kind of situation, although a note is always the best etiquette, I wondered whether I could do something more immediate for them.

The truth is, M. is far more organized than I am, and the notion that I could do anything more than water a plant was ludicrous. Still, I wanted to give him a telephonic hug and make the offer. Naturally, their bags were packed and by the door already.

I gave him my condolences, sent my love along, got a little teary, and asked what I might do. Nothing, of course. They were all set.

But leave it to M., having all his ducks in a row.

Even though I could hear the misery and pain in his voice, his words to me were: "Would you like the tomatoes we just picked from the garden? I can drop them off before we go."

Share your knowledge.

I have two friends, a couple named Jack and Denise—I've known them a long time, and we've been in and out of each other's lives in both business and friendship during most of our adulthood. Recently they took a big and brave step: they have opened an independent bookstore at a time when the economy and publishing are incredibly besieged.

For a long time I was just about the only one to know about their plans. We referred to it only as TSP: Top Secret Project. I swear I was almost as excited as they were. So when the time finally came and books started to arrive, I hopped on the bus to their store and helped them set up (as if they could have stopped me). And today, as I've done on many weekend days this summer, I've popped out to ring up sales in this cute little beach town.

Sure, I work in a different bookstore, but during tough economic times, you cheer for success anywhere and individual competition takes a bit of a backseat. You just want what you love to survive. My respect for my small-business daredevil friends is enormous. If I can be their Guest Bookseller once in a while and give these brainiacs even a couple of tips about what life on the sales floor is like, I am thrilled to do so.

Besides, what's better than being with old friends on a new journey?

Support your neighbors.

One of the best parts of living in the country is farm stands and summer farmers' markets. Sure, cities have them, but there's something special about a transformed field or, in the case of my town, a rectory backyard filled with fresh meats, cheeses, herbs, and bunches of flowers. But in August, when you can get a great tomato in even the biggest supermarkets, I still try to buy local. Today the hunt was on for the best heirlooms, and the choices were dizzying.

I settled on a table of real beauties and was chatting about the bounty with the vendor when another customer sidled up.

ME: Aren't they somethin'?

EVIL CUSTOMER: Ugh. I just came back from a week in Iowa.

ME: Really? So you must be happy to be home.

EVIL CUSTOMER: Well, it's Iowa. All this was so much cheaper there.

Tomato Girl and I locked eyes. "Your heirlooms are magnificent," I said to her.

She replied, with feeling, "Thank you so much for stopping by."

I went out of my way to support local people who work hard; Evil Customer flew across the country to hurl an insult and was too thick even to realize how offensive her behavior was. Right in her own backyard.

Give it up.

I am a ninja about the window seat and it doesn't matter if it's a plane, train, or bus. (I mean, I think that's what I am; I've never actually used the word "ninja" before.) I often take a bus service to the Hamptons for a weekend—of course, since the Hamptons are so fancy, it's not called a bus but a jitney, even though the Hamptons are just on Long Island, not in Great Britain. I always board at the first stop so I can get the pick of the good seats.

Got a really good seat today; it's an art. Not too near the bathroom, not next to one of the windows that blows noisy air, not so close to the front that someone plops down right next to you. Because your next wish, after getting the perfect seat, is that no one sits down next to you. I've been known to place a bottle of Pepto-Bismol on the adjoining seat to silently ward off passengers, and I'm not even kidding.

So now we're at the final pickup stop, and I'm just settling in. I have all my important stuff around me: a book, a sandwich, my iPad, a drink, and a bunch of other items just to take up space. And now the bus is pretty darn full, and here comes an old couple down the aisle.

He asks me, as nice as pie, of course, as he's a sweet old man, "Would you mind moving so that my wife and I can sit together?"

What???

Don't they have any idea at all how much this seat means to me?

They should totally get on at the first stop if they want seats this good!

@#&?%!*

How could *they?*

"Of course. No problem at all."

AUGUST 16

Pass on something useful; don't throw it out.

It's hardly rained at all this summer, and I think because of that, people have gotten casual—lax, really—about not taking umbrellas along with them. Me, I hate umbrellas. In a city like New York, where a lot of your daily traveling to and fro is on busy sidewalks, they become a lethal weapon. If I didn't wear glasses already, I would get a windowpane pair for rainy days, just to protect my vision.

I know, I know: umbrellas don't hurt people—*people hurt people!* The majority of users don't raise them over their head: they use them like a knight on a charger, pointing them ahead to clear their path, and God protect those in their way. It's a fight to the finish. Personally, I find the best way to fend them off is to wear a hat to protect you from the rain instead of carrying an umbrella. You get a better view of what's coming right at you (because the best defense is a good offense). Or you fight them off with flailing arms, like the swarm of stinging insects that they are.

But on this day it had been raining on and off pretty hard, and since I was going out to a nice restaurant after work, for once I brought along one of those little black fold-up umbrellas you can buy on the street cheap, so I wouldn't show up a watery mess. (Yes, I have more than one in my closet. Who doesn't?) The sky still looked ominous on the bus as I neared my destination, but I figured I was OK for the rest of the evening since the report called for clear skies later in the night.

So as I stood to get off, I turned and said, "Would anybody like my umbrella? It's a spare," I added, to assuage the ordinarily suspicious New Yorkers. It was only a few seconds, really, but pretty funny to watch twenty or so people thinking, What is she up to? Is it already broken? Are there drugs hidden in the handle and she's spotted the FBI on the bus? But the fears were superseded by the realization that this was something *for free*, and a hand shot up at last. The umbrella taker still looked wary as I handed over the bounty, though I did receive a murmured thank-you.

Count your blessings. Count them again, because I'm pretty sure you forgot at least three.

"I like your summer hat," I said.

"Why, thank you." He beamed.

I'd never spoken to this man before, though I'd seen him a hundred times over the last few years, and he always had a big-brimmed leather hat on, à la 1960s Bob Dylan. Now he sported a straw fedora.

I wasn't sure if he was homeless; but today I thought I saw him with a cup, and I crept close enough when he turned away a moment to peek in and see that yes, there were a few coins inside. (I certainly didn't want to offend him if it was just a cup of coffee.) Frankly, I guess I had never considered that he is poor, because he always seems so happy. To myself, I've always called him Old Man River—Paul Robeson would be shaking in his boots if he and this man were both *American Idol* finalists, I can tell you that.

Because this man has a voice that would bring you to your knees. It's deep, it's rich, it's mellifluous. I know this because he sings all the time, in a booming baritone. He sings as he strolls down the street. He sings when he's sitting near the bus stop on a milk crate. When the bookstore I work in was in a smaller venue around the corner, he sang in there and made it seem like a cathedral.

"I miss you coming in to the old store," I admitted. "You know we're only just down the street now. I never see you in there."

More beaming. "I used to come in to use the bathroom," he replied, a little sadly. "But there are just too many stairs over there now."

"Well, it's always good to hear you singing, wherever it is." I slipped a little money into his cup.

Beaming to the fullest. "It's good to see you, too. And bless you."

The rest of the day, the same thought kept coming back to me: why does it always seem like it's someone who has the least among us who is blessing us the most?

Good advice is for passing on.

Once in a while, I just like to pass on a little advice; hope you don't mind. Today I was driving down the Cape, and I passed the sign for Brewster; many years ago I did a summer share there with some friends, and when I saw the sign I recalled an incident with my car—and some advice I was given—that had me smiling this morning in my dopey Ford Focus rental.

At the time of the Brewster summer, I owned a fabulous yellow 1977 MGB—wish I had it today. It did have a lot of problems, though, and I had taken to carrying a hammer in the glove compartment so I could crawl under the car to rap on the alternator when it wouldn't start. That worked for a while but was getting less reliable. Then it died again in Brewster—where a guy at the local gas station told me about a miracle man on a back road, a guy who had gone to Harvard but ended up in the woods fixing MGs. Seemed improbable, but when my friends towed me to this godforsaken little garage, sure enough, a hunky guy in a Harvard T-shirt appeared.

I no longer remember his name, but he fixed the MG in a snap. "Listen," he admonished, "this will hold up for a week, a month, who knows. But when you get back to New York..." And he proceeded to give me a long and expensive list of repairs that would make the MG the showpiece it should have been.

I listened politely, but he saw my eyes begin to glaze over. He knew I wasn't going to do any of it. He looked at me and gave me one of the greatest—and funniest—pieces of advice I've ever received, which I pass along now.

"Hey, Erin," MG guy said. "You want to drive like a sport, you got to spend like a sport."

Do it like you mean it.

A recent poll reported that 81 percent of Americans believe they will write a book in their lifetime. And as a publishing veteran, I have been asked by scores of people over the years if I know how to get an agent or how they can get a book deal. They rarely ask what it takes to get to that point. Most of them haven't started at all. "There is no other way," I say, "than to just sit down and do it." No one seems to like hearing this answer much or to be told that writing is really hard work.

Last night I was having a belated birthday dinner with two old friends, and one, who had been reading Eudora Welty, said, "I'd like to try writing short stories." Our companion rolled his eyes and was reprimanded. "You have to just start," said I, as usual. Our friend didn't look very happy. But he's a smart guy, and he has that southern gift of gab. If he wants to try, I'm with him all the way.

So I'm going to send my friend these tips:

- Set yourself up in a nice spot. Maybe a pretty view, good light, a comfortable chair. Writing is torturous enough—you shouldn't be physically uncomfortable on top of it.

- Before you start, get a cup of coffee, a snack, or whatever else you need to make you stay put. No making the phone call you forgot, no getting up to fetch the mail. Pee before you sit down. William Faulkner said the hardest part was sitting in the chair, and he was right.

- Have a regimen. Start by writing just twenty to thirty minutes a day. Put aside the same time daily, if you can, when you're most relaxed and your brain isn't fuzzy.

- Each day, begin by going back over what you wrote the day before. This will help with continuity and get you jump-started.

- If you don't find writing rewarding, then stop. You were meant to do something else.

- Sit and stare at the page. Eventually you'll write something. Maybe not today, but soon.

- Oh, and remember, anything can happen. It did to me.

Many years ago, author Pat Conroy wrote in my copy of *The Prince of Tides*, "For the love of words we write." That should be your motto.

AUGUST 20

Always be thinking: what if that were me?

So I'm out in the country in my friend's car doing an errand—geez, it's a beautiful day—and at the side of the road I see a guy who seems to be having trouble with his bicycle. He's bent over, with what looks to be a punctured tire or a busted chain or who knows what. So I pull up next to him, and just like in the old-fashioned days when people didn't worry about ax murderers and serial killers, I ask him if he needs any help.

The cyclist smiles and responds, "Oh, no, but thanks very much."

But it makes me wonder: When did we stop being Good Samaritans? When did "doing a good turn" become "taking your life in your hands"?

Now it seems like we don't think twice about passing a car on the side of the road with its emergency blinkers on. And you never, ever see a hitchhiker. "No talking to strangers" used to be just for little kids: now it's everyone's motto. I'm wondering how we can wend our way back a little, without losing sight of the fact that, yes, the world is, sadly, a dangerous place.

Suppose the cyclist was in a not-so-nice neighborhood but still was obviously a guy in need. Would it be so hard to lock your car doors, pull abreast of him, roll down your window a little, and offer to call 911? Would that be so terrible?

We have to figure out a way to live like this again, without being so afraid all the time. It just seems we've left very little room in life for Do Unto Others.

AUGUST 21

Walk a dog, make a friend.

I'm visiting my friend Michele and am about to relax with a book while she goes off to yoga class. She usually brings her two little King Charles spaniels along, but it's hot out and she doesn't want to leave them in the car, even with the windows cracked. So she asks me if I'll take the dogs for a long walk while she's gone. (Yes, it's OK if the good deed comes to you—there are no rules about having to chase it down.)

But of course! So the pups and I head off to town, and I tie them up outside the muffin shop while I go in to fetch a cup of coffee. Within moments, kids are circling around like petting vultures. I guess it's because Velvet and Ruby are small and not exactly dangerous-looking creatures. The petters seem to be sort of a starter group, aged maybe two to five, with a couple of stroller-bound kids wiggling on the sidelines. I come back out with my coffee and try to relax and people-watch a bit, but there must be fourteen kids elbowing for dog time within the next ten minutes. Every last one of them touches the dogs extremely gingerly ("Gentle, gentle," parents tell kids), even though Velvet and Ruby stay nearly immobile.

There is even one miracle cure: Mitchell, about three, hovers nervously, clearly torn between his desire to touch the dogs and—from his mother's report—memories of a previous "bad incident." Soft fur wins out, and Mitchell is once again a dog lover. Ruby and Velvet never tire of the attention, but by now I am over the pop-up petting zoo.

Just as I am about to pack up, a woman hurries over to our bench. "Oh," she says with a note of disappointment, "from the angle I saw you, I thought your dogs were dachshunds."

"No, sorry," says me. "But let me ask you something. From the angle you were at, did I look any thinner?"

"You looked terrific." She grins.

Thank you, lady. Good deeds all around.

What means nothing to you could be someone else's memories.

I was just getting a little cone of sweet corn custard at a local eatery when I glanced down and saw a big fat wallet. I mean really big and fat. But not like Daddy Warbucks fat or Diddy fat. This was fat like full of clippings of a daughter's dance recitals, a couple of recipes, maybe some stubs from a baseball game, and a bunch of receipts. Someone was missing some treasures.

So I handed it over to the server behind the counter, and almost immediately the man she was waiting on said, "Hey! That's mine! Where did I leave it?" I pointed to the floor. He was clearly delighted and picked up his dinner order.

"I guess my cheeseburger reward is coming," I prompted.

And he laughed. He thought I was just hilarious. Then he walked off, stuffing that big fat wallet right back into his pants pocket.

Just a reminder that not all good deeds have their obvious reward.

But I'm sure there's a cheeseburger in heaven with my name on it.

"Go green!"

I'm in a little bit of a hurry, and I've stopped at the fast-food place near work for lunch.

"To stay or to go?" asks the server as she rings up my order.

"To go," I say absentmindedly. "But wait, um, just put it on a tray like it's to stay; then I can actually just pick up the hot dog and leave with it, but not use the to-go bags and napkins and stuff you'd give me. Does that make sense?"

I'm not sure I explained it right, and so there's a second where I'm uncertain and the two girls behind the counter are puzzled. Suddenly one breaks into a smile and shouts, "Go green!"

We all laugh, the hot dog arrives, and we part ways. The unwanted paper products stay behind.

Look outside yourself.

I'm trying to learn—almost to train myself, really—how to see outward. A bunch of things, I think, have served to make me someone who doesn't always observe what I should. I'm an only child and played by myself a lot growing up. Also,

I'm a writer, and it makes me kind of dreamy sometimes. I consider myself insightful, peoplewise, but if I were a murder witness, I'm not sure that all my years of considerable *Law & Order* study would do me any good. What color eyes did the murderer have? Age and weight? Any distinguishing characteristics? I would have no idea.

And I'm finding that good deeds don't just drop at your feet, which is probably my first big lesson on this journey, so eyes front! What's going on out there? Tonight I found it was nine o'clock and I hadn't done anyone a lick of good yet.

So I was walking home from my dinner date, and I thought, Take a look around, knucklehead. Stop thinking about laundry and e-mail and your book sales. What's on the virtual and actual horizons? And I spied an opportunity on each.

I knew I was going to my hometown tomorrow for a few days and that my aunt would be lending me her car again. She and I will do some stuff together while I'm there, sure, but I thought maybe I could at least leave a little something behind when I stop by to take her wheels. I dipped into a fancy shop and bought her some nice chocolates—something I know she loves that she never buys for herself. Keep it up, I thought.

I strolled by a supermarket. A small, wiry guy was standing outside, a bored employee waiting to unload a truck. He hopped up and grabbed on to the building scaffolding above his head and hung there.

"You can't chin up on that, I betcha," I taunted.

"What? Just watch me!" he shot back. Then he pulled himself up effortlessly and, with a little flourish, dismounted at my feet.

I laughed, and he offered a fist bump.

And I realized that within just a couple of minutes, everything had changed. I'd asked someone to show off his prowess, and I'd prepared a surprise for tomorrow.

Good day.

AUGUST 25

Help a stranger on his way.

I love to give directions. I practically accost people on the city streets and ask them if they need help.

Today I was on the subway, heading downtown, when a family trudged on board at Times Square. There was no chance that they were not tourists: Mom and Dad and two teens, a boy and a girl, the latter pair complete with bags from the M&M's World store and sullen faces.

I was assured of my keen detecting skills when Dad took a map out of his fanny pack and everyone started to huddle. Ahhh, my moment at last. . . .

"Hi, can I help you get where you want to go?" I inquired, perhaps too eagerly. Did I mention I look trustworthy?

"Well, we're heading to Ground Zero. After that, I don't know. But we loooove to walk," said Dad. The rest of the family remained silent. "We want to see the Statue of Liberty, too." So before they knew it, I had directed them to the Staten Island ferry (free!) for a great view of Lady Liberty, a couple of good places to eat, maybe a walk across the Brooklyn Bridge, and who knows what else. I was on fire.

By now the wife was sitting next to me, asking me all about what she considered to be my swell and glamorous life. I was happy to oblige. Turned out my hometown is only about a half hour away from theirs, and I could almost hear her mind working. She's there. I'm here.

The wife sighed. "I should have moved here. I had kids instead."

Sheesh. And just like that, I'd ruined the vacation.

Note to self: It's nice to help out people when they seem confused. However, it is *not* nice to confuse them about their life choices.

No good deed goes unpunished.

Oh, brother.

Did I do a good deed or a bad deed today?

This is an all-too-familiar story—the question of how to begin caring for an older relative.

My aunt worked as my father's secretary for four decades; she adored him. Toward the end of both my parents' lives, this aunt and her husband were there, helping to find home care, going to the pharmacy, checking in, making doctor's appointments. As an only child who lives quite far away, without their help I would have had to give up my career and return home. I owe her.

My aunt and uncle have no children but four nieces and nephews—two of us in town and the others hours away. There's lots of phoning and e-mailing about what's to be done about Auntie. She is on medication, and her doctor told her she shouldn't drive. Now, she's been a bad and nervous driver for a while, so we were thrilled, though it would mean a lot of calling on us—and it would be tougher on some than on others (like me, two hundred miles away). We realize she is beginning to need care, or at least companionship, but she will not hear of it.

She is determined to drive the old convertible she loves, insisting that she doesn't go far, only to the supermarket and such. Per the doctor's instructions, she has taken a break from driving, but today, after some pleading, I took her to a long, quiet beach road and let her get behind the wheel again. (Still, I'm constantly trying to scare her out of wanting to drive anymore, spinning tales of busy-roads terror. I know she hates me for it.)

This one comes under Awful Life Choices. I understand: we're talking about taking away her freedom. But if my aunt hits someone in the grocery store parking lot because we didn't put our foot down, I might as well have hit that person myself. How would I live with that?

Pay it backward.

"C'mon over. We're going to watch a scary movie."

I'm trying to lure Cousin Mimi into joining us at her brother Leo's for an event Leo and I occasionally get to sneak in. Everything has to align: kid in bed, no wife, Chinese takeout place still open. He owns one of those "order by midnight tonight" DVD box sets—fifty sci-fi and fifty horror films. All classics. Well, maybe not exactly classics. We're trying right now to decide between *The Crawling Eye* and *Santa Claus Conquers the Martians*.

Mimi is on the road, just coming back from a long trip—five hours each way, taking her son back to college. She is both sad and pooped, so of course we want to bring her into our fold. "I can't," she moans. "The first thing I have to do when I hit town is go find Eli's bike, which may or may not be down at the yacht club."

On the ride back to school, son Eli has suddenly remembered that his bike was left by a friend at the yacht club, unlocked and unattended. The friend's vague reply, when Eli called from the car, was, "Yeah. It was there the last time I looked." Typical. We have no idea if this means yesterday, or July Fourth.

But surely I pulled something like this myself on my parents. Many times. So did you. That's why I volunteer to go

down to the yacht club and use my keen investigative pow-
ers. If I find it, we can also avoid getting Eli's dad angry.

I walk onto the club grounds—I don't belong, so I'm
already feeling like I look suspicious as hell and not yachty
at all—and steal over to where the hordes of kids leave their
bikes all summer long. It's nearly Labor Day now, and where
there would have been forty bikes a month ago, there in the
pitch-dark I can make out only five, Eli's among them. I hop
on and ride off, and I feel like I'm getting away with something myself. I have also gotten someone out of trouble, like
someone has done for me once or twice in my life.

So: Eli's relieved, Mimi is so thrilled, she's forgotten she
was mad at Eli, everyone's happy Eli's dad never has to find
out, and I feel like I'm on a joyride, whirling around my little
village in the dark.

AUGUST 28

Try to "save the day" once in a while.

I am an avid nature lover. And when I say "nature lover," I
mean the beach, dinner alfresco, a road trip inside a car. I do
not mean snakes or hiking. I believe that if God really wanted
people to go camping, he would not have invented hotels.
Everyone knows that's why He created the bear: to discour-
age camping. Tonight, I may have reached the pinnacle of my
Nature Girl ways when I saved the Little White Owl.

I was driving home from dinner with the cousins at about ten o'clock, top down, just rolling along the quiet streets. Already it felt like the end of summer: no one was out walking; not one car passed me by. It was as if people were indoors, setting out their school clothes. Suddenly my headlights locked on an animal smack in the middle of the road. Now, it's not that unusual to see a deer or coyote, a possum or pheasant around here. Last year I even saw a reverse skunk: white with a black stripe. (I did too.) So I simply veered left and drove around it. And then I thought, Was that what I think it was? I backed up slowly, so as not to scare the creature, and got him in my beams again. It was a little white owl.

First off: it was just so pretty. Darkness all around, and here was this bird, only about ten inches tall, I'll bet, with his head swiveling around, just like in a Disney movie. How had I never seen one before? He looked at me but wouldn't budge.

I know nothing about owls, so I didn't want to get out of the car and try to shoo him away. Perhaps he would pick me up with his nasty claws and carry me to some owly coven, where my eyes would be scratched out and I'd be left for dead. So I inched the car closer, to try to scare him off. No dice. Closer still. I thought maybe he had a little treat he was gnawing on that he didn't want to leave, but it didn't seem so. I didn't want to toot and scare him. So I just kept at it, inch by inch, really slow, until, at last, he flew off—not injured, as I had feared—and swooped up into some nearby trees.

Did I really save him? I felt like I had, that someone else might have just turned the corner and plowed right into him. Was it a magical, dreamy experience? Oh, yes, it surely was.

Hashtag! #considerothers!

It's all about the hashtag.

For all of you non-Tweeters: What we used to know as the number sign, or the pound sign (#), is frequently used on Twitter as a means to help the user do a search. Or at least, that's what it was supposed to be for. Now it's become sort of a gag, and one of the more amusing parts of the tweeting experience. Let me explain.

Now, the hashtag was originally used so that you could see what folks worldwide were saying about something you, too, were interested in; this way, you could see what people were saying globally about a certain subject. So, if no one you e-consorted with cared about esoteric Olympic sports, you might comment:

WOW! Did you see that awesome run? #luge

Get it? Anyone in the entire world searching "#luge" could see your comment. And vice versa. Cool. But not as cool or funny as when folks started using it as a pretend search tool, that is, one that is likely used only once, and typed in jest. For example, as the writer and chicken raiser Susan Orlean wrote:

> *In a daring move, I just opened the divider between my old chickens and my new chickens and the baby turkeys. #peaceinourtimeihope*

Another Tweeter I know posts:

> *The secret of life? The Hokey Pokey. #thatiswhatitisallabout*

See? So the hashtag thing has gotten so popular that some of the Twitter Greats make it funnier or more interesting than the tweet itself.

Where am I going with this? you wonder. Tonight on my long bus ride back to New York, I was seated toward the back with some . . . well, let's call them revelers. They were a gang of friends, probably in their midtwenties, who had been partying all weekend on the Cape and were evidently determined, judging from the amount of wine they brought on the bus, to continue the funfest. As the miles went by, they got drunker and louder; they were a good enough bunch, but now it was heading toward eleven on a Sunday night, and plenty of people wanted to snooze.

So here's where the hashtag thing comes in—and actually, it was, for a while, kind of a funny sort of parlor game. This gang would start every comment in their conversation by saying "Hashtag!" as in, "Hashtag! #youaresoskanky!"

Or "Hashtag! #ihatemyjob!" and "Hashtag! #whosgotthe-wine?"

Then it got old. Really old. So I thought about my manners, but not for very long, and I turned around and yelled, "Hashtag! #shutthehellup!"

Oh, yes, the passengers did applaud, and the wee party broke up at last.

Take one for the team.

Today the impossible happened.

I received two servings of ice cream, and I gave one away.

I went to a restaurant known for its special revolving array of frozen custards—they change monthly, and there are seasonal flavors that are delightful and surprising. Tuesday is s'mores day. This I was not going to miss.

I ordered a small cone (chocolate with marshmallow and crushed-up graham cracker, if you were wondering), and when it was delivered to me, it was in a cup. "Not for nothing," said I—very nicely, let me add—"but I ordered a cone, and this is the third time this has happened to me."

The server told me to hold on, and in a minute I had my cone and, with a smile, the original cup of ice cream, too.

Well, it would have been impolite to say no.

So I took it, and I did the right thing: though it broke my heart, I offered it to other diners.

There was a swanky Italian couple. They politely declined, though I'm sure they noticed the offer came with a clean spoon.

Parents with a kid. They looked at me like they wanted to kill me when I presented my bounty: they hadn't gotten him to touch his lunch yet. The kid was drooling, and on the edge of tears, when I scurried off.

Then I approached a trio of teenage girls. What was I thinking? Ice cream? OMG! It's so, like, fattening!

I'm sorry. Did I say I gave one away? Well, I certainly tried.

But I'm proud to say I bit the bullet. I ate them both.

AUGUST 31

Help someone look forward to looking back.

I've been e-mailing Anne—all too occasionally—over the last couple of years. Our parents were great friends growing up, and so Anne was one of our gang when we were kids, but as often happens, our paths diverged by the time we were teens. We all went to college; Anne had kids, got married and divorced, and eventually moved away. She finally found someone who truly loved her and, when she got cancer, cared for her. But all those years, she kept in touch with my cousin

Lee, who was her age. And as time went on, Lee reported that Anne was growing more and more nostalgic for our childhood. Then she became quite ill, and Lee said Anne would like to be in touch with more of the family—would I please e-mail her, and just say hello?

Really? Thirty years later?

But I did as Lee asked; I felt sort of foolish but sat down and wrote a newsy e-mail to Anne, reminded her of some funny times, recalled some antics from the past. She wrote right back and was so thrilled to hear from me that I felt bad for not doing it earlier. I wrote a few of those e-mails, and the time between responses grew longer and longer until I didn't hear back again. Today I learned that Anne passed away. Another sad chapter closed, but I am so glad if I helped bring some happy memories back.

SEPTEMBER 1

Be nice.

I felt like I was gritting my teeth from the moment I got up.

I was exhausted from a night of bad dreams, which frequent me when I am anxious. It leaves me with a creepy mental hangover that sometimes takes hours to shake.

So I started the day with a chip on my shoulder and malice in my heart. This wouldn't do. I had to go to work, where I needed to be nice to people all day, no matter their IQ.

I decided this day would be redolent with kindness, lousy with good deeds. I would christen it Be Nice Day. No matter what, I would remain pleasant.

Slow, slooooow line at the deli for coffee. For the billionth time, I wondered why the person in front of me waits for the counterman to tell her her total before she begins to rummage around in her purse for her wallet. Like it's a shock that he asks her for money. Me? Silent.

On to work, where I had three customers who asked for books by titles they insisted were right but were far from it. Don't correct, just deliver, I told myself. Big smile.

I had a cab go in the wrong direction; at today's rates, if the light goes red, and there's a teeny bit of traffic, it costs about a dollar a block. Deep breath.

Only one more stop to get through, thank God. I told the person at the movie ticket window what I wanted to see, and I got a ticket to the wrong movie. Asked the concession person for a Diet Coke, got a regular Coke. Don't complain, I said to myself: you're going to the movies, and they're working the popcorn stand. Thank you, I said to Popcorn Girl.

I spent a whole lot of today thinking, This is life, baby, this is New York. We got to move it along here. So I said nothing. Just took another deep breath.

I crawled into bed feeling like I had saved the world. From me, at least.

Give (it) back.

I have been totally patting myself on the back today, because I finally returned the plate. My pal Joe arrived with the plate about eight months ago, and it had a pie on it. But he's out of town much of the year, and I wasn't very fast at getting it back to him in the first three months before he left and so, yeah, I guess you could say it was my fault.

It was no great shakes, the plate. One of those white CorningWare jobs with the little blue flower in the middle. And of course I had to leave it out on the kitchen counter, because I was going to bring it back any day. I put bags of potato chips in it. Loose change. Peeps, when the season warranted. Once I used it to make a pie.

But this morning I washed it anew and packed it up to go meet Joe. I thought the kitchen counter would look spacious after that, but it seemed empty. Was I making a terrible mistake? No! I had to return what I had borrowed so very long ago. It was not mine—it was never mine! So I trudged, heavyhearted, over to Starbucks and presented to Joe what was rightfully his.

"What's this?" he said.

SEPTEMBER 3

Don't drink and drive.

My good deed today is to tell you a story.

Nine years ago, my family lost someone spectacular. She was my cousin's wife, and we adored her: they had been married seventeen years and had dated since college, so she was long a part of our history. She was funny and smart and had a way of keeping the rest of us in line. I could not really begin to describe her here—she was quirky and indescribably special. Her father had been a top-notch spy in World War II, and she, too, had an uncanny way of ferreting out the odd fact or noticing something out of place. She brooked no foolishness at all. We couldn't remember life without her.

On September 3, 1993, Jeannine suffered a brain aneurysm yet somehow pulled through. I was there for the hours-long operation, and when they brought her out of the O.R. on a gurney, she waved weakly, and our hearts broke, in the very happiest way. Miraculously, she recovered completely.

Labor Day weekends weighed heavy on her, though. While the rest of the family planned cookouts and trips to the beach, she often wanted to spend it by herself. We understood, of course, though I don't think any of us really knew what she went through every September 3. Did she give thanks, reconstruct the whole terrible experience over and over again, pray? It seemed she just desired peace and quiet.

We missed her in our holiday shenanigans, but we would never consider asking her to change her plans.

So it was that on September 3, 2001, we were all spread around at various beaches: I was on Fire Island, though most of the family was in our hometown on Massachusetts' Buzzards Bay. Jeannine was in the Berkshires, gardening, and when a neighbor asked why she was alone for the holiday weekend, she told a short version of her story, ending it by saying, "Aren't I lucky?"

Then she got in her car to go buy some chrysanthemums, because it was Labor Day, and a drunk driver hit her head-on and killed her at one hundred miles an hour at four o'clock in the afternoon.

I have had my own serious problems with substance abuse; blessedly, they seem to be over. But this day, and every day, I am begging you: don't drink and drive.

SEPTEMBER 4

Try to help before someone has to ask.

Over the years working in the bookstore, I've seen a man come into the store again and again—he's probably about thirty and severely affected by what I believe is cerebral palsy. He couldn't be friendlier. I've seen him gab with many booksellers, often drawing out the informational transaction into a lengthier conversation. I don't mean to insinuate that he's a pest; let's just say he likes to chat.

I've waited on him only once or twice, but today he approached me and started to take off his backpack, I assumed to get out some notes on books he might want. Instead, he took two CDs out of a bag and asked me if I would wrap them for him. I automatically asked if he had a receipt. It's just a smart policy. This may sound odd, but more than one customer has slipped the additional item into a bag from the store, or wanted us to wrap things before they've paid for them. (Plus, yes, people have been up in arms in the past—shocked!—that we wouldn't wrap their purchases from Best Buy or the drugstore. Seriously?) He didn't have a receipt. It was merchandise we sell, and he'd just walked in the door—I had no doubt this merchandise had been paid for.

"It's just that I'm not a very good wrapper," he said.

I hated myself. I hatehatehated myself and I was ashamed. With a little foresight and a lot less rigidity, I could have seen what he needed. I could have kept my yap shut and my eyes open.

I wrapped his gift, we talked about music a little, and off he went. I still felt very small. But he hadn't made me feel that way.

SEPTEMBER 5

Shine a light on someone.

Last year I received an award from a local organization. It doesn't matter what it was—by that I mean it doesn't matter to *you*—but I was extremely proud to be honored. This has only happened to me a couple of times, and I'm a little bit of a ham, so I was surprised at what my feelings were at the presentation: a mix of pride and a sort of queasy feeling that it should have been someone else, even though I was not alone in receiving this honor. But like it or hate it, turn it down or have a party to celebrate, there's something special about being singled out and thanked.

Today, almost a year later, I got to pass the torch. As a past honoree, I was asked to make a nomination myself, to suggest someone I thought deserved the spotlight for this year's event. I thought long and hard before I gave a name I was happy with and thought was deserving of this recognition. Anyone who has been a serious volunteer or activist of any kind knows that progress is inch by inch, slow but hopefully steady. It's often hard to see the successes, they are sometimes so minuscule. To applaud this kind of stamina is crucial.

So for me to be able to offer a name and say, Yes, look at what she's done, let's raise a glass to her: well, now, that felt good—no divided feelings about *that* at all.

What's important is that your heart's in the right place.

This may not seem big to you, but I love me my potato chips.

I've just come from buying a new shower curtain at Bed Bath & Beyond, and on my way out—I guess in the Beyond section, since it's got nothing to do with Bed or Bath—I spot a new flavor I've never tried: Chipotle Ranch. This sounded delicious! I snag a bag.

The bus home is taking forever to arrive, and honestly I'm a bit peckish, so when I finally sit down, I rip open the bag. A nice older man sits down next to me. "Chip?" I say in the most beguiling way, but no, he demurs. He's very polite, but I can tell he's thinking, Who the hell are you? And how do I know where those hands have been?

As if I couldn't be thinking the same about him!

Here I am, offering him a *fresh bag* of potato chips, in an *entirely new* flavor—man's perfect culinary invention! Doesn't he know how precious a gift this is? No, he falls immediately asleep. Or maybe pretends to be asleep because he's afraid.

Turns out he was right. There's nothing ranchy or chipotle-ish about them; they are just terribly salty and a sharp disappointment. For the first time in my life, I will throw a bag of potato chips away.

But I did offer to share something I loved. Or at least thought I loved.

There's a place for everyone.

I am a superior parker. I mean I can back into the tiniest space. So when I see drivers on New York streets (or anywhere else) who are having trouble wrangling their way into a space, I often stop, like I did today, to help them squeeze their way in. Most folks are grateful—with the occasional exception of a man with an ego problem. But today I helped a frustrated woman wriggle her way into a nice spot with some professional parking help.

Let me pass on my double-secret parking tip, bestowed on me by my friend Dini in 1975. It is foolproof:

> Line yourself up parallel to the car in front of the empty space as closely as you can. Now start backing up into the space, turning your steering wheel as hard as possible, keeping your eyes on your side-view mirror. The *second* you see both headlights of the car parked behind the empty space, swing your wheel sharply and totally in the opposite direction. *Et voilà.*

Just don't take *my* space.

SEPTEMBER 8

You get what you give.

My friendship with Joe is like no other friendship I have. I feel a little like we operate out of a secret clubhouse with a sign that says "No Grown-Ups Allowed!!!" Not that we do anything *bad* in our virtual fort, but sometimes we like stuff other people might think is weird or eccentric. Or worse, boring. In my mind, we have lots of adventures—not extreme adventures, by any means—but things like a day trip to a cool cemetery is not for everybody. (Celia Cruz's new mausoleum! Look: Miles Davis is right next to Duke Ellington!)

Another example: every outing, no matter how small, includes a search for the best hot dog. We've taken the subway to Coney Island just to go to the original Nathan's; driven off many highway exits on just a billboard's promise. Believe me, we have tried places lesser men (and women) would have passed over.

But my favorite part of being Joe's friend is that we're always trading favors, doing something special for each other. It's not one-upmanship, or trying to pay back, or evening things out. There will be times I won't see Joe for weeks, but today was a perfect example of the way we roll.

I was working at the store and saw him lurking nearby while I was talking to a customer. "Wait fifteen minutes," I said, "and we can have lunch together." I ordered a hot dog, but he was saving his frankfurter experience for the Yankees game he was headed to, so I bought him an ice cream cone. No big deal, just a way to say thanks for stopping by. As he left, we talked about trying to go to the US Open tennis matches tomorrow. Joe took charge. "I'll get out there first, intimidate a couple of tickets out of someone, and give you a call when all is ready," he promised. Oh, boy. And then, as incredible luck would have it, I received a phone call from a friend at 5:01 p.m. as I was leaving work: two free tickets for tonight.

Who'd I call? You got it. We hopped on the subway and started our night's adventure. First stop: Joe bought me a hot dog.

Oh, and if you'd like to go to the Nathan Hale House, or read in the *Moby-Dick* marathon, or check out how a cranberry bog works, come knock twice on the door of the secret clubhouse. Because that's how we roll.

Give credit where it's due.

This summer, there was a contest to see which store in the chain sold the most Frappuccinos—a delish icy coffee concoction that seemed to be flying out of the store practically on its own during this hot, hot summer.

Well, like I said, *practically* on its own. The contest surely helped. The stores that sold the most Frappuccinos were going to get prizes. Now, this meant everybody in the store: cashiers, booksellers, receivers, maintenance people, everyone. That's about 150 employees where I work, and we would each get a fifteen-dollar gift card to the store. So on hot days we urged customers to stop by the café. We slurped plenty of them ourselves. And lo, we won.

But listen: though the rest of us did our part in suggesting to customers that it was a great day for a cold drink, it was the gang working *in* the café who certainly did the lion's share of the selling. And there was one person in particular who I'm sure put sales over the top. She was just a great salesperson: made the product sound irresistible; always cheerful in the face of overheated, cranky adversity; forever patient. And she also treated every employee who came to the café with the same grace and respect. Seriously, this was a girl who could brighten up a day.

But then she left to continue her nursing studies, just days before the announcement that we had won the gift cards, thus becoming ineligible.

I figure I didn't sell those Frappuccinos: she did. I'll bet she sold 75 percent of them. And now she's a student—one who loves to read—without much money. So I went to the manager's office and asked for her address. She gets my card.

Believe in a stranger.

I was helping out my pals at their lovely independent bookstore today. Around midafternoon, just as I was getting a tad hungry, a young teenage boy walked in, attired in a dress shirt and dark pants. This is a beach town, and flip-flops and shades are the rule. But I barely noticed—because he had cookies.

His name was Farad, and in addition to the cookies, he had his mother with him, hanging back and watching him proudly. Farad was selling packages of these cookies, chocolate chip and oatmeal raisin: six for five dollars. And he had a purpose; Farad was raising money for a program he was in (located in a town nowhere near as fancy as this one) where young kids pursue their dreams of becoming chefs. That is Farad's dream, and he spoke excitedly and eloquently about it, handing me a tell-all brochure, complete with pictures of kids in chef coats and junior-size toques.

Who could say no? Had someone told me there was a writers' camp for kids when I was his age, I never would have had the confidence to get out there with my wares and ask for help. Good on you, Farad.

It's not often enough that a good deed like this comes your way, when a person comes along and basically says, Things will get better for me with just a little bit of your help.

And by the way, Farad bakes a mean cookie.

Never forget.

I don't mean to exclude, or sound superior, but it's absolutely impossible to explain what it was like to live in New York City on September 11, 2001. I live about five miles north of Ground Zero, but in some ways on that day it felt as distant as Mars. In the aftermath, the glorious weather that's always described was still intact in my neighborhood, gorgeous and clear as a bell. But daily life was changed. I worked just a couple of miles from the World Trade Center site, and for months there was a time late in the day when the sky would cloud over, and the wind would change, and a sweet, sickly smell permeated much of lower Manhattan. No one talked about what it was. Everyone knew. And everyone looked each other in the eye and said—but silently—Will we get through this? Are you OK? I know, I know, brother. Take care.

Never a word.

Even still, a pall and a kind of silent change comes over the city on 9/11. And I'm going to look everyone I can in the eye today. They know what I'm saying.

Never forget.

If you can't do it yourself, cheer on the team.

Oh, dang, my friend Beth sent me an e-mail weeks ago about sponsoring her on a swim she does every year off the tippity-tip of Cape Cod, the famed little village of Provincetown. I've just remembered and texted her immediately: Is it too late? She thought not and directed me to her cause's website, and I made a small donation. Sometimes you just need to show you care, let a friend know you noticed his or her efforts.

Midday, I see Beth's report on Facebook, along with a wet, happy photo (well, the *photo* wasn't wet—you know what I mean):

> Choppy surf, 64-degree water, jellyfish and shark scares be damned: My father and I completed the 1.4-mile Swim for Life today! Such a great P'town event. Thanks for your support!

Your neighborhood is your home: spread the good word.

A really cool restaurant opened up in my neighborhood last spring. Overnight, it seemed, the crummy, tiny pizza place that had been there, a joint like a million others, metamorphosed into an überfab taqueria. The place is only as big as a living room and serves gourmet tacos and made-to-order guacamole. The first time I went in, the two owners welcomed me like a long-lost friend. Nearly every time I've visited since then, one of them takes me aside and gives me something on the house— if it's not a free drink, it's a dessert to take home or a small dish of something they're thinking of adding to the menu.

No surprise, the place went gangbusters in no time. Soon I had to go to dinner at five thirty to get the seat at the bar I liked and a little time to hang out with David or Elizabeth, the aforementioned owners. Then the best thing possible happened: a much larger restaurant down the block closed and they took over the space. As I was walking by the new location this afternoon, I saw David working inside on the final touches, preparing for the grand opening later in the week. He beckoned me in and showed me around.

After the tour, as I walked out the door, I spied a couple sort of faux-bickering on the sidewalk. "No, it isn't," I heard the woman say to her boyfriend. "It totally is," he retorted.

The boyfriend stopped me. "Hey, do you know if that's the same restaurant that's down the street?" I assured him it was, told him the opening date, and offered the ultimate insider's information: the owners were turning the initial tiny spot into a dumpling bar.

"Ha!" he gloated. "We bet dinner on whether this was the same place or not. And I win."

I tried to shoehorn my way into that free dinner, point-ing out that I had settled the bet. They were having none of it. But when I found out neither of them had previously dined at the smaller venue, I gave a glowing review. By now, a few other people had stopped by to peek in the open doorway, and I repeated my Happy Customer spiel to them. For a few minutes, I became a walking, talking sandwich board, telling folks all about both the old and the new restaurants.

Finally I continued home, thrilled that I had done some free marketing for the restaurant and also brought the news of good food and great hosts to a bunch of hungry neighborhood folks.

But now will I ever be able to get a seat again?

SEPTEMBER 14

Make yourself count.

Loads of people think that primary elections aren't important. Hell, an alarming number of people think registering to vote isn't even worth it.

I have no patience at all for people like this. None.

Call me loudmouthed or pushy, but I am totally ready to give my two cents to anyone who doesn't vote each and every chance they get, and ready to sock anyone in the jaw who doesn't sign up for the privilege at all.

Today I let my opinion on this be known early and often.

You may not consider this a good deed; you may not even consider it my business. Oh, well. Too bad.

Keep the door open.

Howie is my cousin's husband, and I adore him. He's visiting for a couple of nights, which is a treat. Ours is a perfect host/guest arrangement. He comes to the city a couple of times a year for work and stays with me. He has his own business, so no hotel bills is certainly a plus for him—and besides, we have fun. I stock up on the kind of beer he likes; he brings me flowers. We stay out of each other's way or make plans to go out together, whichever is convenient. And always, we meet up at the end of the night and talk about our day. We simply enjoy each other's company.

I'm not saying this is an unusual arrangement or that I'm doing something special. Just that I'm glad he feels at home.

Count to ten.

I feel like this situation happens just about every day.

I'm giving a party this evening, and I'm at the local gourmet food store, ready to pay too much for my supplies, and naturally I'm late for a meeting way across town. Actually, this is my lucky day: I'm using a gift card, so the bill is no skin off my nose.

However.

Right now, at this crucial (to me) moment, the register decides to start having problems. I can't just dump my stuff and leave to get to my meeting on time, because I've put in a special order and have to pay for it now to be able to pick it up later. I'm stuck.

I've been on the other side of a cash register. I've seen the likes of me (on this side), steaming. So now I count to ten—one of life's most useful bromides—and keep my piehole shut for once. I've also willed myself not to fidget, a superhuman feat on my part. This particular store always has long lines, but also about the fastest checkout I've ever seen. So I know it's the machine, not the person. Of course I want to tell her to hurry up, but I also know there's nothing she can do: the damn thing is on the fritz. Not that there haven't been about a billion times I've barked at someone anyway. But maybe, today, I won't.

In the end how long did I have to wait? Forty-five seconds? Two minutes? Did it make absolutely any difference in the way my day went? No, not a jot. Did I feel better for not having been a jerk? Yup. Did she feel better for not having me snap at her? You bet she did.

Sometimes you have to wonder: who's helping whom?

It's my aunt's eighty-fourth birthday, and I wanted to make sure I called her before the day got too far along; I'd have hated to get caught up in something else and forget later. I was a tiny bit worried when I phoned around noon and her message box was full. Had something happened to her, and no one told me?

When I reached her later, I found out that she was out doing a bunch of errands, and by the time she got back she was delighted to find her phone had no more room for good wishes. That's no surprise. Tessie is justifiably popular and beloved. Also, she never sits still. She'll call and say, "I just found an old picture you'd like," or she'll alert you she came upon something you love in a store, and bang! she's at your door with it in seven minutes.

I often use a line, "It's like calling your old aunt," by which I mean something is so dreadful you keep putting it off, all the while knowing that the longer you wait, the more you'll have to pay emotionally when you finally do it. It's a universal feeling, but believe me, I do *not* mean Aunt Tessie. She is a joy. She and Uncle Bud, her husband, were my parents' best friends, and now she is the only one left of the four. Her kids are my best friends, and now I am one of her kids, too.

Calling an old aunt on her birthday is a good deed by anyone's standards, but the truth is, she is our rock, and a ton of fun, besides. She doesn't care to entertain anymore, so instead, she is always Open for Breakfast. For the last several years, you'll find any or all of her children in her kitchen of a morning. Poached eggs on Portuguese bread: that's all she serves, and it's spectacular. This is the family round table: it's where the town gossip is relayed, family meals are planned, and most important, it's where lengthy summer discussions take place about which beach today, whose car, and what kind of sandwiches.

I look forward to these breakfasts more than I can say. While visiting with her one morning recently, I got a little sentimental and said, "Not to be maudlin, but I will remember these years of coming here like this the rest of my life." Tessie laughed and zinged back, "Who says *you're* going to outlive *me*?"

SEPTEMBER 18

Stimulate the economy.

Today was a beautiful Saturday; I'd been working awfully hard; and I really just felt like I wanted to get out, walk the streets, and treat myself. I had a hundred-dollar bill left from a birthday gift, so I slipped it into my pocket and set off, deciding I would try to shop with a rule of thumb in mind:

purchase things from only small businesspeople for the rest of the day.

First thing I bought was a good fake Patek Philippe watch on the street. That probably crosses all sorts of moral lines for a lot of people, but hey, they're still individual vendors, trying to make a living. Then it was a hop up the street to a hip Japanese shop, where I spied a cool little white stapler—just what I needed! (Full disclosure: I thought this store was just a fab one-off, but it turned out to be an international chain. I really think I can't be blamed, since everything in the store was written in Japanese. I guess that should have been a hint, but I thought it was an affectation.)

Next, a walk among the street vendors. Here I bought a hot-looking leather bracelet for a friend's birthday. A little more wandering, and by now I'd gotten hungry. Shoehorned into the oddest little space—the whole restaurant was probably ten feet wide and thirty-five feet long, with a few tables scattered outside—was a taqueria. I got myself an early dinner, sat outside, and watched the world go by. A drop-in at a candy shop on my way home (season's first candy corn!), and my spree was complete. Oh, except for a man I gave some change to on the subway. His wish to me: "Here's to a better day tomorrow. Bless you and your family." How could tomorrow get any better than this?

This was a pricey afternoon for me, even though I came in under a Benjamin at $98.20. But I had helped four working stiffs like me, a person with no job at all, and, mistakenly, one Japanese conglomerate. And that's how the world works. Money changing hands, one dollar at a time.

Take an extra minute with someone.

I had clocked out and was leaving the store tonight when a customer I like a lot waved me over and stopped me. She had a question about a travel guide and needed an alternative to what she had selected. We went back over to the computer to check out other books, had a conversation, then made a decision, and I wished her bon voyage. This all took about five minutes. It wasn't a big deal. But I was really ready to go and had to try hard not to look it.

In a way, I owed this woman nothing; in fact, I had something on her. One of the first times we met, she rushed into the store early in the morning, totally rattled. This is the way someone comes into a doctor's office or police station, but not a bookstore.

"I need a copy of *Eat, Pray, Love* right away," she said breathlessly. "I don't know what came over me," she babbled. "I just lied to a whole table full of people."

"What happened?" I was intrigued.

"I was just at a business breakfast, and people were talking about books, and the woman next to me asked me if I've read *Eat, Pray, Love*. I said yes, and that I, too, had loved it. But I haven't read it at all! This big, fat lie just flew right out of my mouth. So now," she said and hung her head, "I need to read it right away." She felt mortified, and oddly cleansed for telling me, and I loved her for it.

So naturally I've had a soft spot in my heart for this lady ever since. I smile every time she walks in, knowing we have this secret bookish bond between us. How could you not immediately like someone who confided in you like that?

So when she came to ask for a little advice because she was flying to Paris the next day—something I ordinarily would have felt just fine hating a person for—I was happy to stay a few extra minutes to help out.

Now I just have to remember to do the same for everyone who asks, without making a face.

Cajole someone.

Listen, the U.S. Postal Service is never, ever going to recover from that bad rap they got after that guy shot everybody. I mean, really, "going postal" has to be part of our vernacular? It wasn't bad enough when the *Oxford English Dictionary* added "bad hair day" and "bromance"?

People often seem to be in a bad mood at their jobs. It's not fair to buttonhole the post office; bad moods are often just a combination of having to do a repetitive thing a billion times a day and dealing with customers who are crabby. People on the customer service line, the grocery store cashier, a bus driver. They're not like that at home, I'll bet: let's call it an occupational hazard.

I thought I was in for an easy ride today when I walked into the post office: it was twenty minutes before closing, and not a soul in line. Of course, lots of folks are already away for the weekend.

"I should have done all my Christmas shopping today and packed it up," says me to Tina, my post office employee. No response.

I have twenty-five–plus of the same package to send, and I put them all on the scale. Tina gives me the evil eye. "This isn't a super-techno machine," she snaps. "One at a time."

"Sorry—I thought it would be easiest if you had them all at once."

"Nope."

"Then tell me what to do," I plead. "Make like an assembly line and just keep putting them on the scale?"

"That's what I'm trying to say," she says.

I know what to do next. We get into a talk about the Job, what she doesn't like about it, how she always thought, growing up, that she wanted to work there. Why is it so bad? The people are crabby, says Tina, they hate waiting, and they're pissed by the time they get to her. What fun can there be in a job like that?

"Well," I say, "I already knew who you were, because I've been at your window before, and I knew that ordinarily you're really nice."

Tina smirks, because I nailed her a little. We go on to talk about her daughter, my job, customers who are jerks, and what do you know—suddenly it's five p.m. and time for Tina to go home. Me, too.

Do what you can.

Though I am happy to open my wallet when I can if some-one is in need, I don't want this to be the fallback action of my One Good Deed a day—anyone can figure out how to do that. It seems the easy way out, like giving up something that makes you fat for Lent.

But giving is a good way to keep perspective, and I find that since starting my Good Deed project, I've made it an unwritten rule to at least try to find some pocket change for everyone who needs it.

But a chain of grocery stores near me requests an offer-ing for something so frequently that frankly, it can be annoy-ing. And then I feel *guilty* that I'm annoyed. You know how it is: it's not that you don't want to give, but you feel a little like you're always getting hit up. Still, I like to think this super-market's corporate office is a philanthropic one, and that the stores are doing the same as I am on a larger scale, and that's why they're all right with constantly asking their customers to round up their total for donations. But when they've got the same request going on for a couple of weeks, and I stop in for just an onion, I find I want to scream, "You know I said yes yesterday, right? I say yes *a lot*!"

Recently, the ask was for seven dollars—Meals on Wheels, I think. I can't afford right now to stop in four or five times a week on my way home from work and donate seven dollars each time. But maybe I will give, just one more time.

Make a little sacrifice.

One of my best friends and her husband bought a house on Martha's Vineyard a few years ago, and though I have visited a couple of times to ooh and aah, I've never been to stay overnight. But today I've packed my pj's and am on my way.

They bought new everything when they moved in, and green and blue seems to be the color palette. I promised myself that I would be clever enough to remember that when it came time for a host present. So even though I had another gift already wrapped for her, yesterday I set off to a lovely housewares store to fetch them a little something. In green or blue.

It's a great feeling when you can tell that someone has really thought about you when bringing you a gift. Several months ago, this selfsame friend started fidgeting about how she couldn't wait to give me my birthday present: it turned out to be a wonderful pillow with a whale screened onto it, and being a *Moby-Dick* aficionado, I adored it, as she knew I would. But today, as I scoured the store for the perfect thing, I came up dry. I purchased some expensive gourmet salt, because she's a terrific cook, and I've been on a gourmet salt kick. But I felt disappointed.

However, as I was packing tonight, I glanced across the room and saw exactly what I wanted to give them: three beautiful votives I had bought at the beginning of the summer and saved until last week, when I threw a party. Royal blue, turquoise, and frosted white. When I finally lit them they were gorgeous, with a lovely glow I hadn't expected; I was thrilled I had bought them. And now I saw they were what I should be giving Martha.

Sigh. I cleaned them out from their one use and wrapped them up—she would love them, I knew. Now, you may think this is regifting, but you'd be wrong. I will be bringing a treat they'll love, while giving from the heart.

Help someone make a moment to remember.

There are few things I love more than what I call a holiday atmosphere. And by that I don't mean the Christmas Spectacular at Radio City Music Hall or a giant July Fourth fireworks display—though I do love those, too—I just mean anywhere people are all revved up on their way to something fun. Seeing folks packed up, on the move, and ready for some time off thrills me; I love being a fly on the wall, eavesdropping on their plans. They have a little frisson of excitement about them, and it's infectious.

Whether it's at a monument, on the street, or at the beach, I can't help inserting myself into people's fun by moseying up to them when they break out their camera; I offer to take a group picture, so that all of them can be in the same shot. I take great joy in doing this, though it's not always met with the glee I bring to the situation. Like today, for instance . . .

I was lucky enough to be on a ferry to beautiful Martha's Vineyard off the coast of Cape Cod, and it was stunning, the first day of autumn. I figured I had a ripe crowd. But right off the bat, one lady looked down her nose at me as she aimed at a lighthouse we were passing. "Wouldn't you like to be in the picture?" I asked eagerly. "No, it's for a painting," she sniffed. Huh. Excuse me, Picasso.

Next, a woman alone who patted her hair and worried that her inclusion in the photo would ruin the scenery. I convinced her otherwise. A pair of lanky young Russian men. A young family of four. I was on a roll. All these smiles.

See, I'm certain that later on, these people will be happy they're in the photos, whether they look their best or not. It will give the moment, and the scene, context. The photos will telegraph who they were right then, what kind of clothes they sported, what haircut they had, the expression they wore ("I forgot you came with me that day!" "I look tired." "Look how in love with him I was!").

I will never see these people again, and they won't recall who was behind the camera. But I just love being there, hearing that *click*, and knowing I'm helping to make a memory.

Protect your friendships with a designated driver.

It's been almost twenty years since I've had a drink, and though the daily Walk of Shame in my head isn't as gruesome as it once was, there is still a lifetime of payback ahead. Not only am I not drinking while everyone else is whooping it up, I often feel that I should split the dinner check evenly, just as penance. And then, of course, I'm often tapped to be the designated driver.

This weekend, I'm with a bunch of my very best friends, and everyone needs to let off some steam. So I told my girls they should feel free to party: I was set to be the one behind the wheel.

And did I mention we're on a small island, so this should have been easy, right? Wrong.

A big fog rolled in and the night's plans spun out of control.

We had two guests arriving, from different places at different times. And even though we were supposed to be having a relaxing vacation, we had a communications War Room of three computers and phones up and running in an instant.

Tension was high, the beer and wine had been broken out—but we still weren't getting the logistical travel intel that we needed. So we decided to go to the source: the airport. By the time we arrived, we could see the fog had made it impossible to fly, and Guest #1 was, sadly, crossed off our list. But could we save #2? With a barrage of calls to car services, cabs, and friends near her stopover airport of Boston, we micromanaged an arrival that involved a mad one-and-a-half-hour taxi ride with exactly one minute to spare as our beloved hurled herself onto the last ferry.

By now the girls had had a couple of pops and it was time to drive to the ferry dock for the pickup. Designated Driver's second emergency trip of the night, and it nearly killed me. Not because of the weather, but because my copilots were so wound up by then that I was lucky even to get out of the driveway what with all the shouting of orders. "You'll take a right there . . . *there*—do you see it?" "Turn left here—wait! Go to that food truck!" "What are you parking here for? Park closer!"

But finally there was the joyous reunion with lobsters all around and many toasts to our cleverness (mine with a fake beer), and as we locked up for the night—miraculously, there was a perfectly clear sky, with a full moon.

Praise is sweetest when it's a two-way street.

This is one of those things you understand better if you've been on both sides of the fence.

I had my annual job review today, and believe me, I've had plenty in the course of nearly thirty-five years in this industry. I've also given many, because in the years before I was a bookseller, I was a publishing executive. (I will take bookseller/writer any day.) But today's review was the most thoughtful, well-prepared, particular assessment I've ever received. It was so thorough I would have found it comprehensive if I were still senior management and the CEO had presented it.

These reviews are hard to prepare and give, and for what's essentially nearly a minimum-wage job, my reviewer went above and beyond. So when the review was over, I took a couple of minutes to let her know how impressive I thought it was and thank her.

It's one part of my old life I really do not miss. That and giving away holiday bonuses. Wow, that's a nasty day. You'd be surprised how much people love looking a gift horse in the mouth.

Lend a hand.

Walking home tonight, I nearly got run over by a woman pushing a box down the street. A heavy one, I guess, as she was almost horizontal to the sidewalk and giving it all she had; she was concentrating so much she didn't even see me. Where was she headed? I wondered. It turned out to be just a few yards down the street, where her boyfriend was waiting, car trunk open, to wedge in another box. These two were moving.

They were also in a precarious parking space, ticketwise, and it was just the two of them: one to lug, one to stand guard. Slow going.

So I turned around and walked back.

"You guys moving?" Duh.

"Just finishing up," said the boyfriend. "The movers came already, but this is the last of it that we didn't want to send with them."

"Have you got more stuff to bring out?" I asked, nice as pie. "Because I'm happy to stand here with your car for a bit if it'll help." (I didn't offer to actually *carry* stuff. Oh, how I hate carrying.)

They looked askance. They were too polite to say, We think you'll take our most precious belongings. I don't think I looked especially dangerous; I had a bag of tacos and was carrying a novel. Still, they didn't know me, and I was offering to hang on to their car keys in case a cop came along. So I offered to give them my driver's license, and then they were too embarrassed—and exhausted—to say no.

Three more trips for him, two for her, and they had stuffed every inch of their little Camry that they possibly could.

Where were they going? To Brooklyn, to a bigger place and a tiny yard to share with the neighbors upstairs. As tired as they were, they were also clearly very excited. They squeezed into the car, I put one more huge box on her lap, and off they went, *toot-toot*, into their next chapter.

SEPTEMBER 27

Help a friend along his way.

I was having a relaxing evening, watching a little ridiculous TV, when out of the corner of my eye I spotted a big, dark spot on the carpet across the living room. A leaf? A piece of a chocolate bar I somehow overlooked? Upon closer—if reticent—inspection: a cricket. Although a city dweller, I'm on the ground floor of a high-rise and am lucky enough to be the person everybody hates: someone with a yard.

Come fall, the crickets start to chirp in my little paradise (which I refer to as the Shangri-La Surf & Swim Club, because it sports a plastic swimming pool), but they'd never gone so far as to come in for a visit (and how I wish I could say the same about the mice).

But I digress. Now my new roommate started to chirp, which is nice outside, but not so great for *Real Housewife* viewing. So I did what people have been doing for centuries: trapped him in a drinking glass, slid a piece of paper underneath, and let him back out into the wilds of East Eightieth Street.

Believe me, I had learned my lesson with the bad luck that befell me after I had to kill a dragonfly while watching the opening ceremonies of the Olympics in China (I kid you not). You can only imagine the karmic fallout.

SEPTEMBER 28

Never assume your help isn't wanted.

Many years ago I immersed myself in committee and board work. Frankly, my volunteer life sort of dropped into my lap, beginning with a call from a friend asking for assistance chairing an event. In I dove. I had done some stuff here and there before, sure, but this phone call also coincided with my mother's death and my stopping drinking. So now I was sad and I had no idea what people did with their evenings. I was an easy target, ripe with raw emotion and lots of spare time.

Right away, I loved it. I made friends; it felt like family; we did lots of good. Before long, I realized the dirty little secret of volunteering: that you get far more out of it than any organization could ever get out of you.

But after about a dozen years, when I started to concentrate seriously on a writing career at the age of fifty-two, I felt I had to put all my free time into what I call my "cottage industry," and I left the volunteer world behind for a while.

Tonight I put my toe back in.

I went to a party for an organization where I formerly served on the board of directors. I want to become involved again. For several years, I was a member of the grants committee, a vital part of this organization's work. A portion of the money it raises annually is set aside to help local like-minded folks to grow and develop. For example, a tiny new group may send us a proposal saying if they only had three thousand dollars, they could set themselves up with a computer, a printer, and some stamps: with that they could send out a mailing and get more members. The following year, we might get a proposal from that same group. For another five thousand, we could help them rent an office, get a phone; then they are a real organization, up and running, doing good deeds of their own. It's progress you can see, and it's extremely gratifying.

But I had one worry about serving on this committee, as I told the executive director, an old, dear friend. "Remember, I'm a writer," I warned, "and this may be a year with no big donation from me."

She laughed and gave me a hug. "We'd love to have you back," she said. "The beauty of working on this committee is that you don't have to *have* money to give it away."

Pay your own way.

I've said here that as a part of my Good Deed quest, I've begun to put at least a few coins in the cup, guitar case, or whatever of just about everyone I pass who seems to be in need. Today, in omitting a donation, I believe I have performed a passive good deed for a panhandler.

This is the second time in a couple of months I've seen the same setup: a lazy-ass twenty-something sitting on the sidewalk, doing absolutely nuthin', with a cardboard sign that says:

TRAVELING
RAN OUT OF MONEY
Please help!

What, are you kidding me? Stay home if you don't have enough money to go on a trip! Or audition for *The Amazing Race* if you want to see the world. But unless you do a little soft shoe, strum a guitar, or offer to come clean my crib, I am not going to give *you* money to backpack around the country.

Obviously, *he* doesn't realize I'm doing him a good deed—though the glare I gave him might indicate I have *something* on my mind. But in my heart I know I'm teaching him, telepathically, how to be fiscally responsible in the future. If only wishing made it so.

Learn together.

I met an early leaf-peeper today. He came back from the nature section of the store greatly disappointed.

"I can find no book on trees of New England," he said.

That seemed unlikely; perhaps other early autumnal tree lovers had beat him to the punch.

"Gee," he said forlornly, "I just wanted to check and see what a sycamore leaf looked like."

"My grandparents lived on Sycamore Street," I said. "Come on over to the desk, and maybe we can find a picture of it online." He had come to the right girl: few love an October ride in the country more than I do.

So I searched and, sure enough, found some lovely leaves to virtually peep at. We had a nice conversation about the sycamore leaf versus the maple: their similar lobes, the width of the leaf, their color come fall. It was an oddly rewarding conversation; one of those things that was so much more fun to learn together, even with someone you've never met before. Like the smile you give the stranger next to you after sitting together at a movie: a shared experience.

Follow the leader.

Some time ago, I interviewed world-famous breast cancer activist Dr. Susan Love for a book I was writing. At the time, I wrote, "She is adamant. She is kind. She is adamant. She is funny. But oh, she is adamant. What she is adamant about is eradicating breast cancer, and she is determined to do it in her lifetime." And she believes research will help us find the answer.

Back then, the Love/Avon Army of Women initiative was quite new, but I had already signed up and was spreading the word. The plea below is from an action alert for October 1, 2010, and it is directed at women—but women can join any old day, and men can help by urging their mothers, sisters, girlfriends, and wives to add their names to the growing roster.

The pledge they want bloggers to take today is to give a shout-out to women everywhere—on Facebook, on Twitter, on their own blogs, wherever—to help their campaign to reach one million people. So I spread the word, and I know I persuaded at least a couple of women to join the ranks. The goal is to recruit:

> ONE MILLION WOMEN of all ages and ethnicities, with or without breast cancer, to sign up and participate in breast cancer research studies. If we can get ONE MIL-

LION WOMEN involved in research, we are one step closer to understanding the cause of breast cancer and how to prevent it.

The Army of Women campaign is an online initiative, and women can sign up at www.armyofwomen.org. The members are contacted via eBlast to participate in groundbreaking research on breast cancer prevention. They can sign up for the studies online; if they do not qualify, they are encouraged to forward the information to a friend or family member. Every woman over eighteen is welcome to participate, whether a breast cancer survivor or someone never affected.

Together we can move breast cancer beyond a cure and eradicate it once and for all.

<hr>

OCTOBER 2

Be thoughtful.

Now I'm going to say I live in a doorman building, and right away you're going to think that's snooty. But it's not Park Avenue over here, believe me. My building was constructed in the 1960s, and I have the same refrigerator in my rental apartment that they dragged in on the day they gave the first occupant the key. (Only last year did I get a new stove.)

My doormen are a bunch of very nice guys, some of whom have been here ten, fifteen years. They wear uniforms but no hats, no white gloves, nothing like that. They don't always get up to open the door. They start to move a little faster around the holidays, but that's only human nature. If I thought better behavior could garner Christmas tips for booksellers, I'd be all over it.

Still, they perpetually have a warm hello for me whenever I come and go, and as I live alone and write at home, there are days when they're the only people I talk to. I imagine their jobs to be interminably boring, except for the parts where tenants bring home unsuitable people in the dead of night. They've seen me do that, too, and not a peep about it the next day. Plus, they give you your FedEx packages. So, in short, they are invaluable.

Tonight, knowing I needed to work late, I stepped out to the deli to get a cup of coffee and offered to get a cup for the doorman, too. The other downside of his job, of course (besides having to be nice to everyone), is that he can rarely leave his post. You would have thought I'd offered him liquid gold.

And, of course, if now I find I can't fall asleep, I have someone to talk to.

OCTOBER 3

Compassion is always welcome.

I have a friend—more of an acquaintance, really—who is a famous bestselling author. Sounds like a perfect life to me, but tonight I saw that, of course, she's just like the rest of us.

Out on the road to promote her new book, she's away from her family and evidently feeling pensive, even a little blue. Everyone was on Facebook and Twitter saying, "Congrats on your new book!" and "See you in Seattle next week!" and stuff like that. And she was right there with them, updating fans and being gleeful about a great new review. But there was an undercurrent there. Here was the conversation she and I had among the other tweets and posts:

SHE: I'm so excited to launch my book, and so very sad my dad didn't live to see this.

ME: I feel the same. Both my parents. Feel for you.

SHE: Thanks. What a shame, huh?

ME: Yes, sure is. But your friends are very proud, and soon your son will understand [he's about six] and will be, too.

SHE: Now he's just mad at me for being away. Sigh.

ME: Buck up, little soldier. This is the best of times. You're just tired.

SHE: Word. Very tired.

That's all. But I like to think it was a tiny voice in the chaos. Good chaos, but still chaos.

Everyone loves a good neighbor.

I've spoken before about buying local, but today was like extreme locavoring, and I got a kick out of it.

I don't live far from work, about three-quarters of a mile, and I try to mix it up on my walk home every day by taking various different routes down different blocks. And, as always in New York City, there's something around every corner that'll just knock you out.

There's a very cute little Italian restaurant called Vespa, with, yes, a sage-colored eponymous scooter painted with polka dots out front. But for cute, the scooter has lately taken a backseat. This summer, all set up on the sidewalk in front of the restaurant, a model-handsome guy has appeared several times a week selling produce from somewhere nearby. I don't know why, but the combination of the eatery I like plus the beautiful boy and vegetables just kills me.

I stopped today for a five-dollar basket of ten tomatoes ("Next week will be the last ones") and noticed the purveyor had changed from tight Italian biker jersey to corduroy jacket. Guess I may have to put more locavoring off until spring . . . although he did say something about selling Christmas trees.

Those who can, teach.

Oh, this day really didn't look like it was ever going to turn around.

However, when I got home from a particularly grueling day, a fantastic comment was awaiting me from someone who tracked me down because of a children's book I wrote. Elementary school principal Glenn Malone wrote to say he had been chosen as Washington State's Most Distinguished Principal and was heading to a celebration in Washington, DC. Each awardee was asked to bring a "state token" to gift the other states' winners—nice idea. I have written several books for kids in a series called State Shapes—including one for the state of Washington. This was what Glenn wanted to bring to show off his home turf.

I'd like to say money and the fame don't matter to a writer; however, I'd be lying. But if you don't think Glenn Malone's request turned this day—this week—around, well ... you know it did. The publisher, Black Dog & Leventhal, and I were more than thrilled to be asked to help out Principal Malone—the publisher sent fifty copies for the event. I sell books every day, but it's not every day I get to help educate.

Be counted.

Every now and again you'll get an e-mail or see on a social media site that an organization is asking you to vote for them. Don't be so fast to ignore these, please! It's easy to rush for the delete button and count them as spam, but very often they're not. The past few years have seen an uptick in this kind of public popularity contest, and they're often pitting a number of very reputable do-gooder companies or agencies against each other for a grant or cash prize. (For some corporations, doling out this dough may be their self-congratulatory way of giving back to the world, but that's another matter entirely.)

Today I came home and saw one of these pleas, and I happily voted for an organization that I admire. This is a terrific, easy way to support causes you care about, without always having to loosen your own purse strings. As in all contests, political or otherwise, your vote matters.

A little to you can be a lot to them.

I was rushing down the sidewalk to a meeting this morning and heard some odd, haunting music: it sounded like Pan's pipes.

It turned out to be a homeless man, and my guess is that he had no idea how to play—but somehow it still sounded ... so *pretty*. So there I was, now a hundred yards past him, still listening and thinking about the beauty of the music, and I figured, I've got to go back and give this guy a little change.

No change. I had a crumpled single but was headed to the bank after my meeting anyway, so what the hell?

So I doubled back, and he was still playing furiously. He had a cup, but without even a dime in it. I gave him my last dollar, and I realized that now it was his last dollar, too. I thought about the difference between my last dollar and his, and that was when I began to cry, with the trill of the pipes following me down the street.

OCTOBER 8

Failure evidently is an option.

In social media lingo we would call it an #epicfail.

I did good for no one today.

I was exhausted, and I stayed in the house the entire day.

I watched old movies. I didn't answer the phone. I ordered in Chinese food.

So, it has come to this. A day without a good deed. Did I really expect I could make things better, even a tiny bit, every day of the year?

No, I guess not. And surely there will be more days like this. It reminds me of the lyrics from that old standard, "Pick Yourself Up."

I guess I need to start all over again.

It's not like the world can't get along perfectly well without my efforts. I'll just have to see if I can't redouble them tomorrow.

OCTOBER 9

Don't be so sure.

You know how you learn when you're a kid that we use only 10 percent of our brain, but that scientists believe there's huge potential for that other, unused 90 percent? I have long insisted that there's a part of that dormant brain—and it gets bigger and bigger the older you get—which I like to call "Too Late to Ask." You know the section of your noggin I mean. It's stuff you knew, but now you've forgotten. So you wind up asking yourself questions like: Have they gotten divorced? Is her mother dead yet? Is there still a Yugoslavia? Did I date you? For me, the problem with these questions—and so many more!—is that it's Too Late to Ask. The window of opportunity-without-embarrassment is long past.

The kid behind the counter at my corner market falls into this category. My theory is that he's the son of the owner, but I don't know that, because I've never asked him. He's been there about five years, so he's the "new guy" to me: I've been going there thirty-plus years. He's a real card, this guy. His most frequent line, when he hands you your change, is "Enjoy the weather." Dead of winter, middle of the night, it doesn't matter. It's funny because it's old. But the last two Saturday mornings I've been in there around seven, which is very unusual. Last week he said, "Going dancing tonight? It's Saturday." I gave him a half answer; I was half awake. This time he said, "I'm going out tonight. Dancing. Hookers." Now I realized he's been trying to bait me, get an answer, see what kind of stuff I'm made of.

"Sounds good," I replied, "and I'm saying nuthin' about that wedding ring you're wearing."

In this kind of exchange, which we all go through several times a day, it's usually the worker who's in a trance, isn't it? But he's really making an effort. I'll bet it's a game with him: how many people can I snap out of their reverie?

"You know," I finally said, after half a decade of these hijinks have been going on, "I'm sorry to say I don't even know your name."

"Teddy," he replied, shaking my outstretched hand. "And I'm glad we finally met."

Huh. I thought he didn't even know who I was. Guess it wasn't Too Late to Ask after all.

Take a breath.

It's easy to let hours, days, sometimes weeks go by without stopping to be in the here and now. Time is a commodity, and we work hard trying to slow it down—so hard that it's tough to actually live in it.

I pass along here an e-mail from my friend Peter, who was shaken terribly by a tragedy today. He has been working with the government, rebuilding houses—actually, entire towns—in Haiti after the earthquake; but this happened only blocks from his apartment in Miami.

> I go to deco market yesterday. Lady in front of me, a real charmer. Chatting with checkout girl. Great warm smile. She pays and leaves.
>
> I am paying for my stuff and there is a huge ugly wreck sound.
>
> The woman was hit by a car.
>
> Dead.
>
> I am unnervingly unhinged about fragility of life.

Sad as this is—and none of us will ever even know this woman's story, never mind her name—I was pleased Peter sent it along. It made me stop a minute and catch my breath. I hope it does the same for you. I feel like I should read this every day.

Tell your truth.

I understand that not every reader will agree about gay civil rights, about same-sex marriage, but I hope each one of you understands what it means to be frightened: not just by bullies but by people who wish you, and may even *do* you, harm. And take it from me, this is not just teens: as an adult, I've been scared plenty.

For the LGBT population, National Coming Out Day is one of the most effective ways to spread the word that I, and millions of others like me, am not very different from you.

I've seen it work scores of times. This year on National Coming Out Day, I had the opportunity to come out to someone while at work. I had a conversation with a man about several books he was considering taking along on a vacation. We had similar taste in espionage and thrillers, it seemed, until he brought up a book by conservative Glenn Beck. When he asked me my opinion—a personal opinion, mind you, so I deemed my answer appropriate—I took a deep breath and said, "Well, I'm gay, and that's something I would never dream about touching."

He didn't blink; he didn't comment. But it registered. And that was all I cared about.

You don't have to be there to relive it.

Being a creature of habit, every year on Columbus Day I write an e-mail to some old friends of the family. They own a little house in the woods, and when they purchased it many years ago, they blazed some trails, just for fun. And each October 12, because I wanted to feel like Christopher Columbus discovering America, my dad would take me and my cousin Mimi there on a hike.

My friends are now quite old, but they remember it almost as fondly as I do, I think, so every year I get in touch on this day to say hi. If I'm in town, I bring them a pumpkin. It's both a tip of the hat to thank them for all their years of kindness and a sweet, funny memory to share all over again.

Do the best you can under the circumstances.

I was heading for a cup of coffee today in the store when there was a huge *ka-boom* right behind me: clearly a combo platter of a person and an upset table of books. I turned, and there was a man, fallen and flailing around on the tile floor. He was round, very round, and so it seemed he was having a hard time gaining some purchase on the floor. This is said not to make fun of him, but he seemed to keep rolling and not stop; it was hard to know how to help him. Within seconds, however, there I was with another store employee and a customer by his side.

"Are you all right?"

"Can I help you?"

"Let me get you a chair."

In the meantime, I was not so sure this man was running on a hundred percent: he seemed confused, he had a few crumpled bags full of random stuff, and I wondered if everything he was carrying had been purchased legitimately, since a spanking new red plastic purse skittered across the floor. He looked stunned but began to try to get to his feet.

This is where the good deed gets tricky.

Life has become litigious, and most offices, companies, and retail establishments warn employees to be careful about touching people, lifting people, even taking a lost kid by the hand. What if we wrench his back, hurt his neck? What if he or his family comes back and *says* we did?

So we all stood there with our hands outstretched, in case he reached out, praying he wouldn't.

When did doing a good deed start being a money question and not a moral question?

Give what you can.

About twenty years ago I became involved with a foundation as one of its first board members; in fact, I chaired its first fund-raising dinner, as well as several future dinners—including a very successful one where the keynote speaker was the then president Bill Clinton. In recent years the ticket price has escalated, while my income has not.

During these less lucrative times, two friends have asked me annually to sit at their table as their guest. It's a lovely gesture on their part, not just because of the money, but because it's a nod to my emeritus status, and it makes me feel so special, even though I'm no longer directly involved with the organization. It's a really nice good deed on their part, that's for sure.

So I promised myself that on the day of the event, I'd make a donation in the spirit of the evening. I did, and I loved the way it gave me a feeling of being part of the festivities, no matter how small.

Sometimes a gift just belongs to someone else.

I have been hoarding this gift card for months. And it's from Target, my fave shopping haunt.

But this month I've got a million bills to pay, and cash flow is but a trickle. And yet it's Cousin Suzy's birthday, and I want to buy her a present.

Now, I could wait and give her something later, but that's no fun, and it also looks like I don't care, which is not the case. I wasn't in town on the actual birthday, when the rest of the family got together to celebrate, so I'm already a bit of a slacker. Now I'm here, and so is the lava-hot gift card in my hand.

Hmmm . . . There's something she'd love—*I'd* love. And here's the card, good as gold. There goes my treat for myself, and hello to a great birthday present.

She loves it.

OCTOBER 16

Find your own way to join in.

My friend Melissa came to town all the way from Minnesota with a gaggle of women from work to participate in the two-day thirty-nine-mile Avon Walk for Breast Cancer.

I had other obligations, work stuff, so I couldn't have done the walk anyway (I told myself). But still I felt bad.

Earlier in the week I had asked Melissa about her plans and told her I'd come out and cheer her on. At the time, I had no idea how big this event was: these folks do a marathon-length walk on day one, sleep in tents, and get up and start all over on a half marathon. *And* they raise money to participate.

So as Melissa and the rest of her team neared my part of town, I decided to cook up some pesto pasta and dig out a bottle of red. They had been at this eight hours already, and it was pretty cold out. Carbo loading, I figured, and four p.m. didn't seem too early to warm up with a little grape of the vine.

Here they came: I did a little cheer, and they waved happily, if tiredly, stopping for a quick cappellini respite and tucking the wine away for later. They seemed thrilled, and somehow I'd found my own way to help the cause.

And talk about things being returned tenfold. Later on I got this e-mail from my buddy:

> I did this walk two years ago in San Francisco with one friend. I felt a huge sense of accomplishment because I'd raised $3,400 on my own for the charity, and walked a kajillion miles across the Bay Area. Along the way, and particularly at the end, people's family and friends had been there cheering them on and holding signs about how awesome they were and what an accomplishment it was to finish. My friend and I were all alone; no one was there to cheer us on. It was kind of a huge bummer. The friendship you showed today was super-heartwarming and extremely generous.

And here I thought I was a bum. Ain't perception a funny thing?

Charity.

My aunt Tessie tells me tales of her great-great-uncle André. About people gathering in the middle of the night outside her childhood home in New Bedford, Massachusetts, waiting for his annual summer arrival, hoping for favors, some help out of the gut of America's Great Depression, waiting for miracles.

André was a Holy Cross Brother in Canada in the early twentieth century. Today, more than seventy years after his death, André Bessette is being canonized in the Vatican. How I wish I could be there; how I wish I could have brought Tessie there to see *this* miracle happen. A saint in our family! (And though for me, he is a saint-by-marriage, not a blood relative, I could not be prouder.)

They called him "the Miracle Man of Montreal": he was renowned for curing people, especially cancer patients. And though I may have my own problems with being a Roman Catholic, I do believe in miracles. I believe in ghosts, too, if you're asking, and aliens. But when I say "miracle," I mean something wondrous and impossible and life changing. Aunt Tessie says when he arrived every summer, the kids would open the car trunk to get his bags, and it would be filled with the crutches, canes, and braces of people he had stopped to visit along the way.

Think what you like about miracles, or religion, or faith. I know this: a little man who was too sickly to become a priest—whose job it was to answer the door, wash floors, and clean—went on to change countless lives and, yes, become a saint.

I mean, who becomes a saint nowadays? I could do worse for someone to look up to.

In fact, the announcement that André would be canonized was one of the things that made me decide to try this One Good Deed project. It's pretty clear I'm no saint, but I am inspired by him to do a little better, and maybe open a door or two myself.

OCTOBER 18

Be gracious.

Scene from a bookstore:

"I need these wrapped."

OK, not a problem. Happy to.

"They're very heavy."

Not.

"My back hurts, and I don't want to carry them."

Mayhaps you should have stayed home.

Übernice me: "Would you like me to carry these out to the street when we're done?"

"Yes."

Up the escalator, out to busy street. "Shall I hail you a cab?" Sweet. Oh, so sweet.

"Yes."

I get a cab, place her bags inside, hold the door open, help her in.

"All set?" I beam.

"Yes. Thank you," she barks as an afterthought. Not once in these ten minutes has she smiled. Or even looked me in the eye.

And yet I manage to remember: Graciousness always wins.

Acknowledge your life; light a candle.

It's a symbol more than anything else. My religious beliefs are uncertain. Nevertheless, I find it familiar and comforting to be there.

Today I went to church to light a candle.

I don't really know who I'm praying to, or even if I'm praying. I don't know if I'm talking to someone else, or to myself. Many years of therapy taught me that a lot of the work on that couch is about reminding yourself, week after week, to see what your life is really about, not what you wish or imagine or hate about it. The reality of it.

I grew up in a religion that despises gay people, over-looks and undercuts women, and has more than a few pedo-philes. I am ashamed of all of this, yet I find physically being in a church extremely peaceful. Nor can I completely write off my years of religious upbringing; it instilled in me many of the morals and values I turn to today.

So when I light a candle, what am I doing? I say hello to my parents and send them my love wherever they are. I pray that I will do the best job possible in writing this book, and that it will be a success, and that people will admire it and it will inspire them to a good deed, too. I think of all my friends who are unhappy, out of work, ill, lost: I ask that their lives improve. I thank God, or whoever, for any recent good news or successes I am enjoying; rejoice that my life is on track; and hope that it continues that way. I pray that I might be able to pay my bills this month.

I guess I just light a candle and concentrate on what's going on. Stop the world a minute, breathe. Consider the fact that a flame is still burning somewhere.

OCTOBER 20

Share the burden.

This morning, exiting the subway, one woman with a stroller was left behind. Everyone brushed past her, not even paus-ing to hold open the door. So I stopped, kept it open so she could slip through, and offered to help her carry her daughter up the stairs in her stroller.

A warning: Kids are much heavier than they look. Or used to be. Whatever.

Up on the street, I poked the baby. "You," I wheezed, "are much heavier than you look." No response. Kids these days.

Include someone else in your daily chores.

"Grrrrr!" said Nan, pal and coworker. "I'll never be able to find it!"

The elusive Shabby Chic Shower Curtain.

"I've been to three Targets, and they're all sold out," she moaned. "I. Must. Have. it!"

"Let's check the store near my house in Massachusetts," I offered. I was headed up there a few days hence, and frankly, it was no skin off my back. I have a little bit of a Target problem, though I like to think it's an addiction that's under control.

To judge from the website, my chances looked promising, so I took on the project. Telling myself I needed to help Nan out, I headed to the Big Red Bull's-eye within hours of my arrival—and there was the coveted curtain.

I snapped it up. "Mission accomplished," I texted Nan. O happy day.

OCTOBER 22

Nice is as nice does.

I vote in New York State, but even after thirty-four years here, when asked where I'm from, I still say, "I live in New York, but I'm from Massachusetts." I'm a small-town Bay State girl at heart and devoted to my hometown of New Bedford, the "Whaling City" and departure port for Ishmael and the *Pequod* in Herman Melville's incomparable *Moby-Dick*.

In fact, I went to our whaling museum this afternoon for a special event. I also wanted to speak to Barney Frank, my not-congressman whom I much admire and who, I knew, would be there for the ceremony.

You see, the congressman had just done me a huge favor by giving me a quote for the jacket of an upcoming book. I was thrilled, and though I'd e-mailed him and sent him a handwritten note, I wanted to say thank you in person.

So before the festivities started, I tapped him on the shoulder, introduced myself, and thanked him profusely once more. He blinked. "My partner is reading your new book right now," he shot back, naming my last work without missing a beat. I had sent him a copy six weeks before with the thank-you note. But in a congressman's world? A little package like that is a lifetime ago. I was impressed, and so very pleased.

See what just happened there?

Dive in.

Indie Cousin Mimi, that's what I call her on Twitter. That's because she's my cousin, and she's a bookseller, too, at a great independent bookstore in Massachusetts.

I'm home for the weekend, and Baker Books, the store Mimi manages, has a booth up in a tent at something called Bioneers by the Bay, a fantastic weekend event about green and sustainable living. This year's speaker is a bestselling author and people are excited. It'll be busy.

"What time will you be free?" I asked Mimi on the phone, and she launched into the complications of the event, selling books offsite, packing up and closing down the portable shop. I told her I'd come help her and the staff break the set, as it were.

So I drove downtown, and though events were supposed to be winding down, they were hopping instead. So I got behind the table, sold a bunch of books I had never seen before about vegan things and woodstoves, and learned a few things about how a lot of forward-looking people live in this world. Then, at last, we packed up everything and put it in the truck, so they could start all over again in the morning.

(This wasn't all done entirely out of the goodness of my heart. Helping out Mimi meant we could go get pizza a little sooner.)

Help someone stay in the game, because somebody's got to win.

"I need you to do me a favor," said Aunt Tessie. She held an envelope in her hand. A trip to the post office, I thought. So tiny a favor as not even to be good deed–worthy. Easy.

"Sure. Anything for you!" I promised, with a soupçon of largesse.

What a fool I was. She handed the envelope to me, and it was like being served with a subpoena. I'd been had: it was from Publishers Clearing House.

"It says I'm a guaranteed winner." Tessie beamed.

We looked closer. "Actually," I told her, "it says someone in this mailing to about six million people is a winner."

"Well, it still could be me. Would you figure out all this and enter for me?"

But of course.

I let four days go by before I opened this hornet's nest. When I did, I cleared a big table and emptied the envelope. Early on, I found the UltraComboPrize square, which I had to stick on to the main entry form. But it would be some time before I found the Your Initials stamp, buried at the bottom of a Snowman Fleece Throw offer. And it wasn't over yet.

There were thirty-five pieces of paper, plus the envelope it all came in. (Yes, I counted.) The majority, naturally, had nothing to do with the contest: just offers of . . . let's politely call it "crap." Some of the valuable items I could have ordered:

- six-language translator

- set of ten retractable gel pens

- thirty-two-melody wireless digital doorbell

- rosary case

- Bark Off (scary handheld electronic dog trainer)

- *End Time* DVD ("Will you be ready for the Apocalypse?")

- *Great Sex for a Lifetime* DVD (or what's left of your lifetime, before the Apocalypse)

- Civil War historic newspaper compilation

- lucky glass elephant

- and much, much more!

At last I found the final stamp that I needed to process the prizewinning envelope; it was on the Money Machine offer page. It was not what *I* would call a Money Machine—this thing counts coins up to $999.99; I consider a Money Machine something that *prints* money.

No, wait! I hadn't affixed the Bingo card! It could mean an immediate five hundred dollars! What a close call!

I alerted Tessie that the job was done and drove to the mailbox. Only when I dropped it in did I realize that I had no idea what the prize was. A million dollars? A ranch house? A trip around the world? A sun-filled Caribbean vacation For Nieces Only? It better be.

Make something a little easier.

I had dinner with a friend and her son tonight. He's about fourteen years old and has been questioning his sexuality, though I don't *think* he's had any sexual experience at all yet. Still, it amazes me that kids are so open about themselves these days. When I came out to my mother—I was well into my twenties—she actually said, "Don't tell your father, it will kill him."

Anyway, this kid's mom and I were discussing an upcoming event I was attending at the local gay and lesbian center, which in New York City is called the Center and is both vast and renowned. His eyes lit up.

"There's a whole center?" he marveled. I allowed as how there was, and I briefly told him what it was like, and the kind of services they provided, even for teens. "Mom," he said, "we gotta *go* there." Imagine. In my lifetime.

So the next day I e-mailed my friend and just said that any time they'd like to go, if they'd like an escort or have any questions, to just give me a call—I'd be happy to accompany them.

They will or they won't. It doesn't matter: they know I'm here.

Be an audience.

I think it's a toss-up as to who worries more about getting a crowd when an author makes a bookstore appearance. The author, of course, wants to sell books and doesn't want to be embarrassed by an empty room. The event person at the bookstore has the exact same concerns. Believe me, the evenings are few and far between—at both the big chains and the little bookstores—when people are lining up for autographs and need to purchase wristbands in advance just for the promise of a seat. Every night is not Stephen King.

I've been on both sides of this scary street, bookseller and author. When I'm home in Massachusetts, fairly often a bunch of family members arise en masse and go to an event at our local independent store, where Cousin Mimi works, just because. Just because it's someone local who's speaking, just because we might be worried that the crowd might be sparse, just because it's our community, or just because we want to remember that there's good stuff going on out there all the time, for free. Free knowledge!

Tonight once more we rose as one and piled into the car for a bookish outing. We met the author, spoke with some neighbors we didn't know, learned a lot. Total win.

And no, we weren't the only ones there.

Clean up after yourself.

There's piggy, and then there's gross.

Here's piggy:

Today I was at Starbucks and went to pick up my Pumpkin Spice Latte at the end of the counter. I put my hand down and ugh! sticky, tacky coffee spill. OK, that's bound to happen over and over at a coffee shop. I try to clean it up as best I can (yes, people, I did spit on my hand to clean it, but not on the napkin I used to clean the counter). So my companion and I sat down, and not two minutes later did we watch a woman spill a big puddle of milk on the counter, look at it, and walk away. I went and cleaned that up, too. It's Starbucks, and there are a ton of napkins right there, which make it really easy for *everyone* to do. But never mind.

But while I'm at it, may I say a word or two about gross?

There's a certain class of women I call Squatters, and they *really* piss me off (no pun intended). Who are they? They are the "ladies" who think they're too good to sit down on a toilet seat that's not their own, but too thoughtless to clean up after themselves after they squat and tinkle all over the seat. How do they reconcile this behavior? The "I'm so clean" and "I'm so dirty" at the same time? It's a mystery.

Look out for the little guy.

Tonight I popped off to a party for an author friend who's also a devoted mother. She has an adorable daughter named Violet, and I have an adorable new kids' book named *50 States: A State-by-State Tour of the USA*. The book even has a puzzle—Violet and the book seemed made for each other.

At another party where I last spied Violet, she was commandeering a quite messy table of cupcake-making activity with some other kids. I was pretty sure my book would leave no stains in this fancy apartment where I was headed, so I grabbed one to keep Violet company during the party.

As it so happened, this turned out to be a grown-up gig, and Violet was off evidently conquering other horizons. But the book made a hit with some other parents in the house, and I'm sure Violet was happy to get a present at the end of the evening. Bases covered.

Add some extra color.

I was walking along the street, minding my own business, and suddenly spotted a gaggle of folks to my right. What ho? So I sidled over and instantly understood the excitement: a local business was advertising its services by giving away a dollars-off card—and each card was enclosed in a free plastic pumpkin. *And* the pumpkin had candy in it. I looked around; I wasn't the only grown-up taking one, though it's possible I was the only grown-up there without a kid.

There were some Skittles, a bunch of lollipops, and a Kit Kat: it was the latter I was after. And though I could have designed a beautiful tableau with the pumpkin, I decided, in the spirit of the season, to gift it. I walked for blocks and blocks, looking for a kid who might want to call this pumpkin his own, but I was foiled at every turn. Either they were napping in their strollers or they were traveling in groups or they were too young to eat candy altogether. And then I saw it: a scary, tricked-up house, complete with skeletons, cobwebs, ghosts peeking out of the windows, and a fake black cat. Perfect. I opened the gate, snuck in, and left the pumpkin at their doorstep.

Who's tricking who now?

Anything is something.

Though filled with good intentions, a lot of folks are surprised, I think, when they offer to volunteer at a soup kitchen on Thanksgiving. They mean well, but events like this are overrun with offers from people who—sorry to be frank—just want to give a few hours at their convenience. Most agencies that perform services like this want a person to sign up for a particular time slot and commit to it for several months. All those Tuesday mornings or Saturday afternoons when you'd rather be doing something else. They are not there to assuage your guilt.

But there are other things you can do, and I believe in the age-old collection boxes for food donations that your school, church, synagogue, grocery store, and other neighborhood places put out.

So today, and every time over the next few weeks when I shop, I vow to purchase some food for someone else and find just the right box to put it in.

Make a big deal out of something little.

Geez, remember how big a deal it was to get your Halloween costume when you were little? How many times you tried it on (store-bought or handmade) beforehand? And then, the biggest worry of all:

Would your parents make you wear a *sweater* over it?

So here was my promise to myself today: to comment on the costume of every kid I saw.

From the morning until I left in the evening, kid after kid came in the store. I mistook a couple of dragons for dinosaurs, a butterfly for a fairy (and then, a fairy for a butterfly), but all in all, I was pretty accurate. And it was as I thought: these kids just wiggle and beam when you notice them. Often you're complimenting them on one of their very first choices in life, and it's thrilling. Later, going home on the bus, I noticed the bus driver doing the same thing. I was way in the back, and I'd hear him saying, "See you, sunflower girl! Bye-bye, french fries!" I told him I'd been following his lead all day, and his theory was simple: "Well, yeah. You *got* to."

So coming down the street, nearing home, I passed a monster and a devil girl. I said an appropriate "Eek!" and asked a few pertinent questions, then noticed she was waving around a dollar bill. "Are you giving away money?" I asked. Devil Girl was nonplussed. "No. We were in the pizza place, and a man told us he liked our costumes, and then he gave us this dollar!"

Best part of the night: after I said good night to this little family, I heard the mom say, "Vera, do you see how that man gave you the dollar, and asked for nothing in return? Do you think you could do that?"

Hold on to hope.

I tried. I really did.

Knowing tomorrow was an important election day, I decided I would find a candidate who needed volunteers and I'd go out and work the streets the night before the election.

First I e-mailed an acquaintance at city hall. He asked me if I could travel to another borough, and I said yes. That was the last I heard from him.

So this morning, I went online to a group that I heard was organizing volunteers. Clicked on a candidate and was brought to his headquarters. "Contact Susan if you want to help." Ah, good, here we go.

I contacted Susan. "Great," she e-mailed back, "I'm sending this along to our volunteer coordinator, Lauren."

Lauren got back to me. "Actually, now I'm going to forward you right over to the party's central volunteer bureau. Here's the e-mail address." Grand.

"Terrific!" said Daniel later via e-mail. "Can you work both today *and* tomorrow?" Yes! I replied. Just tell me where and when.

And then, I never heard another thing.

I'm sorry, but you know what I'm thinking. Is this the way government works?

I tried today. I really did.

Full disclosure: I did receive a call from my original contact the next day, with apologies and information if I wanted to help on election day.

NOVEMBER 2

Stand up and speak out.

I went to vote this morning, and I got choked up, as I do every single time.

There is no better good deed than voting. None.

And to anyone who doesn't take advantage of this right: you are a fool.

NOVEMBER 3

If you love it, someone else will, too.

I had to have them. But I couldn't have them all.

I'm talking gourds. I went by a fancy gourmet store this morning, and it had a tableau of autumnal splendor—cornstalks, pumpkins, Indian corn, and baskets and baskets of gourds—all colors, shapes, and sizes.

I bought ten, but I felt guilty having them all for myself. OK, I kept three, but the others I gave away throughout the day—I even gave one to a favorite customer and another to a lady on the bus.

I guess it would be overkill to say I was spreading nature's bounty, but it was pretty fun to hand over a gourd on the M79.

"If you believe you're writing a novel, we believe you're writing a novel, too."

This motto comes from an odd yet increasingly popular group. There's a cool thing that's been going on for several years now called NaNoWriMo—you may already know about it. It stands for National Novel Writing Month. Another one of its adages is "Thirty Days and Nights of Literary Abandon," and that pretty much tells it all. It's a self-challenge to write fifty thousand words of a novel in this one month. It sounds impossible to me, but tons of people do it, and it's become a brotherhood; in 1999, twenty-one people got on board; now writers number around two hundred thousand.

If you go to the website, you'll see it's pretty full of fun; founder Chris Baty says he opted for November "to more fully take advantage of the miserable weather." As a participant you can check in online and get a pep talk, confab with other writers, and more. Everyone who gets to fifty thousand words—and once you register with NaNoWriMo, they'll verify your word count—is declared a winner.

I started to find that there were booksellers in my store who were "WriMos," and some of my buddies on Twitter were, too. Now, writing is hard, I'm here to tell you that, and just because you put fifty thousand words on paper, it surely does not mean you're a novelist. However: if you spend this month slaving over your novel-in-progress and put that much sweat into it, I salute you, friend, no matter how good or bad you might be at it.

And I'm not one to talk: I've published lots of books but have had no luck with fiction. So I try to give a cheer as often as possible all month long to all the WriMos I know, whether in person or electronically. I urge you to do the same—it's a hell of a lot of work. Maybe you'd like to try it yourself next year.

NOVEMBER 5

One good deed.

I can't believe I've come this far.

Today I'm one hundred days into the One Good Deed project, and frankly, I'm surprised at both the experience and its results. Most people who know about my blog and book ask the same thing when I see them in person: what good deed are you going to do today?

At the start, I worried that I wouldn't be able to find a daily deed. That I'd be surfing the web for places to give five or ten dollars to and worrying about my schedule and my book contract. That's not what I wanted this to be about. I feared that I'd lose sight of my goal: I just wanted to live my life a tiny bit better than I was doing.

But that's not what's happened at all. I do keep a special calendar for ideas I might have for the future and for days when I know I've got something special slated. It also helps me make sure I don't repeat. It's a shock for me to see the months filled up behind me with kind acts and stories. I'm not driven by the calendar days looming ahead; on the other hand, I've also found you can't wait for a good deed to fall into your lap.

In the back of my head now, when I wake up every day, there is a question. But it's not "How am I going to fulfill my good deed obligation?" It's more like "How can I make this day a little better?" I guarantee this sounds cornier than it feels. But it gives a little extra promise and purpose to life that I hadn't expected. And yes, people do offer me ideas, often from their own experiences, and I love that.

I've found my eyes are open to my surroundings: to people who have too much to carry (I help); who look confused (I ask); who have a cup out (I give). But the very best part of One Good Deed so far is the people I see each day who say to me, always sheepishly, "Hey, I did a good thing today." Inevitably—and I mean every single time—when they tell their story their face lights up. Like me, you can just tell they're a little surprised at how good it felt.

And that's enough for me.

Pass the baton of giving.

My friend Lisa very kindly asked me to be her guest at a fund-raising dinner and dance, and I was thrilled. It's an event I love to attend. The story gets better: a couple of weeks later, I got an exhausted e-mail from her: "I'm tired of being the boss of things. Why don't you just take the table and invite some friends. It's all paid for."

Well, a treat like that doesn't come along very often. So what I did was call a bunch of people who had done something nice for me. Mary, who had lent me money when I was broke; Ariel, who had helped me develop my blog; Liz, who had given me a great quote for a book I wrote; Joni, who had treated me as an eternal guest at the nightclub she owned in the 1980s. Not because I felt they were people I needed to pay back, but because I was thrilled to have the opportunity to treat them for a change.

And when the dinner speaker made a plea for donations, I watched all my friends open their wallets and take out their checkbooks and credit cards. It was a trickle-down evening of giving: from Lisa to me, me to my friends, my friends to the charity.

Some things are better left unsaid.

Lest you think I'm ignoring them, I want to mention something that I haven't brought up in these pages, and that's the Big Deeds. One Good Deed is a project about "doing a little bit better in life," and because of that I haven't discussed the kinds of things that are happening in our lives all the time: staying up through the night listening to a friend's story of heartbreak; spending time with someone very sick; lending money, one of the most trying requests of all on a friendship.

Today I'm off to help a friend in a situation like one of those mentioned above, but it's not something I would ever speak about here. Many of our days are filled too much with the big stuff, too. A tip of the hat to you for doing these things with grace.

Time is the best gift ever.

I have started to wonder if I could volunteer in my city, but in a way that might let me try a few things on for size. Would such an organization exist? In New York City (and now in more than two hundred other locations around the United States), the answer is yes. Here in Gotham it's called New York Cares.

Tonight I went to an orientation for new volunteers; New York Cares offers these sessions several times a month, and on a cold, windy night, about forty folks showed up.

Tripp, our host for the evening, went through an exercise of asking people to stand if they had any prior volunteer experience: a majority of people stood again and again. Worked with kids? Seniors? Food kitchens or meal delivery? Not-for-profits? The list went on. The young woman next to me stood up a half dozen times. Impressive.

And here's the happiest statistic of the evening. Want to guess how many people in this city stood up and *showed* up as a volunteer for New York Cares in the last year? Over forty thousand. Maybe just once. Maybe a bunch of times. Wow.

But I've buried the lead. Here's the greatest part about New York Cares. You go to the website, and it's a veritable Chinese menu of choices. Read to a kid on Tuesday. Walk a dog for someone ill on Sunday morning. Help paint a mural and plant some bulbs at a school. That's what I'm doing on Saturday.

Like New York Cares, the HandsOn Network, which reaches around the country, offers incredible opportunities to help. Spend an afternoon, a semester, a summer helping others. There's no excuse to say you don't have the time anymore.

In New York, it's www.newyorkcares.org. To see if there's an organization like this near you, go to www.handson network.org.

And if not, think about getting a few friends together around the dinner table and figuring it out. That's what the folks at New York Cares did, way back in 1987.

Feed a furry friend.

Ohhh, that's nice!

Today a friend on Twitter supplied a link that led to a site called www.theanimalrescuesite.com. Right up at the top of the page is a box that says "Click to give free food and care!" And when you do, it leads to a page that says you've given the value of 0.6 bowls of food for rescued animals. Sweet! Yes, I, too, wondered whether it was legit, but I scouted around on Google, joining others who had asked the same question, and it seems these guys have been doing this since 2003, with some major sponsors footing the bills.

Now, if you're pet crazy, the site is for profit, and there's plenty of stuff to buy. So don't try blaming me if you get frisky with the credit card.

Create a tradition.

I'm sad. I'm really, really sad.

One of my oldest and best friends is moving out of town, and so I suggested we get together and have a private screening of one of our favorite movies, *Love Actually*. It's a little early in the season for it, as a lot of it takes place around the holidays, but I introduced it to Steve, and it has become an annual tradition.

So we sit, and order Chinese food, and we watch, and cry as usual, though I'm not really sure what the crying's about this time. When it's over, I pack it up and give it to Steve.

We'll watch it again, somewhere else, another year.

Share your friends.

It started about a year ago when a woman named Delia was coming to town from Boston. "Anyone want to have lunch?" she queried on the social media site. A bunch of "bookish Tweeps" as we had begun calling ourselves, were fast becoming friends—writers, agents, editors, bloggers, booksellers, or just people who like to talk books. Five folks piped up right away, and then the question was, where to go? The Algonquin! The site of the *New Yorker* magazine's Vicious Circle and their daily boozy luncheons during the halcyon days of Dorothy Parker, Robert Benchley, George S. Kaufman, editor Harold Ross, and others would be perfect. So, my friends Bethanne and Denise and I got together and planned our own "Virtuous Circle." We put the word out, and within two days we had over fifty people signed up for lunch a week hence.

It was like old home week—except in most cases, most of us had never met each other in person before. Introductions, recognition, delight, all at once. What a funny scene. We had bonded together through a common interest on Twitter, the world of books, and now it was like one gigantic blind date.

And how'd the date go, you ask? Well, today we had the *third* Virtuous Circle Round Table. As usual, we swapped books, found new friends, made connections. (No business pitches of any kind are allowed, by the way.) We actually have found an electronic way to make new friends in person.

What's lovely is that everyone goes home (and today that included all the way to Baltimore, Boston, and Minnesota), settles back in behind their avatars, and spends the next day or two talking up the event and thanking us for putting it together; and then new folks starting inquiring about the Virtuous Circle.

And so on, and so on, and so on.

NOVEMBER 12

Be of good cheer.

I don't think it matters what your religion is; when the holidays near, things get dicey. In my family, we primarily celebrate Christmas, but there are some Hanukkah events thrown in, too. And gifts are central to all of our hoopla. Like a lot of big families, we have devised a Holiday Gift Pull: a fifty-dollar gift for one person whose name is pulled out of a hat. I have put myself in charge.

Now, I love a holiday. Any holiday. I *love* a decoration. My personal cache of various holiday lights nears five digits. But see? I digress, just thinking about holidays.

I took over the Holiday Gift Pull because it was getting out of control and rife with unholidayish feelings. Things like, "I can't give to him; he brings everything back." "I *must* have *her* name, because I like to give her this special thing every year that she loves." (Read: it makes it really easy for me.) Soon the exceptions list was longer than the list of participants. Look at this, I said. Everyone agreed that it had become Not Much Fun.

Plan A was put back into effect. Put the names in a hat, period. I repull if it turns out they're married, but that's it. Not your favorite person in the family? Well, then, maybe this is a good time of year to make an effort.

There's still an occasional:

"I got her last year!"

"Will you switch with me?"

No. And no. Happy Holidays.

Join the crowd.

The auditorium at the Mahalia Jackson Elementary School, PS 123, was populated with about 150 grown-ups this morning, a Saturday, and they were juiced. Pumped. And *everybody* was nice. That defies any odds. We had all signed up through

American Express's Member Project, New York Cares, perhaps a local group, or we simply lived in the neighborhood. Face it, there just aren't that many places you go where everybody wants to actually be, come a Saturday morning. This was different: we were here to clean up a school.

Armed with coffee and croissants, water bottles, T-shirts, and even digital cameras to chronicle the event (and then post the pictures online—courtesy of the folks at American Express), we were offered our choice of chores: organizing the library, cleaning storage closets, planting bulbs, revamping the playground, painting murals. I wouldn't clean out my own closet in a blizzard—why would I do it here on a sunny sixty-five-degree day in November? I chose the murals, without giving full disclosure about having lifelong trouble staying inside the lines (about almost anything).

I'm shy when entering a crowd alone. And it seemed lots of these people painting near me knew each other already. But this bunch of kids I was near—all in their twenties—were volunteer maniacs. They were talking about raising money, other volunteer gigs they had done, mentoring. And lucky, lucky me—they took me in for the day.

PS 123's principal, Beverly Lewis, was on hand to thank each of us at the end of the day. "All this"—she beamed—"all you've done today? It would have taken us two years to do."

By the end of the day I was beat, but I can't remember when I had such a spring in my step.

Oh, and on the way home I ran into some folks who asked me for quarters for the parking meter. "That's a lot of different paint colors," they said, laughing and checking out my clothes, my hands. Next thing they knew, I'd whipped out the pictures, and I was spreading the One Good Deed word once more.

What a day.

Your extra could be someone else's essential.

Dang.

I forgot I had no half-and-half, and here it was, bleary-eyed morning. I had just enough time to get something delivered before I had to go to work. So when the guy came to the door with my order of a blueberry muffin and small coffee and said "That's $4.90," I was surprised. OK, outraged. When I opened the bag, I realized why: two coffees.

I put the bag by the door to return the extra coffee on my way to work. It was the principle, damn it! (And the dollar.)

But as I neared the corner I saw a familiar sight. Every morning I see the same hefty, middle-aged man sitting on one of his three black bags. If I go by even an hour later, he's always gone, so it seems like he must get picked up each day to go . . . somewhere. Where he goes, I have no idea—day work? A shelter? I am reluctant to offer him money or anything, because he never asks.

This morning, there sat the bags—but no owner. I left him my extra cup.

Don't forget the people who didn't forget you.

Over the years, dozens of people save you. For me, some of them are friends in my industry who know I'm reliable and call for some freelancing help. Sometimes it's a quick couple hundred bucks; sometimes a long-term freelance gig; occasionally even a short book.

Tonight I had dinner with a couple of women who have shepherded me through several of the latter. One of them was a client of mine over twenty years ago, when I was in advertising. Laura became an editor and hired me to write a short children's book; Judy took over the project, and now, though they have both moved elsewhere, I am discussing book number seven with their former boss. We are all friends, good friends, and get together several times a year for lunch or dinner.

I have had a lean few months, but yesterday I received what these days passes for a sumptuous check. One of my first thoughts was: I can take the girls out to dinner when we meet tomorrow night. Someone had picked a joint that was loud and fun and not particularly expensive, and I was thrilled to be able to tell them that it was on me. And even though none of us are working together now, I think it made us all feel good. We've played a part in each other's lives and supported each other along the way. We likely will again. So here's to Laura and Judy, and all the other Lauras and Judys to come. Cheers, and thank you once more.

Buy two. Give one away.

I talk about books a lot here. Sorry, but I love them; they are my passion and have been the basis of my career for over thirty years. And, well, this is a book, isn't it, so you probably like them, too.

Today I'm going to mention books yet again, but it could be anything—food, clothing, toys, whatever.

In my store, we run a holiday book drive. It doesn't cost the store a thing. At every checkout, there is a selection of inexpensive kids' books, and you are welcome to plop one into your pile of purchases (I know, I know, I've already spoken about how stores' constantly busking bugs me, but this is a little different). The organization behind this is Reach Out and Read; it promotes early literacy by "prescribing" books to kids at doctor's visits.

There are lots of drives like this around the holidays: there's even a box out in the lobby of my apartment building to donate food items for Thanksgiving. All I'm saying is that it occurs to me that it's a great idea, and if you own a retail establishment, it almost doesn't matter what you sell— lightbulbs, toilet paper, juice, toys, pie, books, fruit, movie tickets, tacos, towels—you should put a box out and make it easy for your customers to choose a selection from your wares and give. If you're a customer, urge your local shops to start this practice. Make the first donation.

Tell it like it was.

One of life's unavoidable sadnesses is the writing of a sympathy note after someone's death. But I have found a little bit of a way through the pain—both for me and, more importantly, for the family.

It started many years ago, with a distant family member who died very young. What to say in a terrible case like this? I had already delayed too long writing this note. So I sat down and told some stories: I mentioned how the last time I had seen him, he had charmed his way in front of me in a long buffet line at a family wedding before I even noticed. How he was always a bit of a rascal and could talk his way into anything. I added a couple more examples, which seemed at the time endearing to me—but an hour after I'd mailed it I worried if I'd gone too far or been disrespectful.

Just the opposite. I got a phone call saying in the midst of all the sorrow and letters and flowers and just plain awfulness, it was the one thing that made the family laugh. Since then my funereal tone has become a little bit of a trademark, I guess. I just try to make the memories of someone a bit more devilish and a little less saintly.

Listen: I just think people like to remember why they got such a kick out of somebody. So that's what I wrote about today. One of these times I may get the cold shoulder—but so far, so good.

Call a friend. Do it now.

My friend moved away today.

He recently mentioned he was going to stay in a hotel for a few days between the time the movers came and his closing. The hell you are, I said. Come stay with me. (Frankly, I think that was what he was *hoping* I'd say, and yes, I rose to the occasion.) But how do you count a tiny good deed like that in the recipe that makes a friendship?

When you hit midlife, stuff happens: people move away, lose their jobs, retire; some die. You start to make your world smaller because you want to surround yourself with the people and things you care about, and then it gets even smaller, all on its own. And you don't have any say in it.

So today was one of those days. We grilled some hot dogs, because they're our favorite thing, and watched some bad TV, and laughed a bunch, and then I walked Steve to the corner and put him in a taxi to the airport. Good-bye.

Steve and I had mutual friends, so I knew who he was way before we actually met. That was twenty-five years ago. When we did finally cross paths, we were on neighboring chaise lounges in Key West. Within a couple of days, he had me move out of my hotel and into the house he was renting so we wouldn't miss a minute of fun. And we've had lots of it—fun, that is—over the years. We also could drive each other crazy, like brothers and sisters do. But he's the kind of guy you could count on to keep your secrets and laugh at your jokes, over and over again. I guess that's what a friend is: invaluable.

Will I see Steve again? Of course—he moved to Florida, not Mars, and I love the beach. But will we fight about what movie to go see every week? Will I have someone who knows you have to vote for the previews as you watch them, and that the first one there gets the tickets and the other guy gets the soda and popcorn? And who also knows what my movie candy treats are?

No. No, I will not.

NOVEMBER 19

Sometimes work isn't work.

I'm headed off to one of my favorite nights of the year. It's a big fund-raiser, but this time I'm one of the volunteers. And what do I do all evening? Sell books. Why, oh, why, you may think, is this any different from any other day?

This organization provides all kinds of incredible aid to people in our city who need shelter, food, and education. It does this—and does it well—365 days a year. But each year on the weekend before Thanksgiving, it holds a big book fair. And it's no ordinary book fair.

All the books are donated by the major publishing houses around the city—and not their leftovers, either. Big bestsellers and annual favorites are here, and everything in the room is 50 percent off. Most of the volunteer booksellers are from the publishing industry—in fact, folks from publishing started this event over two decades ago. The money raised goes specifically to college scholarships for underprivileged kids.

Tonight is the big-ticket preview night, with food and drink and raffle prizes all donated by neighborhood businesses. For me it's sort of the opening of the holiday season. I love this night, because when I look around I see a roomful of people, some I've known twenty, thirty years, all still dedicated to books and learning—and you can practically see the scholarships adding up.

I give just a few hours—some have worked on this for months. But for all of us, it's a pleasure to help change students' futures, one book sale at a time.

NOVEMBER 20

Somebody has to take the runt.

The "Holiday Fair" sign had been up outside the church on my block for weeks, and I was determined to make it there this year.

If I actually attended church, St. Monica's would be my parish. I do stop in now and again, because it's beautiful and peaceful and it feels right to visit because it's on my block. I occasionally see the stained-glass windows lit at night from my backyard, and can even hear the choir practicing. For the record, my mother didn't think that was enough. "The only time you've ever been in that church," she sobbed, "is to vote!"

But it was the bake sale I was after today. I wanted to support all the work these folks from my neighborhood had done, and it was a good way to get some goodies. I opted for a delicious-looking baked bread (pumpkin, please) and some cupcakes. Oh, the cupcakes. Decorated with so much labor and love, and not so much talent. And really, not so tasty, either. But when I picked the ugly duckling, the parishioner manning the money box beamed. That's what a bake sale is about: clearing the table, counting the crumpled singles.

(Oh, and I bought three raffle tickets there in the Catholic church basement for a Broadway play starring a famous gay actor. That made me feel naughty, but nice.)

NOVEMBER 21

Tip as if you were tipping yourself.

Now, I always tip around 20 percent in restaurants, and at times when I'm flush or the service is spectacular, I tip bigger. But there are a couple of tipping things that stick in my craw.

One in particular is tipping at Starbucks. Perhaps you feel the same way. Their coffee is expensive already. And the truth is, I work hard at bookselling, too, and *I* don't get tipped for working behind a counter. So it's clear I'm just being selfish. But I've been going to my around-the-corner Starbucks a lot lately (I'm stuck on the Pumpkin Spice Latte—even more expensive), and the gang there is really nice, and they sort of know me now.

So I'm thinking to myself: *they* make hardly any money, *you* make hardly any money. Just because booksellers don't get tips, should I punish the baristas? Shouldn't there be a sort of camaraderie among us instead? Plus, they're really nice and helpful. Probably nicer than I am.

Several years ago I taught my nephew what I considered a valuable life lesson—he was about nine at the time. "Simon," I said as we stood at the ice cream window, "always make sure they see it when you tip." Now I'm thinking that was sort of cheesy. But still good advice.

NOVEMBER 22

Bag 'em yourself.

You do this, right? I mean, everybody does. Right? Please tell me yes, or I will lose heart.

I stopped at the grocery store tonight on the way home from work, as I often do, and of course it's the busiest time, because everybody in the world leaves work at the same time and comes to the grocery store.

I got my stuff and stood in the checkout line. As the checker ran things through, I started to pack the bags. I always pack my own bags. It saves either the checker from having to do it (which, of course, also makes the line move faster) or the bagger, who often is working two registers. And they're grateful. Tonight, just a few days before Thanksgiving, I got exhausted thank-yous from both of them.

Anytime you make someone else's job easier, well, that's a good deed.

<hr>

Help the lonely traveler.

It was really early at Port Authority Bus Terminal, which, while not as dangerous a place as it was twenty years ago, is still rough.

The line for my bus was short, which is unusual—it's one of only a couple of ways to get from New York to Providence, Rhode Island. Second in line was a man who was either fast asleep or dead. Flat on his back, unmoving. There was some luggage parked next to him, and only an empty plastic bag under his head, presumably for cleanliness. When the driver came out to board us, a lady in front of me had the same idea I did: she stood over him and said, "We're getting on the bus now." No response. Then the first person in line got on, and she took with her all the luggage that was beside Inert Guy. So evidently it wasn't his. Maybe he'd been there for days! All he had were the clothes on his back, a trucker hat, and the plastic bag.

But I was going to give it one more try. I, for one, would be loco if my fellow passengers didn't alert me. So I nudged him in the leg a little with my toe. "Hey," I said quietly, "did you want to be on this bus?" His eyes flew open, and he was on his feet in seconds. "What? Yeah. Yeah."

I was not so pleased with my rescue hours later when he had draped his legs across the aisle into the opposite seats and I had to go to the bathroom. And wake him up again. And on the way back.

Plus, he didn't say thank you. You *know* how I hate that.

But I should just be happy he didn't have a gun, right?

Friendship is timeless.

This story is kind of long.

It starts in the 1930s.

My grandmother Agnes Kavanaugh hooked rugs with a group of ladies on Wednesday afternoons back then, and they called themselves "the Hookers," which is probably about as racy as my family's ever been, including now.

When Agnes died suddenly in 1949, in her midfifties, my mother, who had just graduated from college and was set to go to graduate school in journalism, decided to stay home with her father instead. Her two brothers were close by, but newly married, and it just seemed right.

One of the Hookers was named Hazel Atkinson, a longtime friend of Agnes's, and Hazel's daughters were pals of my mom's and her brothers. Hazel and Agnes used to speak on the phone every morning, just to check in, relay a tidbit from around town, whatever women have talked about *ad infinitum*. The day after Agnes died, Hazel called my mother, and then she called her every morning, always before ten o'clock. One of the most frequent refrains from my childhood became, "Ha! Wait'll I tell Hazel."

Hazel called my mother every day until her death at ninety-four.

Now Hazel's daughters, Hope and Ruth, are in their late eighties. We don't speak every day, but Hope and I e-mail, and they are adamant that we stay in touch. This family friendship has now gone on for over eighty years, and I cherish it.

"The Girls," as they are known about town, are the personification of Yankeedom. Yoga and tai chi are staples several times a week. Where they stand on a subject is never a mystery. "We don't like a dessert with a mint chip," they told me recently. Or, "We don't really read fiction." They are pillars of the community, annually decorating the whaling museum Christmas tree with their own vintage collection, serving on the library board, helping with the annual church clambake. I am crazy about the Atkinsons.

For their Thanksgiving dinner this year, the Girls were down from their original gang of thirteen to just one guest. Likely they would serve a dessert with Hazel's hot fudge sauce, which is the recipe everyone I know in town still uses.

I value this friendship so, and I can never, ever repay what their mother Hazel did for my mother during such a lonely time.

So when I made a Cranberry Surprise Pie for my Thanksgiving dinner guests, I made two, so I could bring one to the Girls. Where this recipe came from originally, I don't recall, but certainly it's been kicking around between our families for half a century. So I rang the doorbell of their perfect house in the woods, and when Hope opened the door, her face lit up like I'd never seen before. "Ruth," she shouted back into the living room, "it's the Cranberry Surprise Pie!"

That one's for you, Hazel.

CRANBERRY SURPRISE PIE

2 cups fresh cranberries
½ cup walnuts, chopped
1½ cups white sugar
¾ cup butter, melted
2 large eggs, beaten
1 cup flour
1 tsp. vanilla extract

Preheat oven to 325°F. Butter a 9½" pie plate.

Pour the cranberries into the bottom of the pie plate and sprinkle evenly with the walnuts and ½ cup of the sugar.

Mix the eggs with the melted butter, 1 cup sugar, the vanilla, and the flour. Pour over the cranberry mixture.

Bake for 50 minutes at 325°F.

Eat early and often.

Give thanks.

If it's not enough to gather your family around you and show them love and thanks for everything they mean to you, well, then, I don't know what One Good Deed is.

Happy Thanksgiving for all that you are, and all that you have.

Keep your family close.

My family is large. Not the biggest Irish family you ever came across, but numerous. In my generation there are twelve cousins just on the Kavanaugh side alone, and I adore them all. Though fewer than half of us still live in our tiny hometown, most of us have a second home here—and we do like to hang out together. Trouble is, it's three different sets of cousins, and spouses and offspring, so it's hard to rally everybody at once.

But every few years I get a bee in my bonnet and really want us all to gather together; tonight, the night after Thanksgiving, always seems to be the best bet. We still think of ourselves as the kids, and it's a shock to see that it was years ago now that my cousin Jim became the oldest male family member, still in his midfifties.

After an early dinner, folks start to arrive, kids start to career around, drinks are served up, desserts are laid out. No matter what I do—set a nice fire, put out plates and plates of food, turn up the music—I can't get anyone out of the kitchen (although everyone knows that is the benchmark of a great party). But when the crowd swells to forty or fifty people, as it occasionally does, that old house rocks. Literally.

Sure, it's a little bit more work than I wanted to do after having everybody over yesterday, and every time I decide to do it I want to kick myself beforehand for such a harebrained idea. But we're not kids anymore, and this is my family. The minute they start coming through the door, I am thrilled I made the effort to do this just one more time—and, from the sound of it, so are they.

NOVEMBER 27

Learn from the elders.

Sometimes you just have to observe a genius and take a page from his—or in this case her—book. A good-deed genius.

My aunt Tessie (she who just had her great-great-uncle canonized as a saint) is a master at making people feel good. Today I followed her around and got a lesson.

First of all, she made me poached eggs. She will do that every single time I show up at her house, no matter how often. Some might think me pesky. Her take? "It's our one-on-one time."

She is never, ever still, even for a minute. Today we are off to see her aunt Bernie at the nursing home. Tessie goes the long way and points out the old homesteads of friends and relatives, where she and her brothers ice-skated as kids, where her uncle had a barbershop.

In the car, on the street, she waves to everyone. It takes me a while to realize she doesn't actually know them all. When I comment on this, she has a simple rejoinder: "I love people!" she laughs.

We arrive at the nursing home, and here's a delivery guy dragging in a new mattress from a truck. Tessie runs to hold the door open, then asks if she can help him carry it down the hall. He is about thirty-two. She is eighty-five. She greets every employee in the halls, introduces me, and then tells me something complimentary about each of them. ("She's been here forty years! Doesn't she look young?" "She is *so* nice to Aunt Bernie.")

At last we head home over the local bridge at low tide, and the smell is pretty pungent. There's construction going on, so there are workers everywhere, and policemen, too. "Stinky, PU!" says Tessie, holding her nose like we used to do as kids, looking right into the face of the cop we're passing. He gives her the death stare, because of course he thinks she's talking about him; but we manage to escape, unarrested. Close call, though. It just goes to show—even the good can be misunderstood.

Share beauty.

Sometimes it seems I am only able to keep hold of my parents' house by the skin of my teeth. There are years when it's a scramble to pay the taxes, the guy who mows the lawn (badly), the heating bills that are exorbitant in This Old House, even when I'm away and the thermostat is turned way down.

The cost of visiting for a long weekend isn't cheap, so it's hard for me to get there as frequently as I'd like. And then the minute everything feels copacetic, with a full larder and enough firewood and a plan for the night—it's time to go back to New York, and closing up the house again marks the reentry to everyday life. Change the sheets. Did I turn down the heat? I'm out of garbage bags. Is there enough time to give this food away? Do I toss the food? What about these flowers?

I decide the flowers, which were given to me only yesterday, are coming on the bus back to New York—until I remember how annoying carrying the cheesecake on the train was only a mere five days ago. Toss them. No, too beautiful: give them away. Also not so easy. I close the flue in the fireplace, set the timers on the lights, and balance the flowers on my knee while driving one-handed to my aunt's to present them to her. I tell her where I got them, she oohs and aahs and picks a spot near her favorite chair, and I feel like I've saved beauty for two or three more days.

Nothing beats a kind word.

Sometimes just a really good compliment is enough.

I was on the bus tonight and spotted a woman sitting in front of me, in a seat facing the middle aisle of the bus, which allowed me to see her entire outfit.

She was very slim and dressed fashionably, and for a second I thought she might be in her twenties—though when she turned it was clear she'd probably passed seventy some time back. (That wasn't the compliment. That would have been too much.)

But she wore this big, incredible, cabled cream-colored sweater. It had a fur (real or imagined, I don't know) collar and she cinched it at the waist with a wide faux-alligator belt over her skinny black pants. This broad looked like a million bucks. I had on a brown parka with a gigantic grease stain on the sleeve.

As I got off the bus, I stopped and said, "That is one fantastic sweater."

She shot right back, "Ten years old. I went shopping in my closet. We all have to. Thank you *so* much."

Now as I sit here writing about her, I realize she'd been waiting all day for someone to notice.

Happy to oblige.

Raise a glass to good health.

I have a friend who's been ill. I haven't known her too long, and we're not confidantes, nor do we chat for hours on the phone. But she is wise and helpful and fun, and I respect her opinion. We enjoy each other a good deal.

She has just gotten a clean bill of health after a rocky time with cancer, and she's been a sport and a half throughout the whole thing, hiding nothing about her health on places like Facebook and Twitter and in personal e-mails. She's been brave and funny and I think she's taken a bit of the fear out of illness—for both herself and everyone she knows.

We're so busy checking up on people when they're ill—and I'm not saying that's not great—that I'm not sure we take time for properly celebrating the return of good health.

But at dinner tonight, that's what my pal and I are going to do.

Remember the fallen. Stop the loss.

Today is World AIDS Day.

Working at the Gay Men's Health Crisis office was my very first job as a volunteer. It was the mid-1980s, and my friends were beginning to die. I wanted to help, and I didn't know how, so I signed up to work there on Wednesday nights.

Almost everyone you saw in the elevator looked very ill. Actually, everywhere you looked, people you knew well were suddenly unrecognizable. When you returned to your beach share in the spring, you asked after last year's buddies anxiously: if you didn't see them right away, you feared they were dead. So once a week, I spent three hours in a room, mostly alone, filling requests for information about AIDS. These all came in by snail mail or phone: there was no Internet or e-mail in those days. The envelopes bore stamps and queries from around the world. There wasn't that much information to send out: a flyer about using condoms; some tips on safe sex; a few other hopeful pieces. There were no drug cocktails to hold HIV in check.

In later years, I would work with and become good friends with Tim Sweeney, who was one of GMHC's founders and served early on as executive director. I asked him a way-too-simple question: what was it like to have that job back then, at the height of the epidemic? He grew quiet and finally said: "Some days I could barely put one foot in front of the other. I was going to a dozen funerals a week." Running GMHC, which was—and still is—the largest AIDS organization in the world, meant you could not stop trying to end this epidemic, not for a minute. Alone down in that room, stuffing envelopes, sending out tiny rays of hope, even I could see that. That was twenty-five years ago.

New York City was my corner of the world then as now, and it was where my friends were dying. Now people—at least people with good health care—are staving off the disease for indeterminate amounts of time. But on World AIDS Day—and every day—7,397 people will still contract HIV. I posted this statistic today on Facebook, and on Twitter, just to remind myself, and everyone I could reach, to remember their friends, and the people around the world we don't know, and help to fight for a healthy future.

Welcome someone into the fold.

A couple of days ago, knowing we would all be at the same event tonight, I received an e-mail from some friends saying they would be bringing along someone new, a woman I had never met before. The scrivener called her an ingénue, which was a nice way-cum-dig of letting us know she was much younger than the rest of us.

By the time the event rolled around tonight, I was exhausted, and now I had to head back to a part of town I had left only a few hours earlier. But it was for a good cause, and I wanted to support everyone, so of course I scrounged around, found an outfit, and headed off.

As is always the way, at least with me, I had a great time and wondered why I had ever dragged my feet to come in the first place. And then as I made my way over to the coat check to call it a night, I remembered: I hadn't met the ingénue. I turned around and set off to find my pals, whom I had not seen all evening.

Ah! There they were. Introductions were made, and our little group spent the last chapter of the party getting to know each other. Ingénue was lovely, of course—I knew she would be, because I know my friends. But that's not the point. I can't take credit for making the introductions, but I surely did my best to make her feel welcome—just like these same friends did nearly twenty years ago, when they took *me* under their wing.

DECEMBER 3

Do your duty.

Several times over the last few weeks, I've dropped in at a local West Elm store to sniff around. I kept hearing the tinkle of a little bell over at the register—I figured it was some sort of promotion where a random customer got a special discount. Whenever the bell rang, everyone around clapped, too. Whatever it was, I liked it.

Today I discovered what the bell ringing was all about, because I actually bought something. When I got to the front of the line, the cashier asked me if I'd like to donate to St. Jude's Hospital for Children. Sure, I said, add two dollars to my bill. The woman behind me, clearly more of a West Elmer than myself, piped up. "Hey, you didn't ring the bell!" she said to the cashier. The woman at the register to our left had been ringing hers pretty merrily.

But my cashier just looked at us and said flatly, "I don't have time for the bell."

Really? Did I mention that it was the middle of the morning and not very busy? (And that she had also mistakenly shortchanged me a dollar?)

You're asking me for money, and you can't even give me a musical high-five?

Ouch. Come on now.

DECEMBER 4

Spread the light(s).

I'm a lights nut. I love a holiday, and if there's a light that goes along with it, I'm in. I mean, I'm not someone the neighbors take to court because my decorating is a public nuisance, nothing like that. But I do love a display.

So today I thought I'd put up a few strings. Really—not a lot. But first I needed to take down the nice orange lights I had in the yard for the Halloween and Thanksgiving season. It's just a simple line of lights wrapped along a fence, but it does the job and, I believe, makes everybody happy.

That's where the good deed comes in, you see. I really believe that part of putting up the lights is for others to enjoy them. OK, I'm not sure I really believe that, but it's what I tell myself.

Having a yard is already an anomaly and makes me the envy of all my friends. I'm on the first floor of an apartment building, and my yard is in the middle of the block, at the bottom of a canyon of surrounding high-rises. No one—among hundreds of apartment dwellers—has anything to look at. Think *Rear Window*. Think about how nice it would have been if there were some lights down there where Thelma Ritter was digging for Raymond Burr's wife's body.

See? *For others!* And even though it's not spectacular, it took a couple of hours to string some white lights along the fence and decorate the laurel bushes with just a few hundred colored lights. Pretty.

And really, who's to say I'm the one who enjoys them most? In fact, one of my most successful decorating projects was surprising my former boss with a snappy set of blue dreidel-shaped bulbs in his office one Hanukkah when he was having a bad day. Because I am also nondenominational.

Check back in February. I have some swell red heart-shaped stuff, too. Or, c'mon over. Enjoy!

DECEMBER 5

Soothe the soul.

My buddies, the girls from the rock group BETTY, were advertising and talking up their concert online. Get tickets fast, said Amy, we're going to sell out. And of course, they did . . . but not before I snagged me a deuce.

I didn't have anyone in mind to go with, but it seemed a good idea to get two. Something would come up, I figured.

And it did. A friend whom I hadn't seen in too long was having a bad week—and she was also old friends with the girls in the band. Pick you up at seven, I said. I brought along her belated birthday gift, we had a chance to catch up, and we went to hear some music.

As they say, it soothes the soul. Meanwhile, I supported my friends, hopefully reminded my pal that I love her, and, I gotta admit, had a fabulous time myself.

Besides, once again it proved one of my double-secret mantras: concerts keep you young.

DECEMBER 6

Go ahead, take a bite.

This evening, a little early for a party I was attending, I found myself wandering around Grand Central Station, instead of rushing through it like the rest of the world was doing. That stunning celestial ceiling, the fantastic restaurants and beautiful shops. What a treat.

And speaking of treats, I still had an hour until the fete, and I was famished. And pooped. I needed a sugar fix, and I needed it bad. So I stopped into the gourmet market, where I found the answer: a gigantic éclair. I mean, this thing was as big as a hot dog on a bun. The server was a little taken aback when I insisted he not wrap it but hand it right over in a napkin, but he complied.

Delight. So obviously delicious that a man passing me became a little jealous.

"Mmmm, éclair," he moaned.

"I know," I replied, mouth half full. "I couldn't resist."

We smiled at each other and kept on walking. But now, things felt unright. I turned around; he was still in sight. "Hey!" He looked back. "Want a bite?" I asked. "I'd love one," he said without hesitation, and came and took a mouthful.

We laughed, beamed at each other, and went our separate ways.

Made my day.

Somebody's going to pay.

If you tell me you've never been tempted in this situation, I will call you a liar.

It's a busy time of year in shoppingdom; the checkout lines are getting long and the cashiers tired. Also, lots of customers are doing their best to irritate, and doing a pretty good job of it, too. I was trying to put on an extra coat of cheer, in my do-gooding way, and so evidently—and unwittingly—distracted the woman at the register where I had just purchased a couple of gifts.

I walked away, barely glancing at the lump of change and bills she had hurriedly put into my hand as I took my bag and departed. But on second thought, it *did* have a generous heft. Out on the street, I paused and counted: she had given me five dollars too much.

Does it really matter? I wondered. Do I really want to head back into that hellhole and insert myself into a line of angry shoppers?

Will they take it out of her pay?

Man. There goes my free, fancy hot chocolate from Starbucks. I headed back in.

But I *do* feel pretty good about myself. Righteous, in fact. I'll toast to that instead.

DECEMBER 8

Mum's the word.

Today a friend told me a secret. She told me another, some time ago, and I kept it for over a year until it came to fruition, everyone found out, and joy was spread throughout the land. That's why she could tell me this one.

And I won't tell this one, either, no matter how much you beg me. Because nothing makes a friend trust you like keeping a promise.

Keep someone warm.

I've been trying to find the perfect winter coat. To give away, that is. An organization hosts an annual coat drive for the homeless every year here in New York, though I'm sure there's something like it in everyone's hometown: you drop off your cast-offs at a firehouse, a store, or a church. Our local event is accompanied by very effective public service ads on TV showing a shivering, huddled Statue of Liberty. These ads have been running for years, and yet I had never even opened my closet door.

So today I took a look and found a terrific fake shearling that was, as they requested, gently used. I bought it eight years ago, gained a bunch of weight, and of course saved it for that fictional time in the future when I would diet it away. And this coat was warm, too warm: way too hot just to wear in and out of a movie theater or a mall, but not if you lived on the street. So I searched on Google for my closest drop-off spot, and off I went.

The store that served as the drop-off point wasn't open, and that seemed karmic: the instructions *did* say "freshly laundered." Miraculously, there was a dry cleaner's next door, so I asked the proprietor if he would just wash and dry the coat and bring it over. He inspected it for about fourteen minutes, and then said "Twenty dollars," which I'm pretty sure is highway robbery. I'm also not sure he wasn't just inspecting it for his daughter. Later on, I realized I should have asked him to donate the laundering costs. Dang. Clearly I still need some One Good Deed practice.

I'm trying not to think about the twenty bucks, but when I figure I haven't even worn it in over eight years, I'm prepared to call it a two-dollar-a-year storage fee. In my own closet.

But I felt great being able to give away something that was still in such good shape and would help someone else so much. Plus, it's the *only* time ever I've gotten something that positive out of eating too much.

Act as a guide.

I guess this is one of those good deeds where everybody wins, but frankly, I feel like I'm getting a free lunch—or in this case, breakfast.

The whole setup is sweet and sort of funny. My friend Susan's husband was offered a gigantic promotion, but accepting it would mean spending two or three days a week in the New York office. They live outside of Boston, and they like it that way, thank you very much. He hemmed and hawed and finally said he'd consider taking it, but *only* if his wife would agree to come for part of each week.

I reminded Susan that most men would be saying, "Wahoo! Bachelor pad!" Her husband wants to take her out for a weekly romantic dinner after thirty years. Sheesh. So they rented a place in Manhattan, and off they went on their new adventure.

I was thrilled with the news. I hadn't seen nearly enough of Susan in the years (OK, *decades*) since college. Suddenly we're having breakfast together once a week—and every time, she picks up the check. I tell her this is some terrific good deed on her part—feeding the starving writer.

"Are you kidding?" She laughs. "Every week you teach me something new about this city and make it exciting for me. And my husband is so happy that *I'm* happy coming down here every week that we figure we both have you to thank."

Well, this is the craziest thing I ever heard, but . . . two poached eggs with a side of bacon, please. And more coffee.

DECEMBER 11

Offer shelter.

It was a close call.

I was prowling around Twitter earlier when I saw an acquaintance—someone I've met now in real life but was introduced to originally through Twitter—recounting her fun shopping trip in New York City. Her latest update, however, had her cutting it close getting her train home. Not to worry, said I. If you miss it, just tweet me, and I'll give you my address. You can stay over with me.

This would have meant a last-minute crunch of dusting, scrubbing, sheet changing, and ice making. Just for starters. I held my breath and lo, at last, up came a tweet that she was homeward bound. And a thank-you, of course.

I'm a terrible housekeeper, so she was taking her life in her hands as it was. But at least I got the laundry done.

DECEMBER 12

Power to the people.

Damn. I've run out of money on my transit card. So I scrape together some change and figure I'll fill up a new card when I get to the subway: but first, I have to take the bus. So I get a transfer from the driver, and then—crap! I remember the transfer works only on another bus, not on the subway, where I'm headed. Now I'll have to pay twice.

So I get off the bus and take the transfer out of my pocket to throw in the garbage.

But wait! What about all these folks waiting at the bus stop? I look for someone underpaid-looking. "Hey," I say to someone as young as I was once, "you want this transfer?"

Now, what do you think: sticking it to the man, or stealing?

A little goodwill goes a long way.

You might not consider this a good deed, unless you're down with tattletales like me. This is really Carlos's story.

I braved another visit to West Elm (see December 3), because frankly I cannot resist its wares and it has a great do-it-yourself wrapping counter. When the inevitable request came for a donation to St. Jude's, I said yes again but decided to dive in and tell the story of my last visit to today's much merrier sales associate at the register, Carlos. His response:

"I think *you* should ring the bell."

Carlos gets it. Carlos saved the day. Carlos made me feel goodwill toward West Elm again.

Refrain.

I am pooped. Not only do I work in retail, but it's in an industry where about 75 percent of annual sales are made during this month. So close to the holidays, people are beginning to grab almost anything off the shelf. Several customers I would like to have bitten.

But I did not. Nor did I push an old lady down on the street. Or steal. Or call any exes when I got home in my foul mood to tell them they treated me like crap. Though at some point in the day, it would have been really easy to do any of these things.

So, a good day all around. Because sometimes No Bad Deed is a Good Deed.

Be as generous as you can.

I admit it: even though it's the holiday season, this is a time of year when I have a problem with giving. I know, I know—we've talked about tipping. But now it's out of control. Tipping the postman? The paperboy? Really? And yes, part of it is that, like in the case of the postman, he's already making more money than I am, and getting a government pension when it's all over. He's in a way better place than I am.

But what puts me partly back on track is tipping the people in my building. If you live in an apartment instead of a house, you know what I mean. When you receive the annual holiday card (a.k.a. the list of people who expect to get some money), I find there's inevitably a person or two whose name I don't recognize. This used to irk me, until I realized that, as in any business, there are people behind the scenes that keep things humming—in my case, throwing out the garbage, fixing the boiler or my shower, and plenty more. Then, naturally, I felt like a heel—but it made me step up.

So I still will not tip the postman, even though I like him, because this has to stop somewhere. Today I have put hundreds of dollars in envelopes to thank those in this building who keep my life comfortable.

But I cannot tell a lie. I still wish booksellers got tips.

Share, and you see something for the first time again.

Many years ago, I decided to give this opera thing a try. I am a big fan of classical, jazz, and disco and dance music, not a lover of blues, reggae, or hip-hop. (So sue me.) Opera seemed like it might be a good fit for me, especially now that they were translating the lyrics onto little screens on the seat in front of you—otherwise, I would not even have attempted it. It would have been over my head.

But I loved it right away and began to go quite often: with clients on my expense account; in ten-dollar SRO seats; in nosebleed seats, scrambling down to a better location after the first act; once, even in a private box. I didn't care. Much of it was the pageantry; I still always go in person to the Metropolitan Opera to buy my tickets. It seems to have become my touchstone for living in New York—every time I walk in, I tear up, and my thought is always the same: I cannot believe I grew up and moved to New York City and am a person who is lucky enough to go to the opera.

And then, an incredible thing happened: I made a friend, and it turned out she works at the Met. She is given seats for the dress rehearsals, many of which are on the mornings I don't work. Every year, she offers me a few. They are terrific seats that aren't for sale, and it's an amazing thing to be able to bring a friend to experience these special performances. Like today.

Elizabeth told me she'd never been to the opera, though she's been a successful musician her entire life. I offered to take her, and this morning was the day: velvet seats; golden walls; we watched the Sputnik crystal chandeliers ascend to the ceiling, the iconic signal that the opera is about to begin that never, ever gets old.

I've seen *Tosca* a dozen times, and hope to see it fifty more, but only once will I see the beatific smile I saw today on Elizabeth's face. Thank you, Suzy, for the tickets; thank you, Elizabeth, for introducing me to the opera, for the first time, again.

DECEMBER 17

Remember a few of your favorite things.

My One Good Deed quest has a certain path to follow: to show that there are a lot of wrongs that need righting, people who deserve more or need a hand, tiny things that can be done to make life a little easier all around. I try to keep my eyes peeled and to do something a little different every day.

But just a reminder that there's nothing wrong with doing something over and over that particularly touches your heart.

Today I spent $14.11, which is not a huge sum, but not tiny, either. I felt I had fallen behind. A few weeks ago I spoke here about Reach Out and Read, and trying to donate a book to this great organization whenever I purchased something at my store. I simply hadn't bought anything lately, so this evening I picked up three inexpensive books and brought them over to the register. Total, with tax: $9.11.

It was cold when I walked to the bus, and I spotted my homeless baritone friend I told you about last summer—you remember, I called him "Old Man River." Turns out his name is Thomas, and I shook his hand tonight and palmed him five dollars. No snooty maître d', he checked out the bill right away, and he actually gasped.

Just $14.11. Four happy souls. I've got to remember to do that again.

DECEMBER 18

Give the people what they want.

On the weekend before Christmas every year, the bookstore has a little . . . well, I don't know what *they* call it, but we employees call it a holiday potluck. The company supplies food and drink. And by "food and drink" I mean a pretty gruesome six-foot submarine sandwich and a few gallons of soda. It's not exactly a party; it's just food on the table in the back room for employees to enjoy on their break. Not a lampshade-on-the-head holiday bash by any means.

It's the potluck part that makes it any fun at all. A bunch of us bring dishes and desserts, and when they're laid out, you see and smell the New York melting pot: rice and beans, Latin chicken dishes, Yugoslavian cookies and sweets, lasagna, fried chicken, and more. Every year it changes, just as the pool of booksellers does. And every year I bring the aforementioned Cranberry Surprise Pie, because New Englanders are stubborn and unrelenting and hate change, as everybody knows. Besides, it's a crowd pleaser.

DECEMBER 19

Do the right thing.

It's a Sunday, and I have to work, but I'm honored to have been asked to attend a party for my friend Paula, an LGBT activist, lawyer, and someone I've worked hand in hand with and long admired. Paula became sick with cancer this fall; she felt puny—she thought it was the flu—later she began to feel some pain, and then, just like that, she was told she would live only six months.

Paula has been through chemotherapy and radiation this fall and is going to have an operation after the holidays, all in hopes that she can beat this illness. During this respite, while she's feeling somewhat better, she wanted to have a party and see all her friends who have been calling, praying, writing, and thinking about her these last months. I want to go desperately, but I am torn: the open house lasts only until six p.m., and I get out of work at five. It will take me more than a half hour to get there, so I will arrive just before the party is slated to end. What if Paula is too tired to see friends by then? I don't want her to feel she has to be polite and chat me up. I start to head in the direction of home, but I turn around abruptly and head off to the party at the last minute.

I am eager to see Paula, be there, give her my love, and show her I care. The real truth is, I am afraid I will never see her again. How many times in life have we lost someone and thought, "If only I had ten more minutes. If only I could say 'I love you' one more time." I am being given an opportunity to show how I care, and I am not going to miss it. I will support Paula now, and hope for the best in the new year.

When I rush in, the party is slowing down, with some people putting on their coats, but there is my friend Paula, waving and flashing me her one-of-a-kind smile from across the room. Oh, I am thrilled that I came. I sit at her feet and hold her hand and we talk.

Sadly, this was indeed the last time I saw Paula. After a brief, heady few weeks when her doctors thought she was cancer free, she succumbed, at the age of fifty-six.

Do unto others.

Whether you live in a city or town, there's always some kind of rush hour, and in my world, it often involves traffic and scouring for a cab. Today I was in a rush, and carrying a bunch of packages, and I was careening down the street, searching desperately for a taxi. I was just about to board the bus (assuring certain tardiness), when a cab stopped right in front of me and unloaded.

I hopped in, and when we got to the stoplight, I looked to my left and saw another man getting out of a cab (two miracles!). To my right, a woman scowling, arm waving.

Let me be clear: I had not cheated her out of a cab—I'd gone to a different location and lucked out—but I do remember seeing her there before I arrived on the scene.

I rolled my window down. "Hey! Cab on your three o'clock!" She smiled, and her wave turned into one of thanks. Ah, how easily a day can be turned around!

Don't be so stingy.

My very favorite customer stopped in today and, as she so often does, brought me a treat—this time, some fancy, gorgeous-looking meringues.

I started off to stash them in my locker, and then thought, ah, what the hell.

So I shared them.

That is all.

Even merriment has its limits.

I cannot take one more step. Smile one more smile. Wrap one more gift. I was nice, not naughty, festive all the while, and working full tilt.

Don't get me wrong: I adore working during the holidays, I really do. But is it OK if we just think of it today as one big good deed?

There is sheer joy in creating joy.

I was waiting to board the bus in the Providence terminal tonight, munching on some Charleston Mini Chews; this tiny boy had his eye on me. I looked at his mom and got the nonverbal high sign that it would be OK to hand over a bit of my booty to her son. I called him over and shared. It was hardly even a morsel of candy, but it brought me to one of my favorite childhood memories.

Her name was Clemmie, and in the 1960s, she was our goddess.

Not to look at her. She was short, quite round, with a decided limp and a lift in her shoe. I remember her as quite shy, with a wardrobe entirely of black dresses, which many of the older Portuguese women in our city wore at the time.

Every Saturday morning in the summer, Clemmie opened up her garage to all the kids. Mind you, this was a beach community—we were inches from sea and sand, swimming and sailing. We were already the luckiest kids we knew. But as far as we were concerned, Clemmie's garage had it all: a pinball machine, shuffleboard, a bowling machine, *color TV*. Best of all, Clemmie's husband owned a grocery store, and they had moved in a commercial freezer, filled with Popsicles and ice cream sandwiches.

As many as you wanted! All you could eat!

I know! Doesn't it sound too good to be true? Clemmie had no children, which is I guess why she invited all us kids over every week. She didn't bug us, never intervened unless someone got out of line. I guess she just got a kick out of kids.

In the countless great memories I have of those summers, why is it those mornings are so important still? A grown-up letting us do whatever we wanted? Having too much of a good thing and discovering its repercussions? A near stranger offering gifts without expectations?

All I know is this: I have wished many, many times for one more Saturday morning at Clemmie's. I wished it today.

My original sin.

I guess it would be easy to say that Christmas Eve, like other happy religious holidays this time of year people everywhere enjoy, abounds with good deeds. All season long we're on our best behavior, and if there is a time of year when all we're doing is concentrating on making others happy, well, then this is it. But for decades there has never been a Christmas Eve when I don't think back to the one long ago, and with great shame.

I must have been around nine, and my mom and I were doing some last-minute holiday shopping. Dusk was falling outside and the shop was about to close for the holiday when a little boy came in alone, younger than I was. I watched him look around carefully, finally pick out an apron, and bring it to the proprietor. He held out his hand, and the shop owner looked down. "That apron's one dollar," he said. "You need twenty-two cents more. You don't have enough money." The kid was crestfallen, put the apron back, and left the store without a Christmas gift for his mother.

I had twenty-two cents in my pocket. I knew I had enough to help him out, and I didn't. I knew it standing there, I knew it when I didn't run after him down the street in 1961, I know it as I write this, fifty years later. I know this has the ring of a corny fable, but it has broken my heart every Christmas since.

I wonder sometimes whether we all have one personal original sin. I believe this one is mine. So whenever I think of this twenty-two cents, I try to remember: mistakes can be corrected.

Play your part.

"The house looks so beautiful!" "You've outdone yourself yet again!" "It's so great that you do this."

These are just some of the things my extremely nice family says to me on the holidays. We get together many, many times over the course of the year for any number of real and imagined holidays and fetes. Just happens that my house is built for parties, and I love being in the thick of any kind of event, so lots of the larger hijinks happen at my place.

The truth is, I'm certain I have the easy part of the deal. Though there are exceptions—like tomorrow, when I will have to clean up the holiday mess and take down the Christmas tree so I can get on the bus and try to beat a blizzard home—I have not been completely honest. It so happens that every woman in my family involved in these celebrations has a culinary background—catering, chef-ing, running a kitchen, whatever. Oh, sure, I make a mean deviled egg (and, as you all know, Cranberry Surprise Pie), but these guys are pros and it shows. They should make a holiday documentary of this well-oiled machine: it is truly awesome to watch, from beginning to end. I would be the one in the movie doing something dumb like choosing the cocktail napkins.

So, amid all the "Thank you for doing this, Erin!" hallelujahs, I always feel like I'm getting away with something. But as we know: there are many pieces to the pie. Be one.

Keep your word.

They say a blizzard this big comes around only every decade or so. This time, it had to come the day after Christmas, and on a Sunday, so together one of the biggest travel nightmare days of the year.

My plan was to take a late bus and wring every bit of fun I could out of my holiday weekend, but it was not to be. I practically hurled my Christmas tree out the front door, leaving furniture askew and yesterday's wineglasses unwashed. Pine needles everywhere—no time to vacuum. I managed to squeeze on a bus at eleven thirty a.m. And oh, do I mean squeeze.

The trip took forever what with the snow, but even though it was cramped, it was warm, and the drive didn't feel too dangerous. Then I started to think, never mind about the first two hundred miles. How was I going to get the five miles from the bus station to home?

You don't need to ask: of course the streets were empty, even in Times Square, and the snow was falling hard and fast. A few cabs came by, all filled or with off-duty lights on. After about fifteen minutes, one lone off-duty taxi stopped at the light and gave me a glance, me and all my bags and holiday gear.

"Please," I begged, telling him my address, "could you take me home?" He was heading home himself after only three hours of driving, and I was out of his way. He shook his head no and inched off. I half ran, half fell toward him. "Please. I'll give you a good tip."

He nodded his assent and I poured myself in. It wasn't the worst driving I've ever seen, but it was slow going on the icy roads, and we sort of talked each other through it. It was pretty, that's for sure, but I was glad when I was home, and a little worried that he was not yet.

Now, I'll never see him again, and I could easily have stiffed him. But I tipped him 100 percent and was thrilled to do it.

DECEMBER 27

Find a new way.

What a great idea for us social media nuts.

In this case, it was for a terrific organization called Reading Is Fundamental, but it could be anything—including something you make up yourself.

The idea is to announce that you offer a donation to the cause for every new person who follows you within a certain time period. This way, you make new friends online (this was on Twitter) who are interested in what you're interested in, while helping out with something you believe in.

I'm in!

The offer can be as good as the deed.

Just because someone doesn't take you up on a favor offered, it doesn't mean you haven't done something nice.

In the subway tonight, I ran across a man with two suitcases, trying to arrange himself and his gear before trudging up a couple of long flights of stairs. Having recently been in the same situation myself during the holidays—plus trying to balance a cheesecake, though I have no clear memory of why I would want to do that—I decided to lend a hand. Actually, I had hurt my back, and was a little achy, but his situation looked like a total drag.

"Can I help you with those?" I asked.

"Oh, no, but thanks," he answered, but amid his mess and the throngs of commuters bumping by him, he smiled up at me happily. Guess it was just enough for him to know that it was going to get better, if he ever actually got home.

One man's garbage is another man's gift.

It was my aunt Tessie I first saw doing this. We always kid her that she loves a trip to the dump. ("I do!" she inevitably responds.) A couple of Diet Cokes, a few beer cans, and off she'd go with a little plastic bag, tied up with her treasures inside. It wasn't really about being green: it was the five cents a can. She would screech up to the little hut where the guys who worked at the dump sat (the same men who, when Uncle Bud complained that it seemed crazy that the dump was closed on Sundays, said, "Hey, mister, we like a nice hot meal, too") and hand them her bag of cans. She figured they might as well get the deposit money, never mind recycling them. They loved it.

It took me a while to realize folks here in New York City were doing the same thing. I live near a large supermarket, and they have a specific time of day when people come with huge bags and grocery carts, filled with hundreds of cans to redeem. The majority of the cans must come from corner garbage containers, but you can walk down the prettiest little block in Manhattan and see tiny plastic bags tied on wrought-iron fences. Cans for the collectors. I put mine together today and left them by a city garbage container on my corner—not quite as prosaic, but the same result.

Toss a coin in someone's e-wishing well.

Kickstarter. What an incredible idea!

I'm so in love with this concept I hardly know where to start. Maybe everyone else knows about it by now, but I just heard about Kickstarter a couple of weeks ago, when I got an e-mail from my friend Jesse. I knew he'd been involved in making a movie recently, and it had seen some success, yet had a limited release. Now he and his partners wanted to spread the word, and hopefully get themselves in the black. A DVD release seemed the answer . . . but where would they get the money? Jesse's e-mail explained it all: how they could get their DVD seed money of ten thousand dollars, and how I could be their angel. It was all about Kickstarter.com.

When you need money for a creative project, you go to this website and fill out a proposal to start your fund-raising. Set giving levels, offer rewards to donors, make your dream sound irresistible. Have a time limit: folks pledge their support, and if the goal is not reached, the money is never collected.*

As I look on the home page, there are some incredible projects that need our help: a design studio that came up

---

*If the goal is met, Kickstarter charges a 5 percent fee of the funds raised. Amazon, through PayPal, also charges a credit card processing fee.

with edible cups for a Jell-O mold competition now wants to bring this sustainable invention to the world. It's looking for ten thousand dollars. A woman plans to buy a used truck and make it a mobile printshop, crossing the country and teaching her craft. A New Orleans street band is trying to produce an album: you can pledge as little as one dollar to these guys, but if you give them ten dollars, you'll get a CD when it's done.

Kickstarter calls itself "a new way to fund creative ideas and ambitious endeavors." Will I start a new project of my own on Kickstarter in the coming year? I have no idea right now. But I do plan to make it a website I visit often, and I hope to give (even if it's a tiny amount) to lots of creative people who need a little help from their friends—and some friends they've never met.

Oh, and as for Jesse and his partners? They passed their ten-thousand-dollar goal, and for the thirty dollars I donated, I'll get a DVD of the film—and I'll be listed in the credits!

DECEMBER 31

New year, new you.

It may be the end of this particular year, but it's just nearing the middle of the One Good Deed project for me. Aside from everything else, embarking on this path has made me feel better about myself as this year comes to a close, and though this is not the goal, it's a wonderful side effect and certainly makes it easier every day to move forward. I think it has made me build on myself, like working out at the gym.

So I welcome the new year.

On this particular day I guess I could recount my favorite and memorable moments (and the not-so), but that seems either self-aggrandizing or self-deprecating.

I'm doing what I can, and next year, I'll try to do better. That's all.

Connect.

It does seem funny to start the new year talking about booze, since January 1 is pretty much considered National Hangover Day, and I don't even drink anymore.

However, January 1 is also my friend Bob's annual International Vodka Tasting party. It's been going on for twenty-one years, and now that we're all a couple of decades older, the event seems to be more about the fabulous dinner spread he puts out than about the quaffing.

Also: I have a great friend named Ann who started a small distillery in Lake Placid a few years ago, and what do you think she makes? Vodka. One brand has special Lake Placid water; another is made from nearby potatoes. Terrific locavore stuff.

What better way to say thank you to both Bob and Ann for all the nice invites they've proffered over the years than to buy some of Ann's wares and send Bob a private stash for when the party's over? Everybody wins!

Sadly, except for me. Oh, well: Diet Coke, please.

Resolve.

I didn't talk about New Year's resolutions yesterday because I was busy thinking about the vodka, but today, as the new year fully settles in, it's time to consider.

This year I simply want to feel just a little better every day about my place in the world, and inspire others to do the same. A little more from everybody = a lot.

The advice I give myself every year on the resolution front, and that I'm happy to pass along to you, is to remember that resolutions are like diets. Don't dream too big; you'll only be disappointed. But inch by inch, pound by pound—that's in the ballpark.

Send good thoughts.

There are days, like today, when nothing unusual happens. I take the bus. I work at the store. I'm a writer, and lots of times I have deadlines, and so I just come home and write.

Sure, I like to think I do something nice every day, even on the really boring days. Maybe I don't bite someone on the bus who bugged me. *That's* nice. I'm extra friendly to the cashier at the grocery store on the way home. And I'm always trying to help customers find the very best book for themselves: but who wants to hear about that every day?

So at some point in the day, I try to do a little thing, even if it's just in my head. Sometimes it's only a plan I can do for someone later. Sometimes it's just, what, a prayer? A message sent out into the ether? Good energy on another's behalf? A positive thought?

Maybe just thinking outside your own box is good deed enough.

JANUARY 4

Top it off.

I ask you: Who, in what city or town in the last half century, assumes that a bus driver gives change on the bus? Who? Or that dollar bills will suffice? What dopes! And then there's that smaller subset who know perfectly well that they don't have the right change when they get on the bus, but, equipped with the knowledge of their fabulosity, assume that riders will rush to take their crumpled singles and come up with the correct change or a dip of their transit card.

I know, I know ... when do I get to the good deed?

Tonight, on the way home from work, a lady who looked as tired as I was got on the bus just before me. *Clink, clink, cl...* well, turns out not quite enough clinking: she had miscounted her change and was short fifteen cents. Of course I was happy to lean in and say, "Here, I've got it." Why? Because anyone can miscount; she didn't do it on purpose. And besides, what's better than when you see a stupid hassle coming, and someone steps in and makes it just go away?

JANUARY 5

Prick up your ears.

I got a text from a friend today: "Hey, Happy New Year! Wanna grab a drink tonight?"

No, not really. I'm exhausted; I'm still reeling and fat from the holidays. I want to go home and watch cheesy TV.

"Sure!" I tap back. "When and where?"

Telecommunication cannot dull the sixth sense that your friends have something on their minds, that they're feeling low, that maybe they just need to talk. Too many exclamation points. An urgency in their cheery patter. Last-minute requests, disguised as fun.

This is an unusual request from this particular friend, and so of course I say yes. I'll find out soon enough what's up.

Hold your tongue. (Except for dumplings.)

My favorite deeds have become the ones where the Good Guy role changes several times during the story. Tonight was one of those times.

You may remember my shilling outside the local taco restaurant a couple of months ago, telling passersby they simply must stop in for a bite. Now the same owners have taken the first, tiny joint they were in and turned it into a dumpling den. I couldn't wait for it to open.

But it did, at last, this evening. And the newspapers had been given a taste, evidently, because the reviews were already in: fantastic. So I trundled over to pay my respects. Jammed. And the place had been open only two hours! I kissed the owners, found the last seat, a stool by the window, and squeezed in.

Well, no one could have seen this coming—seems, as kitchen people say, that they were "in the weeds" a little already. Things seemed sluggish, some diners agitated.

Here's the tale of what transpired, and how we each tried to out-good each other:

1. I order, and I wait. And wait.

2. Waitress offers me free drink. I decline but inquire about my food. I am told it went to the wrong table.

3. I continue to be a delightful customer. And wait. (Did I mention this was just dumplings?)

4. Another half hour passes. I am told my meal will be comped. (I love free food—who doesn't?) Now I'm excited.

5. Dumplings arrive. Scrumptious.

6. I tell waitress to bring me check, regardless of boss's orders. "OK." She shrugs.

7. I sit and feel good about myself.

8. Waitress returns. "No go on the check," she reports. "Still free."

9. I give her a huge tip and thank her.

JANUARY 7

Give with your whole heart.

Let me tell you what I hate. I hate sitting next to people. I believe the best reason in the world to have a significant other, besides having help to move furniture, is that you have someone you like in the adjoining plane, train, or movie seat. I adore an adventuremate; but if I'm traveling alone, I'd rather *be* alone.

Today, I had two fantastic seats to a morning dress rehearsal at the opera, given to me by my very generous Met friend. At the last minute, my musical date had to cancel. This left me with an extra ticket, and a conundrum: would I make a ticketless opera lover ecstatic, and give away the seat *right next to me*? Or throw it away, with the knowledge that I could languish, stretch out, and surround myself with all my stuff? I put the ticket in my pocket.

It was a freezing day, but there were a few hardy souls outside the opera house, hoping for the best. I've done the same myself. Now my better side was in gear and I was excited to give away the ticket, because I know how thrilling it is for someone to walk up to you and offer you a chance to see something spectacular.

So here was a guy with a photocopied sign that said "Need Ticket Please," which made me suspicious that he might do this every day, but he was older, and had a cane, so naturally I caved. I got a pretty perfunctory "Thank you," not one worthy of fourteenth-row orchestra, if you ask me, but OK. After I walked away, I turned around, and there he was, showing his bounty to another man. I flew back over. "Hey," I said, "you're not *selling* that to him, are you?"

"No, no, no, we are friends, not scalpers," they replied in unison. I apologized, of course, though they did seem a bit too savvy at this.

I felt like the schmo that I am, but still, when I sat down next to some ladies whom he evidently knows, and he plopped himself down in front of me (not the seat I gave him), I offered to switch so they could sit together, because I felt creepy about being accusatory. "No, I want to sit closer," he said.

Never another peep from this joker. Not a "Thanks so much again," or "Wasn't that a lovely show," not even a "Have a nice day."

But at least he didn't try to sit next to me.

Give the earth a break.

Mulchfest! Who wouldn't want to go?

Sometimes I get to mark my calendar in advance, knowing a good deed is headed my way. Like Mulchfest. There's a grand little park nearby that hosts all kinds of things year-round: concerts, bulb-planting day, and my favorite, the Halloween Howl, an autumnal doggie dress-up contest.

But this was an event new to me, and it piqued my interest. You could drag your Christmas tree to dozens of spots throughout the city, they would toss it into a chipper, and it would exit as wood chips used to nourish trees and plants citywide. If you were lucky enough, as I am, to have outdoor space, they would even give you a bag of mulch to take home with you! I slung my tiny, dried-out, apartment-size tree over my shoulder for a second time, and off I went.

I love this idea. It's green and all, but mostly it lets you keep your tree up way past the time your mother would ever allow.

Stand by your friends.

I felt pretty crummy today, but I went to work anyway, since I didn't have a fever, and tried not to breathe on or kiss too many people; I had a ticket to see an old friend play music tonight way downtown, and I was really dragging my feet. It's not that I didn't want to go, I did—but it was so cold, and I felt so puny, and I had no one to go with.

So after I got done feeling sorry for myself, I got on the subway.

Though I'd known this woman for twenty years, I'll bet I hadn't heard her play in nearly ten. She has been an extremely supportive friend all the while, performing for free at fund-raising events when I've asked her, and buying my books when they were published. I would not miss this night. I ordered a tea with honey at the bar, which came with a side of snarly glare, found a seat, and settled in.

What a difference a decade makes! It was almost as if I were listening to a different instrument altogether: confident, strong, as honeyed as the tea. I left feeling worlds better, and I doubt it was the libation.

Now, if we could just figure out a way to repay every extra effort we make with beautiful music.

Rise above it.

I'd like your opinion:

If I hold the door open for several people in a row, and not one of them says thank you or even glances at me, and then I am resentful, does it still count as a good deed?

Because now I feel like I want to trip a couple of them.

Not the old lady, though.

Waste not, want not.

It wasn't a big deal. But it was nice.

I was peckish, and doing errands, and all that was in my sights was a McDonald's. But they do have those scrumptious little wraps for a buck, so in I went. As I finished paying for my order, the teenager behind the register started to walk away with a cup of coffee in her hand. She eyed me and said instead, "Want this? I got the wrong drink, and I'm just gonna throw it away." Not the most beguiling offer, but it tickled me somehow. I had no desire for a cup of coffee, but it seemed only right to say yes, the way you do in some countries because it's customary, and terrible manners if you don't.

I thanked her profusely and slipped her a dollar. She just looked at me. The magic was broken. Plus, I'd actually paid now for the cup of coffee I didn't even want or order.

So why did I leave feeling so good?

Make it a little easier.

Sometime in the dead of night—like Santa, nobody actually knows when—the newspaper is delivered. (Never even mind the entire mystery of how they manage to get them off the press and into the trucks and to the right door in the space of a few hours. That I can't fathom.) I don't have a subscription, but the people across the hall from me do. And they surely keep different hours than I do, because I've seen their *New York Times* plenty, but I don't think I've ever seen them.

However, the last few weeks it seems their paper has been getting tossed a shorter and shorter distance, or farther and farther from their apartment. So now part of my morning ritual has become to kick it down to their door, so they can just put a hand out, like Thing, instead of having to come down the hall in their bathrobe and scare the neighbors.

Everybody wins.

You have something valuable to give.

A woman I had just met—but in the company of others I knew a little better—told me that she was going to try to write a book. I thought it was a good idea, would have an audience, and be helpful to lots of folks. So I told her to let me know if she needed any advice starting out, and she said yes.

So tonight we met for a drink. I've written lots of books; I'm no millionaire, but I am a professional. As often happens in a situation like this, people don't always want to hear some of the truths you're going to tell them. For example: it's really hard, it's going to take longer to write than you think, you have to organize the entire book before you try to sell it. But I think she was grateful, though it may take time for her to realize it was a lot of useful advice, like a one-on-one workshop over a couple of chardonnays—at least for one of us.

As I say, I didn't know her, but I believed in the idea. And at one time, not so long ago, some people I knew believed I had good ideas, too. My first editor, my first agent, are good friends. So yes, I was happy to help.

Pass the word along.

It couldn't be easier to do, and it might mean the world to one family.

This morning, one of the people I follow on Twitter has lost her dog somewhere in New Jersey. I can't go look myself, obviously, but she's loaded a picture and description online. The more of us who "retweet," or send the message along to ever-widening circles, the better chance Maggie will be returned to her owners. All I did was hit a button. Come home, Maggie!

Maggie was spotted the next day by her owner, who drove around looking for her. A local woman had found her and taken her in for the night, and they were going for a walk. Happy ending!

There's a cover for every pot.

I get a lot of free books, having been in the industry for so long, but every so often I get a surprise box of treats from a pal of mine at a major publishing house. It's always the same feeling. Ooh! Free books! New stuff! Each beautiful to gaze at and touch. I take them all out of the box and line them up. I zoom in on what I want to read first, put a few to the side, read the jacket copy on some I'm unfamiliar with.

There are always a few I know I won't read, but still, there's a crazy desire to hold on to them all anyway. But I resist the selfish book hoarder in me and make a pile and a list in my head of where some of these will find happy new homes and I take them there, whether it be the library or a friend. So from Karen, to me, to unsuspecting recipients, here come some great books.

Put a mind at ease.

Sometimes a good deed is just in the offering. My cousin tells me that an old friend of my parents is in the hospital here in New York. Her two daughters live quite far away, and I know at least one of them has come to town, but here they are, away from home. It's hard enough to be a patient and be away from home, and a whole other to have none of your friends around. So I e-mailed the daughter and said, Hey, I'm available for bedside companionship when you need a break. Just say the word.

Because there's nothing like having a familiar face on call.

Help a kid learn about fund-raising.

Anyone out there got somethin' to say if I claim that buying six boxes of Girl Scout Thin Mint cookies from an adorable little girl named Ruby is a good deed?

Anybody?

OK, then. Good.

Keep it to yourself.

I'm home, sick. Coughy, dizzy, exhausted, feverish sick.

I didn't go to work. I can barely sit up to write this.

What's the good deed? I fully believe that if at all possible, when you work in close proximity with people—both coworkers and customers—you owe it to them to stay home and not infect them.

But geez, if this is really a good deed, why does it feel so *bad*!

And by the way, if you share phones or computer keyboards with other people during sick season, wiping them off with disinfectant now and again is your best defense.

Sometimes, just say nothing.

A reenactment from the gift-wrapping station at the store this morning:

FAKE CUSTOMER: Oh, my God! I bought this camera? Across the street at Best Buy? And they don't wrap? And I couldn't find anyplace that sold wrapping paper?

ME: Really? There's a drugstore right next door, and another one across the street.

FAKE CUSTOMER: Yeah, well, but then the camera was so *expensive*.

ME: (Mute. But what I want to say is, "Then you should have bought him socks.")

FAKE CUSTOMER: You can't wrap this?

ME: No. We don't wrap people's gifts from other stores.

She looks incredulous. Shocked! And pissed off, too. Now there's another person—someone who actually bought something from the bookstore—behind her.

I give Fake Customer the stare of death, tear off a bit of paper for her, roll it up, and proffer it. Wordlessly.

FAKE CUSTOMER: Well, *that's* not going to do me any good. I have to get on the subway!

ME: (more mute)

She grabs it out of my hand and storms off. Real customer behind her wishes to give me a medal.

This is the kind of thing I like to call the Good Deed of Omission, like a Sin of Omission we learned about in catechism. Because the good deed was that I *didn't* spit.

Help the poor.

At a party before the holidays, my friend Connie said, "Everybody got a pair of goats this year." Was she drunk? Did I mishear? And then just today, I found a pamphlet in my house I had evidently overlooked back in December: Heifer International.

Turns out that was *exactly* what Connie meant.

You know, I sort of set aside a little cash each week for good deeds; as I've often said, I don't want this journey to be about just handing over money for whatever comes along, but things do come up that I just can't resist. And today, though I won't go so far as to purchase the entire animal, I will buy a share in a sheep.

Heifer International, by the way, has been around since 1944, working with agriculture and livestock programs to alleviate hunger and poverty. Hence, the goat, or sheep, a flock of chickens, some honeybees. If it helps, think of it as a pet you don't have to come home and walk.

So today, for ten dollars, I will help buy someone very far away a little lamb. You can do it, too. Check it out at www.heifer.org.

JANUARY 21

Don't be a jerk.

Of course there are days when I'm awful. (You had to ask?) Today was one.

I had a meeting I was afraid I'd be late for, so I hopped in a taxi. I told the cabbie the way I wanted to go, and he waved his hand and said, "No, no, no. No good. We'll go this way," and proceeded to tell me the route he had chosen. I decided to keep my mouth shut, but as time got tighter and traffic got slower, I lit into him—I was sure my route was better, and I told him so. Oh, yes, there were four-letter words. And the maddening part is that they never yell back at you. They've heard it all; they just keep driving.

But then, as it became clear that we might screech up to my destination in time, I grew quiet. Besides, now I was getting myself all riled up and sweaty before my meeting. I relented.

"I'm so sorry," I said to the driver. "You were right, and I apologize for being such a bitch. I'm nervous is all, and it's my own fault I left late." They never say anything to this, either, just expect a big tip. He got one.

Does the apologizing count as a good deed? Oh, no, I think not. I'm simply trying to assuage my guilt by telling myself that at least I tried to right my wrong.

Maybe that's worth something.

Recycle.

You know you have them. They're all over your house—cell phones, broken computers, your old Palm Pilot. And there's a way to get rid of them. In my case, there is a computer service center that sponsors events in different neighborhoods where you can drop off most of the stuff that right now is taking up an entire shelf in your closet. Your town has a place for this junk, too, so you should look it up. Today, I'm ridding myself of three old phones, a VCR, an old video camera, and a lot of guilt. Have I ever slipped the occasional battery into the trash? Yes, I have, and I've not lost sleep about it. But this is a lot of e-waste to just toss down the chute, so today I'm going to toss it where I'm supposed to. Now, if only I could find an emissions-free taxi to take me over there....

Don't let a minute pass you by.

Today marks the halfway point of my One Good Deed proj-ect, and as a special nod, I thought I'd share a little some-thing different. Last month, my friend Susan and I had a day on the town before the holidays. Susan doesn't live here in New York but is in town regularly, so that day, we did all the touristy things—the great things you never get around to doing, wherever you live, until guests come to visit. In our case, it included seeing the tree at Rockefeller Center, high tea at the Plaza, taking in the shop windows. Just a great day. For fun, I went home that night and wrote a list of all the things we did, from start to finish, and e-mailed it to her, just to point out exactly how much fun we had crammed into a few hours.

"Thank you, this is so great!" gushed Susan in a return e-mail. "I printed the list out, and it's going right in the Grati-tude Drawer."

The what?

She explained that for years she's had an empty drawer where she just tosses every piece of paper that will some-day be an important memory. (I know. I just have a junk drawer.) Party invites. Birth announcements. Report cards. Pencils from the racetrack. Maybe parking tickets, too, I don't know. Every few years, the drawer gets transferred to a bigger box. And there are boxes for her kids' stuff, too—

the things they don't care about now but will just love having later on.

"It's nothing formal," Susan says, "but it's fun to dip into every once in a while."

I love the idea. No one I know keeps a scrapbook with dance cards anymore, but I was thrilled to hear that Susan enjoyed our day so much that she wanted to treasure it.

So, may I suggest here, as we keep on the good deed trail: empty a drawer and keep a place for all the nice things that are happening to *you*, too.

Make it prettier.

A job is hard enough without having to kowtow to others' thoughtlessness; especially jobs where you have to pick up after others. People think, Oh, that's what they're paid for. But to me that begs two questions: one, paid how much? And two, do you really think that means you don't have to clean up after yourself?

There are jobs that people look down their noses at constantly, and a little help or a smile could give it some dignity: sanitation workers, bus drivers, checkout line folks, maintenance people, the guy in your building who compacts everyone's garbage and then takes it to the curb. Ick.

Today I decided to make it my job to pick up junk everyone else left behind. A can rolling around on the floor of the subway car (which is also just so damn annoying); napkins and tissues dropped on the floor at the store (so gross, I know, so I used a buffer tissue for that work); empty water bottles sitting just about everywhere; bags that missed the trash can on the corner. Does it sound demented? Maybe. But every time I picked something up and tossed it in the right place, I kept picturing what it would be like if everybody did it, just for a day.

The rest of the time I spent washing my hands. It's entirely possible that the amount of water I used offset my good deed.

Reach out.

It was a slippery, slidy day on the streets, and everyone's eyes were focused on their feet. Mine, too. But as I was scanning the slush and puddles at the corner, trying to pick the best route, I heard a plaintive little cry: "Help! Will somebody please help me?"

And there she was, trying to make her way from the street to the sidewalk: she was in no danger, just sort of stuck. An older woman, bright yellow mittens sticking straight out, hoping for a hand. A couple of people slowed, though others ignored her altogether—probably they pictured her bringing them both down.

I figured what the hell—I'm still a little too young to break a hip, but she wasn't. So I tossed my bag down into the snow, reached across to this trembling little lady, and pulled her ashore. It was next to nothing on my part, but you should have seen the relief on her face.

Just listen.

It sounded interesting: volunteering at a mystery book club—for blind people. I showed up at the appointed time and was directed to a small, sparse room with a snack bar. I bought a bottle of water and sat down. Eventually everyone arrived, and although it was three volunteers to four club members, it was clear these regulars looked forward to this weekly rendezvous.

Our volunteer leader offered up this week's selections: some British short stories. Our group preferred a recording, I learned, rather than one of us reading. The room grew quiet and we began. Strange but true, I'd never listened to an audiobook. It didn't take but a minute for me to realize I didn't know how to do this. How to stop looking around, to concentrate just on hearing. After a while I settled in and started to get the hang of it, but I was unnerved; for the first time in my life it became obvious to me how much I relied on all my senses, always working together in perfect harmony.

I glanced at the man sitting at the next table. He had fallen asleep. I immediately lost my concentration. How do you stay awake when everything is dark all the time? This would totally be me! If I were blind, I thought, I would always be asleep. I would be in a constant state of napping. I realize this is surely one of the lesser problems of being sightless, but still. This group was so cheerful. They had no idea of their drab surroundings, they didn't care who we volunteers were, what we wore, who we were when we weren't there with them, listening.

There was banter, discussion, great insights, plans for the next week. I had fun. I learned about a whole new way to read. I learned about listening, which is never bad. I intend to go back and learn more. Once again, I seem to have gotten the sweet end of the good deed.

JANUARY 27

There are some things there's always time for.

I hate to be ignored. So do you.

So I never, ever pass by any of my doormen without a wave or a hello. Often, at the end of a long day, their smiles are the thing that has made me feel best all day.

"Hello, Ram. Am I glad to see you."

JANUARY 28

Your heart learns from observing.

I think I'm learning from One Good Deed. Because this is getting very meta.

I've mentioned the mysterious man who sits on the corner with his bags, and disappears every morning. Tonight I was walking to the movies, and he was there once more— the first time I'd seen him at night. Just as I was wondering why, a guy turned the corner and handed him a cup of coffee. "Here you go," he said and waved, while the man with the bags thanked him profusely. Nice, I thought.

And then, wouldn't you know it. I was walking home in the snow, post-movie, and found a woman sitting outside a nearby drugstore. As has become my custom, I gave her some change from my pocket. Exiting a few minutes later, I took a few steps before the lightbulb went off. I backed up.

"Can I get you a cup of coffee?"

JANUARY 29

Celebrate anything.

I'm disguising this as a good deed, but really, I did it to make myself feel good.

I'll make it short, but the story actually starts in 1957. I was five, and my mother got it in her head that before I started first grade, I should contract every childhood disease possible (seemed she had rheumatic fever as a kid, and developed a lifelong problem with fractions because she missed so much school). So she kept her ear to the ground, and whenever she heard about another kid home sick, whoop! there we were, hanging out at their house, sharing sippy cups and germs. Over the years I've retold this, and people think it's awful; but I think it's pretty smart. I got mumps, measles, German measles, and chicken pox, all in the course of a few months. I also got to lie around a lot, something I still excel at. The downside for my parents was that they were running out of ways to entertain me: books, puzzles, TV, finger paints.

On one of these endless days my mom realized it was my half-birthday, so as a way to entertain me, she made a one-layer round cake, cut it in half, put one layer atop the other, and frosted it. How cute! A half cake, and I loved it.

But, oh, no, I wouldn't let it go; I insisted on a half-birthday cake every year; then she found the Wine Cake recipe, and that became the annual treat. It actually *does* have wine in it, and these days I suppose parents don't go for that, but times were different. In those days, you were also smoking while you were baking Wine Cakes. College, Boston, New York, home or office, the Wine Cake arrived every January 29. It ain't fancy, it weighs about six pounds, and it has the shelf life of a Twinkie. It doesn't even have frosting! But wow, what a cake. Before she died, my mother asked my cousin Mimi to carry on the tradition, and she's done a pretty good job. Sometimes the cake shows up today, sometimes another random day during the year.

So tonight I came home and made the Wine Cake, and I'll take it to work tomorrow and share it. It's hard to tell which goes over better—the cake or the story. They're both delicious.

WINE CAKE

1 pkg. yellow cake mix
1 small pkg. vanilla instant pudding
4 eggs
3 Tbsps. butter
½ c. vegetable oil
1 c. cooking wine
¼ c. hot water
1 tsp. nutmeg

Preheat oven to 350°F. Combine all ingredients in a bowl and mix with electric mixer on medium for about two minutes. Pour into flat cake pan or Bundt pan and bake for 40–45 minutes.

JANUARY 30

Try, anyway.

This place bugs me. But I actually wanted something I knew this store carried, so I headed over and was met by the usual "Big Sale" signs, including, this time, "Lost Our Lease." What bugs me about it is that this chain, which shall remain nameless (Pier 1 Imports) advertises sales, and they are never very good.

Nevertheless. I get my one thing I came for, and I go stand in line. A woman comes over to the lady in front of me and says, "How much you spending there?" which I think is odd, because they don't seem to know each other. Lady glances into her basket: "About a hundred dollars." Lady #2 says, "Take this coupon, then. You get a free candle if you spend fifty dollars." Much thanks, nice words, and then Lady #2 hands a coupon to me: she has a few. I'm thrilled, even though I'm spending twelve dollars, and did I mention I hate this place? But free is free.

Come to find out when Lady #1 gets to the register, nobody gets to use the coupons because this branch is closing, though we have two more days to go to another branch and spend fifty dollars before the coupon expires.

So now we all scramble around and ask everybody else around us if they might be going to another Pier 1 in the next couple of days, because we have coupons! coupons! coupons for them! Now it's a group effort—a groupon, if you will. No luck.

I can't stand it anymore. I finally say to my posse, "You know what? I hate this place anyway. They should be ashamed to call their sales sales." Lady #2 whips around and looks at me, wide-eyed. "I thought it was just me! Their sales are awful. It's barely the sales tax!" We all concur that it generally makes us feel worse than no sale at all and head out into the night, resigned but happy to have tried to help each other out.

Always offer.

Had the cable guy here this evening.

I'm sorry—is there any sweeter transaction between two strangers than someone who tries to tip, and another who refuses, but offers a warm thanks?

I don't think so. It's one of those restores-your-faith-in-humanity moments.

Rejigger.

"Where do you live? You want some help with those?"

I was speaking to a woman on the street who looked like she was about to drop one of her several bags. She laughed—she could feel she was losing her grip—and let me at least help her rearrange her packages. With a heartfelt thank-you, she moved on and so did I.

That's all. Felt nice, though. And I'm pretty sure I saved an expensive bottle of wine.

Politics is a two-way street.

I have a friend I've known for many years. I am hoping, and I am not alone, that she will become the next mayor of New York City.

It's a couple of years until the next election, and as yet she has not formally announced that she's running. She needs a war chest, and some public support, and I am 1,000 percent behind her. That's why I sent a contribution to go to this event and squeezed into a bar with hundreds of other people who believe in her like I do.

This early on, I suspect this is just what a candidate wants to see: that interest is high, that the community is behind her, that everywhere in the room she looks, she sees a face that's eager to help. This was no big-ticket event. I gave her a hug, was careful not to take up any of her valuable time tonight, had a drink, and left for a bite with a friend.

This is part one of helping the candidate you believe in to win. There will be more, and I will be there. I am happy to help her now, or anytime. With any luck, she'll be working very hard for me later.

Think positive.

When I heard a friend had been let go from her job, I winced. It seems these days, we've all been through it at least once, and even if it's not your fault, and you really hated that job anyway, there it is every morning, the first thing you think of when you get up: I'm jobless.

So I asked her over for dinner and was pleased when she accepted. We are not close enough to be cry-on-your-shoulder friends, but I know that after the initial round of surprise and calls from people, it's easy to feel absolutely alone. Also easy not to leave the house.

We had fun, she got to vent a little, and I was happy I'd made the call. It brought to mind how I felt when I lost a job many years ago. I was glad not to be at that job anymore and was even getting paid for a while, but I was blue, no doubt about it. I said to my girlfriend, "I don't know. Whenever I go out in the daytime I feel like everyone on the street is looking at me and thinking, 'Why isn't she at work? She must have gotten fired.'" And she replied, "Maybe people think you're just taking a stroll, trying to figure out how your novel ends."

That changed everything.

Send some love.

Somehow I got in my head recently a picture of the old-fashioned valentines that came in a cellophane package that we got as kids. You gave them out at school to your class-mates. My mom made me send one to everybody, which spoiled the entire idea—how would my true love know he was special? One of your first lessons in being kind.

These are the selfsame valentine cards Charlie Brown never gets.

I know it's a little early in the Love Season to talk about valentine cards, but I thought maybe you'd like to do what I'm doing. I went to the drugstore today to suss out the card choices. Things have changed some, of course—now they're all tie-ins to something else. Barbie, SpongeBob, lenticular Star Wars. Oy. I settled on a set of twenty-four Olivia cards, because she is an irresistible pig in any season. (A warning: these cards no longer come with envelopes, so go buy your-self a box of cheap ones.)

My mission: if you're old, if you're alone, if your heart is broken, expect an old-fashioned valentine from me and Olivia this year. Sealed with a kiss.

Clean up your mess.

Today I prevented a major personal hygiene embarrassment. I was meeting someone for lunch and stopped into the restaurant bathroom to wash my hands before sitting down. What a mess. All around the sinks were puddles of water splashed by previous customers: clean hands, wet, soapy sink. I leaned toward the mirror and whoa! just in the nick of time avoided adding a huge wet stripe to the front of my outfit. Sheesh. So I got a big wad of paper towels and had just set about cleaning up the counter when another customer exited a stall and came over to the adjoining set to wash up as well.

"Hold it!" I dove over like I was going for a line drive. "It's all wet." Suffice it to say she had on a much nicer outfit than mine. I sopped up the rest of the mess, and we went on our way, she leaving with a grateful thank-you.

You can save a tree, one branch at a time.

Without fail, every Saturday and Sunday morning, swarms of parents arrive at the bookstore with their kids in tow. What do they have in common, aside from frayed nerves?

No present for the birthday party.

Because it seems like that's where most of them are on their way to—and late for: a kiddie birthday party. They come to our store because we have books and toys. And we wrap for free. It's a very smart and inexpensive way to boost sales, that's for sure.

Eventually there's a heap of paper scraps. Our M.O. is to put them to one side and call upon them when the right present comes along. Some of our gift wrappers are less than scrupulous; to me it's a personal competition to try to utilize what I can.

I do have scruples. I figure as long as I can control myself and not put the leftover Happy Birthday paper on the gift from the "Death and Grieving" section, I should be all right.

FEBRUARY 7

Put your signature where your mouth is.

I was livid.

So livid that I wanted to sign the petition I heard was going around.

Signing a petition is a great good deed, because it means you're really standing up for something you believe in. Literally putting your name on the line. This is why when you look at a petition-in-progress, all the signatures look so angry; if you run your finger along them, you can feel that anger in the indentations the pen has made in the paper. I love that.

And why was I so mad? Patty's Taco Truck was gone! Oh, sure, this may mean nothing to you, but this mobile Mexican eatery serves the best taco I've ever had in my life. Like, twenty-three times better than the best taco I'd ever had before. For three dollars. Lovely people, clean kitchen, top-notch ingredients. But now they have been towed twice. *Towed!* Right there as they were busy making burritos! The neighborhood association wants them gone, because the business and restaurant owners think they're cutting in on local business. These people employ folks, pay a city vendor's license, pass health inspections. Plus, they offer the superior product.

I'm sorry, I thought this was America!

I signed the petition. Next, picketing, if I must.

Toot someone's horn.

Here's a two-parter in Good Deed–dom.

Chatting the other day with Alason, who works with me in the bookstore, I discovered that she's an actress. Not an "actress," but an actual actress—in fact, she excitedly told me about an upcoming part she has on a new Oprah Winfrey Network show. Me, I would have been taking out ads in *Variety* to announce that, but Alason is very shy.

I was so totally excited for her that at our daily morning meeting I brought up Alason's coup—everyone seemed to be as in the dark as I was about her parallel life. And, of course, equally happy. Alason stood at the edge of the group, embarrassed and thrilled. Did I do the wrong thing? Somebody's got to toot her horn.

One good deed deserves another.

I was busy with a customer this morning when out of the corner of my eye I spotted Alason. You remember Alason, the actress from yesterday? She's very polite, so she just lurked around for a while while my customer yakked on and on. At last I was free, and she dove over, clasped my hand, and said thank you.

I looked down, and in my hand was a receipt. Working in our store's café, Alason knows that every day, I eat soup for lunch. (Yes, every day. Because I'm Irish, and the Irish hate change. And no, it's not the *same* soup every day.)

Alason had bought me lunch. So I hadn't mortified her by touting her success yesterday! I had done the right thing after all, and she was tickled.

Support what you enjoy.

I went to the gift shop in my favorite local museum the other day and found that my membership had just expired. Unfortunately, I didn't have my credit card with me, so I couldn't re-up on the spot. Dang.

Now a week has gone by, and I had forgotten all about it. But I can promise you, the second I finish writing this, I'm off to the New Bedford Whaling Museum website. You already know how much this museum means to me—has since I was a little girl. Now, many of you have likely both made use of some local institution and maybe also volunteered somewhere, so you know what it's like from both sides. It's great to have a park or museum or public beach or whatever to take advantage of, and if you've ever done some fund-raising, you know how tough it can be to meet payroll or avoid cutting corners or even shutting down something everybody enjoys. And every once in a while, if too many people like me miss a membership renewal or delay a planned donation, well, it can make all the difference. A few too many lean months can mean the end of the line for small institutions.

FEBRUARY 11

Take the wheel.

I had a guest who arrived yesterday from out of town and is staying with me, and we were discussing whether or not to take a little road trip today. "Ugh, I don't know if I can stand getting back in the car," she said. "I'll drive," I said, though I do enjoy watching the scenery instead on most occasions. "C'mon, it'll be fun." (An aside: A friend once said my tombstone should say, "C'mon, it'll be fun." Seems like I'm always trying to cajole someone into something.) She relented, and we had a ball, as we both knew we would. It was just the getting going of it.

It wasn't a big deal, really, and I didn't mind driving. But it reminded me that we all work so hard and get so worn out that sometimes taking the wheel in one form or another makes all the difference. Nah, let me go to the grocery store. Don't worry, I'll pick up the wine on the way over. I'll put the steaks on the grill—you relax.

Sometimes, you just need someone else to drive for a while.

Look outside your own world.

It's true that I have no children and thus, I am willing to admit, often have a less-than-patient attitude toward tots. Add to this an increasingly looser (in my humble opinion) parenting and nannying style, witnessed all day in a bookstore with a large kids' section, and I can become unpleasant in the face of bad behavior.

But when you let your child stand on a counter in the shoes he has walked around in all day, gathering dog poop, old gum, and a billion other miscreant germs—the very counter where I am standing to pick up my coffee and a Rice Krispies bar—well, yeah, sister, you're going to hear it from me.

Take the extra steps.

My back was killing me.

Standing in the bookstore for eight and a half hours usually doesn't take too much of a toll, I'm happy to say, but today, for some reason, *Ow.*

So I couldn't wait to get home. I suited up for the cold, got out to the street, walked to the corner to catch the bus, and there she was: the taco truck.

The (now-famed) truck has always seemed to have a Never on Sunday rule: at least, I've never seen it there on the Lord's Day. Which was just what I'd been telling my friend Christine at work. She, like nearly everybody at the bookstore, was upset about the recent taco truck tragedies, and had recently cut her days at the store down to one: Sunday. I had already offered to try freezing a burrito for her.

But my eyes deceived me not: there was the truck! What could I do? I wanted nothing more than to get home to two aspirin and a hot bath. But I walked back to the store, down the stairs, and into the break room and found my friend. She knew I had already left for home.

"Christine," I said simply.

She knew. Oh, she knew instantly. "It's here, isn't it?" she breathed.

FEBRUARY 14

Go paperless.

I thought for Valentine's Day I'd have a heart and help out those beautiful forests across this great land of ours. So I sat down and went through a bunch of bills sitting on my desk, got online, and went paperless.

I've dragged my feet about this. I'm all for the idea, and I already pay most of my bills online, but I've used the arrival of the bills on my doorstep to act as reminders. But that's stupid. I'm a grown-up. I can figure out how to remember to pay my bills without killing something, I suppose.

And so, I'm sending a little Valentine's tree-hugging love to all the forests out there today.

Don't complain!

I was pretty crabby this morning, I won't deny it; I felt like I was grousing about everything. It caused a certain old memory to come flooding back that was so silly it cheered me for the rest of the day.

Several years ago I was with some friends on a day trip to Martha's Vineyard. They were all southerners, and this was their inaugural visit. We had driven way up to Gay Head—now called Aquinnah—to see those gorgeous views and browse around at the little Native American shops. Ready to leave, I thought it a good idea to take a bathroom break before continuing our adventures. Everyone was still shopping when I headed down the hill to the public restrooms. I couldn't hurry back fast enough.

"You guys," I squealed, "you gotta come see this."

So off we all raced, me trailing close behind so I could catch their reactions. For right in front of the restrooms was a huge, cross, mean-looking woman perched on a chair next to a little table with a fishbowl. Taped on it was a hand-printed sign:

BATHROOMS
50¢
DON'T COMPLAIN!!!

Too hilarious. And did anyone complain about the fifty cents? No, they did not. How could you? All you could think about was how you should be shutting your yap. Well, that and the prison matron at the door.

So, my good deed, as I like to do occasionally, is to pass on some advice to myself and you today: heed the signs.

Allow yourself to hear.

Tonight I went to a meet-and-greet for a health agency, because a friend asked me to.

That would be enough right there, good deed–wise. We should support our friends' endeavors and causes if we can. And this one wasn't about money (at least not tonight); this was about spreading the word. And I'm happy to.

It's called Health Leads, and as is often the case, it's a simple idea, executed brilliantly. Some years ago a Harvard student named Rebecca Onie volunteered at a medical clinic, and she realized after several weeks that she kept seeing the same low-income patients over and over again. They would receive medical care, but then go back to a home with no heat or no food or other essentials to help them stay well.

She had an idea: why not get other volunteers to help at clinics and hospitals around the country, eager young students like herself who would ferret out ways to help these patients? And the pièce de rèsistance: the doctors began to "prescribe" what these sick people needed—and the patients were not to leave the office until they'd visited the Health Leads volunteer and gotten it.

I could go on; it was impressive. Doctors, volunteers, and staff spoke that night, and their enthusiasm about Health Leads's success was contagious. I'll be spreading the word about this fantastic venture often.

I'm not asking you to give money or volunteer for Health Leads (though you should check out this genius idea at www. healthleadsusa.org). But it's a great example of what you can learn when you say yes to someone.

Remembrance is vital.

I had a meeting today in a section of town I'm not very familiar with. New York has been walloped with snow this winter, but today it was an anomaly: sunny and sixty degrees. I checked my directions and was surprised to see how close to the World Trade Center site I was. Today, I thought, I would stop into that famous church nearby and say a prayer for the fallen.

I hadn't been to the site for a while, so when I rounded the corner, I was shocked to see how little had been accomplished. Nearly ten years later, only one office building was rising in the corner. I had the incredible good fortune to be in the pit as part of a documentary crew when the first concrete was poured in November 2005. It felt like little had been done since. Here came the tears: I was angry, and more than that, ashamed.

I entered the little chapel across the street. In over thirty years of living in the city, I'd never visited this spot, built in 1766 and the oldest public building still in continuous use. It was here at St. Paul's that workers, visitors, family, and brokenhearted people went in the days and months after 9/11 to say a prayer, as I was doing now. Only hundreds of yards away from the World Trade Center, its tiny graveyard had been severely damaged and filled with debris after the towers fell. I stepped inside the church: it was minuscule! How could such a small place have held so much sorrow?

It turned out I had some help paying my respects. There were just a couple of people wandering around, viewing the incredible memorials left behind, the most moving being a mannequin topped with a London bobby's hat, completely covered with badges left by police, firemen, and other responders from around the world. More tears.

And there was the choir. Right there, at that moment, a high school choir, complete with robes, was singing at St. Paul's, at one thirty p.m. on a random Thursday. I sat and listened to a couple of hymns, and the director announced they would finish with two last pieces. They sang "May the Lord hold you in the palm of His hand until we meet again."

Tears: lots of them. They finished with the "Hallelujah Chorus." By now I was a complete mess. How had I happened upon this? There was hardly anyone there but me! Turned out the choir was some kids from Michigan on a school trip who were just eager to sing in this hallowed place, audience be damned (pardon me).

By now there was nothing for it but to finish the afternoon by walking across the Brooklyn Bridge, where so many fled on that terrible day, which is such a monument to industry and invention, whose view is so vast and so purely American that you could swear you see Peter Minuit in the distance. I've walked the bridge only a couple of times, and have made sure to reread Walt Whitman's "Crossing Brooklyn Ferry" when I go. Tonight, I'll do that before I go to bed.

How did this plan to stop off and pay my respects turn into this amazing day? I'll never know, but to experience again the pain and brotherhood that was New York after September 11 was unexpected, and it felt like a private miracle.

And if you're wondering? No, I wouldn't have traded living here in the aftermath of that day for anything in the world.

FEBRUARY 18

Tiny multiplies.

Could this be any tinier of a good deed? Maybe not. But it's something that bugs me. I was on a long-distance bus—they would call it a luxury liner, but that's their opinion—and it was a beautiful morning, bright and sunny. I sat down and was nearly settled in for my trip: drink, muffin, music. But then I looked up and saw about a dozen overhead lights on. Ah, geez.

I couldn't stand it. Up I got, and I went and turned off every unnecessary light (no, not the ones where people were sitting!). What kind of energy could I have saved on this behemoth of a bus with such a small act? Am I OCD, green, or just a good girl? Who cares?

Someone wants what you don't.

You know you do it.

Regifting.

I have to go to a party tonight and thought I'd take a quick peek in my closet to see if there was anything there that might suit.

Not really. Boxes of nice soap, books I would never read, stationery, an expensive candle I hated the smell of (that one was my own mistake), even the Clapper, which I didn't know they still made. I mean, some good stuff, but perhaps not up my giftee's alley. But I figured somebody would want it. So I packed it all up and brought it to one of the many thrift stores dedicated to a good cause in my neighborhood, where they were thrilled with the windfall.

And the good news is, I now have almost a whole new shelf to fill.

Make a family.

You know by now that I have a large family, that we're very close, and that we very nearly invent scenarios in order to cook up a celebration. I'm extremely fortunate, and I know that. It's what has made me so good at keeping in touch with old friends—I think that my positive feelings about my relatives make me want to surround myself with satellite families. Folks I've worked with over the decades, college friends (I've chaired nearly every class reunion since 1979), other activists and groups I've volunteered with, whatever. Being gay has mushroomed my family-forming, too. Any minority knows that when the chips are down, it's other people like you who come forward to help and listen to your fears and dreams. I love a family.

Today I was speaking with a friend whose husband is ill. They are both often included in our family's festivities, but now we want to make sure she knows that she is always part of our family, without making her sad. Of course, that's impossible, but we say, jokingly, "If you hear we're having a party and we haven't called you, just show up. Show up if we're not having a party. Just come on over." There's no easy way to say, "Don't be sad and lonely, come be with us." We'll never be her real family, but we'll try our damnedest to make her feel loved.

Scrounge around.

Who ever has stamps? Who ever needs stamps when you happen to have them? No one. Never! And yet today, for some once-in-a-lifetime reason, I had two first-class stamps with me. Sort of left in a jacket pocket like a piece of gum.

In fact it was a lot like that, because they were a little bit the worse for wear, sort of linty on one edge. But when someone at work asked if anyone had three stamps, I jumped at the chance to be the savior. Naturally everyone was shocked: because everybody knows no one ever has stamps.

So my offer was quickly accepted, though I could tell the recipient was a little tiny bit annoyed that I didn't have the requisite three she wanted. (Another lesson in human nature: no one is ever satisfied.) But it did turn out that two of the bills in her hand absolutely had to go out today, and this less-than-a-dollar gift from me saved that day. Tomorrow, she would go to the post office. (And tomorrow we'll see if she offers those two stamps back.)

Try another door.

I don't know how to knit. OK, that's a *tiny* exaggeration. There was a summer sometime in the sixties when it was all the rage among us kids, so we bought this big thick yarn called Scandia, because you could—well, most could—whip off a hat or mittens in a flash. Ends up Cousin Mimi inherited the knitting gene in the family and has it still. I took up tennis.

At my bookstore, at the bookstore where Cousin Mimi works today, plus loads of others across the nation, knitting groups have become the subgenre of the book clubs that meet in stores for the benefit of folks who don't have their own group. I didn't get it for a while: I thought the members read a book and discussed it, plus knitted. But I came to discover that lots of these knitters come for an entirely different purpose: they're knitting for charity.

Maribel, the store manager who hosts our knitting group, mentioned an upcoming get-together recently, announcing that they were making hats for premature babies. Now I wished I had continued my paltry efforts all those years ago. How could I help? I wondered. So I asked. "Some of the yarn, the nice stuff, is expensive," she said. "And we do have a homeless woman who occasionally comes." And there's where I came in. If I can't knit, I can help someone else do it by donating some yarn.

Makes me think of the ladies' auxiliaries you heard about in wartime: sewing, rolling bandages, writing letters to soldiers. And in truth, I suppose it's not much different.

Show you care.

Ran into a friend tonight whose sister has been ill for some time. This is one of life's toughest times, of course, and if you're a friend who's not in daily contact, keeping tabs on the state of someone's health can be difficult.

This isn't the only person I ask this of—as life progresses, friends begin to lose their friends, their parents, their siblings. So I always want to ask how someone is doing, because I care, I do. But I know from experience, with both my parents gone (and neither deaths were quick ones), that my mood changed by the second. I didn't want one more person to ask about my mom—I needed to have an evening, an hour away from it, on my own. Ask me ten minutes later, I'd need to vent, maybe even cry.

There's no good way to approach it, really, and so very often the answers, too, aren't very good. But if you think a friend ever forgets that you asked, you'd be wrong. No matter how painful, it's always appreciated.

So I asked, and not for the last time: "How's your sister doing? I've been thinking about you."

Save a memory; relive it later.

Another piece of advice—hope you don't mind.

I saw an old friend tonight. Not a very close friend, but a woman I have just always liked so very much. She was as happy to see me as I was her—it had been a couple of years, and even then, it's always a cocktail party kind of thing when we *do* run into each other.

I've known her a long time, but part of what makes our brief encounters special is one night in the past. We were in a car together going to a funeral home for the wake of a mutual friend. It was a long ride, and we sat in the back together while the boys were in the front—the age-old division of automobile seating—and we had a long chat. About our deceased friend, about trouble in her marriage, about dreams for our careers. Here's what it was: just a situational closeness, but it was real, and it was a night I've never forgotten.

I know when we saw each other this evening that we both immediately thought of that night. It's our context. In fact, I asked after her kids, and then said, "You're still married?" She laughed, not because she's still married, but without my saying another word, she knew I was following up on a conversation from nearly twenty years ago, and that I cared.

That whole evening of the wake was special, and oddly, I remember almost every minute of it. That's the funny thing about life: you rarely realize at the time when something is happening—often something very ordinary—that it's going to be one of those offbeat times you remember forever. Sometimes, if the view out the car window is great, or somebody says something unexpectedly hilarious, or a night just turns into something totally unexpected, I try to remember to say to myself, right at that moment, Oh, put this in that memory bank. Save this. Because when I hugged my old friend hello tonight, it was like having that whole night back, all over again.

FEBRUARY 25

Wait a minute.

Today I decided to end a very bad habit.

All right, it's not exactly a *habit*, but years ago some jokester pointed out to me that when you're in an elevator, if you lean over and press the wall right next to the "door open" button, the poor slob running for the elevator thinks that you just gave it your best shot. You have to make an "oh, no" face, too. And yes, I've done this a few times.

Today, I actually did press the "door open" button for a grateful someone, pissing off an entire crowded elevator.

And that's how I'm gonna roll from here on in.

Respect someone's decision.

My cousin's son (nephew? second cousin? whatever) made his confirmation today. He's twenty-seven and getting married in the fall. Though he was baptized a Catholic, he was never confirmed, and now that he's marrying into a Catholic family, he decided to take the next step, presumably so that they can raise their children in the church. That is *my* assumption—I don't feel it's my place to inquire.

When I heard he was doing this, I asked if I might come to the ceremony, and I think he was pleased. I have plenty of problems with the church I was brought up in; still, that doesn't mean I don't occasionally go, and when I do I still receive communion. But the point is that I was extremely proud of him for coming into this as an adult. Normally a confirmation is at fourteen, years before most people seriously ponder theology and the place of religion in their lives. His was a huge decision: I wanted to show my support.

It was a lovely ceremony, and when his fiancée stood by him, her hand on his shoulder, declaring herself his sponsor, I teared up. When he surprised us by taking as his confirmation name his beloved late grandfather's, I cried.

Then I knew that despite my misgivings, I'd done the right thing: supporting my family.

Cheerlead.

I was talking to a pal from work today about her studies. Lots of people who work with me are also going to school, and though many of them are not young, this one is. "I've applied for an internship," she confided, "but I don't want to talk about it. I could jinx it."

"You can tell me," I prompted her. "I have a saint in my family, so I'm a really good person to tell stuff to, as I have connections."

Her eyes widened. "You could say a special prayer!" she breathed.

So she told me a little about the internship, and I asked some questions, and allowed as how she seemed a perfect choice, and that they'd be lucky to have her.

I'd like to think she walked off with a little spring in her step. Because we could both pray all we want, but nothing beats giving someone a jolt of confidence.

Keep your opinions to yourself.

Really, lady. That is a terrible outfit. Ooh, ouch. The worst. The maxi leather coat from 1991? With the cowboy hat? And waaaay too much perfume—no, let's call it just "scent"—

for anywhere outside of a brothel. The colors don't go, and there's too much jewelry.

In my heart I want to scream out and say, "I can help you!" With even the tiniest fashion advice—and I shop more frequently at Target than Saks Fifth Avenue—I could help right this wrong.

But she's got a little strut, and I do believe she thinks she is rocking this getup. So I know that though I think (and from the glances of others, I am not alone) that it would be a good deed to set her straight, the polite thing to do is just look away. It's another one of those Good Deeds of Omission.

I'm joking, of course—I'd never want to hurt her feelings. But I do sometimes need to remind myself to keep my pie-hole shut.

MARCH 1

Friendship is a lifelong good deed.

It's always the same trick with Lorraine. Alwaysalways-always. She'll e-mail and we'll make a dinner date. I'll say, "I'm paying: I still haven't taken you to dinner for your birthday." Or something like that. I try to think up any old reason, because she's paid for the last eighteen dinners.

"OK, fine, it *is* your turn," she'll say, and then we fight about the check when it comes. She always wins.

Lorraine was my assistant many years ago. I begged her to leave the position she had at the ad agency where we worked and come work for me; she was terrific and rose quickly. She says I was a good boss and am a good friend, and now that her life is more lucrative than mine, she apparently wants to make sure I have a good steak now and again. It's been many years of watching out for each other, with many more, I hope, to come.

Twenty minutes ago, Lorraine called and said her dinner date had canceled and she was in the mood to go to our favorite restaurant. Could I meet her there in half an hour?

Of course I could. Because I am holding the power tonight, I ruled that I could come only if I could pay. She reluctantly agreed. We'll see how that works out.

MARCH 2

Honor a person's wishes.

Here's something I hate. I hate it, and I think it's disrespectful: when a sincere request is ignored.

I got an e-vite last week to a friend's fiftieth birthday bash. At the bottom, she asked that in lieu of presents, she'd like people to donate to a charity—in this case Equality Now, an organization that works to end violence and discrimination against women and girls. She provided a link. Today, she sent a reminder about the party and reiterated that even if you weren't coming to the party, please don't send a gift. So I did what she asked and clicked to the site.

She means it. Because she knows people don't listen. They figure you don't mean *them*, and that the gift they have planned for you is *different*, and better.

It reminded me of when my mother died and I requested—in the newspaper and through word of mouth—that in lieu of flowers, all donations go to a women's homeless shelter. I love flowers, but I knew my family would be supplying more than enough for the service. My mother had had a rough childhood, shuttled around among family and strangers both, and was finally taken in by her aunt, uncle, and two boy cousins. It was a family made in heaven. But if this hadn't happened? No home, no future, no Erin, that's for sure. It meant a lot to me for people to do what I requested. And the shelter got some donations, sure. But what did we get more of? Flowers, flowers, flowers.

It's a slap in the face. If people gently prod you to turn your generosity elsewhere on their behalf, do it. They don't want your bottle of champagne or a cashmere sweater. They want you to do what they asked.

MARCH 3

Support means everything.

I could never do a deed as good as what all my friends did for me tonight, so I'm going to write about that.

I have just published a book, and tonight was to be my first appearance reading from it, with a little cocktail gathering beforehand.

Or that's what I thought was my night ahead. It seemed like everyone I knew showed up—and lots that I didn't know. There were well over one hundred people crammed in the room. New York's city council speaker—the second-biggest job in this grand metropolis—introduced me, and when I read from my book there were laughs, tears, and lots of applause. And yes, I also sold a bunch of books. A swarm of my very oldest pals carted me off to dinner afterward, where we laughed so loud and so long that nearby people moved to another table. (I'm sorry, folks.)

I've had few nights like this in my life, and I just thought it a good reminder to myself to see, and pass on, how the effects of one hundred good deeds brought together can make someone feel.

MARCH 4

Like.

This is what social media has brought us to.

A few weeks ago I asked a bunch of people I know on Facebook to "Like" the fan page of one of my books. Lots did. But not the person who asked me to be a fan on *his* page today. The nerve.

But I am bigger than that. I Liked his page. I was supportive.

And I hope you see this and know who you are. Because it hurts not to be Liked.

Say it.

Took a walk on the beach this morning with an old friend. Still wintry, no doubt about it—even a little snow in the parking lot. I wouldn't say the smell of spring was in the air, but on the other hand, I didn't have to wear a hat and gloves.

My pal had much to talk about—a lot was on her mind. Big things, life things. I listened, we mused, we parted not knowing a whole lot more than when we arrived.

It's funny, isn't it? I find it's when you see someone a little less, rather than more, that you find yourself trying to catch up on the major stuff when you get together. I don't think I caused any big lightbulbs to go off for her, but opening up to a friend is always a little bit of therapy, and it's the rare day that you don't both come out feeling a little better.

MARCH 6

Go out. Have fun.

It's a Sunday night, and though I hate to admit it, I am no longer eager to go out to a nightclub at ten o'clock. But a friend is having her fiftieth birthday party, and she's a musician, so there you are. They don't punch a clock at 8:45 a.m. Monday, now do they?

She is a cancer survivor, and the friend who insisted on no gifts, suggesting a charity to give to instead. I made sure I did that, but I also wanted to celebrate with her. We're not terribly close—frankly, I was thrilled to be included. I wasn't sure I'd know but one or two people, so I was feeling shy, but off I went nonetheless.

Whoa! The stuff that happens when you do the right thing! One of her band members had produced a whole show with people singing their congratulations to Elizabeth, all using a word that reminded them of her as their theme—and it ran the gamut from famous people to friends who couldn't carry a tune in a basket. And all the while, Elizabeth, standing at the side of the stage with the biggest, cancer-freest smile you can imagine.

And I was going to stay home and go to bed? Lesson learned.

There is such a thing as pennies from heaven.

Everybody's done this, and I've talked about it before, but it always gives me such pleasure.

Today I went to the deli to get some tomatoes, which it didn't seem to sell. How that can be, I still don't understand. Evidently, all the tomato space was taken up by cut flowers, so I bought those instead, which changed my culinary plans dramatically.

So there I was in line, and I was so lost in space that I didn't notice at first that the lady in jogging clothes in front of me was counting out the change from her jacket pocket, penny by penny. "What do you need?" I asked her, smiling and taking a bunch of coins out of my own pocket. (The smile was so she would think I was nice, and not a jerk hurrying her up. Which was possibly also true.) Turned out it was thirty-seven cents, and I was happy to hand it over.

Of course she thanked me profusely, then commented on the beauty of my flowers, and I left with a fistful of daffodils and a grin.

They call it a job because it's work.

Oh, what a good deed I did today. One that may not be appreciated for some time—or, if the recipient of the good deed doesn't wise up, ever.

I was standing at the information counter at the bookstore this morning when a young woman came in and told me she had a job interview at ten. We had a very short conversation; here's how it went:

ME: OK, who's your interview with?
HER: I don't know.
ME: You don't remember their name?
HER: I think it was a guy.

Pause. I paused because it made me feel really old to say the thing I said next, and I paused because I tried very hard *not* to say what I said next. But I couldn't help myself.

ME: Wow. That really seems like something you'd want to remember.

Disagree if you like, but I do believe I may have given someone the first—and perhaps most valuable—business advice of her quite possibly hapless career.

MARCH 9

Do extra.

At Holy Family Grammar School, where I spent what seemed like every second of my formative years, nothing put the fear of God into us tiny children more than Lent.

It was like a contest, and there was no way we were going to win. In the 1950s, Lent—starting on Ash Wednesday and lasting for forty endless days until Easter—was for giving something up. Of course, we were kids, so it was candy, or not hitting your sister, or ice cream. And as much as we hated it, we all wanted to be the best little sacrificial lamb in the class. As we got older, some of the more progressive nuns started suggesting that we should do something extra instead of giving something up, that this was a more productive way to teach kids about sacrifice. Groundbreaking!

So, today being Ash Wednesday, I thought it a good time to remind everyone that spring is a time of rejuvenation and new beginnings. Like maybe doing One Good Deed.

Besides, I'd rather do anything else than give up candy.

MARCH 10

Be polite.

This winter is eternal. And I am getting crankier. How many times over the last week have I held the door open for an older person, a woman with a carriage for twins, a lady with a walker, a person simply with a lot of stuff. How many gifts have I wrapped beautifully for you for free? A whole bunch, that's how many. And how many have said thank you? Four? Out of what, nineteen, maybe?

I know, I know: everybody else is as cold and cranky as I am, too. Still. Would it kill you to say thanks so I don't have to negate my good deed by yelling after you, "You're *welcome*!" Because I'm about to go into Negative Deedism right now.

MARCH 11

Don't waste a minute.

Today is one of those days. And, at least as my life goes on, it seems they are coming closer and closer together.

Last night, a ferocious earthquake, followed by a devastating tsunami, hit Japan. I often say here that it's not about giving money as a way to perform good deeds.

But today it is.

While they are saying on the news that hundreds have died in Sendai, I can't believe it won't jump into the thousands before this is over. Earlier today, it looked like our own citizens, people from Hawaii and California, might also become victims of a tsunami. The danger seems to have passed, but in that moment, in those hours you thought it might be you, or those you love, you knew a little of that fear: that you might lose your home, your life, your family.

There will be plenty of benefits and ways to help. I wanted to start helping now. I texted 90999 on my phone, and in the message box, typed "Red Cross." In seconds, I got a message back that they had tacked ten dollars on to my phone bill. Big deal.

So do it, or something like it, and do it now. What if no one did the same for you?

Personalize.

Damn. I'm about to walk into a radio studio as a guest on a show to talk about one of my books. I've been informed that the assistant will come get me in the lobby.

Now what the hell is that guy's name? They change so often here, and yet I've met him once before. . . .

But I think I've— Ah, yes, here it is. I rarely disappoint myself on this. In the notes section of my phone, I keep a list. It's called "People." I'm fairly good with names, but this list is filled with folks I don't see very often and yet expect to run into again. I don't want to hurt their feelings in case I forget their name (like now) when I say hello. Here's what part of the list looks like:

ALBERTO—taco truck
DALE—postman
DEBORAH—diner waitress (mornings)
TEDDY—bald kid at deli
MATTIE & WILLIE—old twins at store who just moved
     back to NYC
TODD—bus driver
MARTHA—bartender at Al Forno

Ah, and there it is, just as he comes through the swinging door.

"Hey, there, Shaq! Thanks for fetching me."

MARCH 13

Send a memory.

I've been worried about a good friend who has written that he is ill. I believe he'll be OK, but I don't really know that, plus I'm not the one in his body, fearful. He is a religious

249

man—his father and his mother's father were both Episcopal bishops—and when he lived in New York City, his favorite church was St. Thomas's, a stunning cathedral and home to the world-famous boys' choir.

This morning I walked down Fifth Avenue, where the most gorgeous stores in the world nest cheek by jowl next to some of the most beautiful places of worship. I started to pass St. Thomas's but took a second instead to step in out of the cold and snap a picture of the altar on my phone. I sent it off to my friend. He cried.

MARCH 14

It's the sentiment.

Few are more Irish than Aunt Peg.

Except for me, she is the last of the McHughs, the baby of six kids and now eighty-eight years old. Her mother and dad were both from Ireland—in fact, Grandpa McHugh taught me the Irish jig as a little girl in the living room of the house he built with his own hands.

So Peg loves St. Patrick's Day. In years past, there was always corned beef and cabbage and Irish records to play; still there are special green wreaths on the door, tiny shamrock plants from the supermarket, a sparkly green sweater. So when a shamrock scarf caught my eye (and how could it not?) on a street vendor's cart last weekend, I knew it was bound for glory under Aunt Peg's winter coat.

Five bucks and a couple of stamps later, it was winging its way to her. So I was not surprised to arrive home from work tonight to a joyful phone call: "It's beautiful! I don't know where I'm going on St. Patrick's, but now I've got to go *somewhere!*" This sort-of-awful scarf probably brought back loads of bittersweet memories. But that's what being Irish is all about, isn't it? We do love to shed a tear.

MARCH 15

Sometimes you just can't give it away.

There has been a lot of talk over the last week or so among my gang on Twitter about a fund-raising effort that I will leave unnamed—a silent auction where writers offer their wares as prizes. Signed copies, agents donating services, bookstores offering promotions—that sort of thing. It was a nice idea, and when the earthquake and tsunami hit Japan this week, their efforts became even more important.

I looked at the list of authors, to see if I'd fit in. I've written a wide array of books, and I thought it might be fun to offer a gift bag full of them. Turns out the gift donors weren't only mega-blockbuster authors, so I jumped in and e-mailed my offer to the committee.

The reply was swift and sharp. They had quite enough prizes, thanks. "Maybe next year."

Ouch.

Keep at it.

I don't know if it's mind control or just a chance remark, but here's what happened today in the store. . . .

A lady approached me and told me she had an acquaintance in the hospital and wanted to bring her a book. The parameters were these:

- not too expensive

- a hardcover

- not too hard to read, because she's sick

- not something dumb, because she's not

I knew right off what to suggest: one of my favorites, *An Uncommon Reader*, a tiny gem about a fictional Queen of England who suddenly becomes obsessed with books. My customer agreed that it seemed the very thing.

So off she scuttled to pick up a copy, and as she was leaving the store, she came over and touched my arm. Here's what she said:

"Today you've done a good deed!"

Gasp! It's working!

Put someone else first.

How many St. Patrick's Days have I lived in New York?

Thirty-four.

How far do I live from the parade route?

Six blocks.

And how many times have I been to the parade?

Zero. Zero!

Why this year? Why did I suddenly decide I had to go? Oh, I don't know. It was a lovely, sunny, springish day, and all this Good Deeding has got me thinking about time slipping away, and—well, Jesus, Mary, Joseph, and all the saints: my name *is* Erin McHugh, after all. It was time.

The truth probably is that it's too drunk a day for me out there, and living close to where the parade ends is a neighborhood hazard. You can only imagine. But I figured, maybe I was missing the point. All these years I'd been watching it on TV (I know, crazy), and it looked swell. Maybe I just needed to avoid the parade aftermath.

Well. That'll be the last parade I miss. It was, as we Irish like to say, grand. Proud, emotional, fun, full of Irish people! I wedged into a perfect spot right up front in a crowd that was four deep. I couldn't believe my good fortune. But after several minutes, I spotted a tiny old lady right behind me, sporting an old green blazer pinned with a fresh green carnation. She couldn't see over a large dog, never mind the rest of the parade viewers.

"Ma'am," I said, "sure and begorrah, you should come stand right up here in front of me," and I gently navigated her into my prime position. She was thrilled, naturally.

OK, I didn't say "sure and begorrah," but I thought it. After all, she could be a McHugh. And any minute, *I'm* going to be that little old lady.

Also: Erin Go Bragh (Ireland forever)

MARCH 18

Be a good scout.

At last, at last, the Girl Scout cookies have arrived. You all remember when I ordered thirty-nine boxes for myself and a few friends back in January from the famous Ruby. I may not have mentioned then that the troop had also offered an option to donate a box or two to City Harvest, whose mission is to rescue food from places like restaurants for New York City's homeless. I made a donation, and today Alyson, Ruby's mom, sent this lovely note along to the cookie purchasers, which made me cry on the bus on my way to pick them up. Thanks for this, Alyson.

My Dear Friend,
　　The Girl Scout Cookies came in this week!

On Monday, the truck from City Harvest came to pick up the stacks and stacks of cases of cookies that our Brownie Troop's generous friends like you donated to those in need. Troop leader Laurie was thrilled to be able to see her living room floor again. Curious about the delivery process, she chose to ride along with the driver to the distribution center.

When the truck pulled in somewhere on 10th Avenue, there was a line of people waiting. Bundled in coats and blankets against the constant chill from the Hudson River, they clutched the plastic bags of their possessions tightly or kept shopping carts near, stuffed with sleeping bags, broken suitcases, and more bulging plastic bags.

The big driver lugged the first cases of Thin Mints to the table where food was being shared with those in line. An old man stared at the box, then stepped forward, eyes alight. He told the driver and Laurie that he was a veteran who had been homeless for a very long time. He had given his life to his country and found he had nothing left afterward but time. Hands trembling, he picked up a box of cookies.

He told them how much they reminded him of being a kid. "This is the first time in a long time," his voice broke, "that I feel like a person again."

A fat tear ran down the burly driver's face. Everyone cried.

Thank you from the bottom of our collective Troop 3260 hearts—young and not-so-young—for the sweet kind of kindness that touches the souls of strangers.

I love you,
Alyson

Prepare to be ignored, even when you're doing your best work.

Such a dapper gent sat next to me on the bus. Have you ever noticed that in a Richard Gere movie, nearly his entire wardrobe plus the set—cars, couches, cats—is all in gray? If you don't believe me, add something like *Intersection* or *Nights in Rodanthe* to your Netflix queue. Anyway, that's how this guy looked. Silvery gray hair, wide-wale charcoal corduroy pants, a light gray cashmere sweater, a houndstooth gray and white scarf cinched around his patrician neck under a gray wool jacket. Brown shoes.

I looked at him, I looked at me. At his shoes, at mine, which were a sporty high-top sneaker, but in gray flannel. Unusual, and very fab. I leaned over and said, "Imagine how perfect your outfit would be if only you had on these shoes." I thought he would be grateful. I was about to let him in on where I had purchased them, and the happy accident that they were on sale, but the look he gave me—which conveyed at once his opinion of my sanity and my wardrobe—dissuaded me.

I was in the right, no doubt about it, and would have helped make his near-perfect outfit *GQ*-ready. But some people just don't know a good deed when they see one.

Put your friends together.

Someone says in conversation, "Hey, if you hear about a cheap studio apartment to sublet, let me know, will you?" The subject is interchangeable: it can be "someone who wants a kitten," "a rich boyfriend," "a friend getting rid of a bureau," "an angel investor." You promise to keep the request in mind, but it's impossible: it all gets mixed up in your head. You can never remember who asked you, how recent it was, and who went with what. Did Sally want the secondhand bike, or was it the fake ID? Did your brother say he was looking for a cocktail table, or was it a grill? Did he ask you at that party at the beach, or was that last Thanksgiving? Because all these requests have a shelf life, too. By the time you hear of a cheap apartment, that person is on his or her second home.

But today, worlds collided—in a good way. My friend Kiki was subletting her apartment for the summer, and a friend had an internship here in Manhattan. I got hold of both of them, explained the parameters and supplied phone numbers, and let them have at it. I just got word that it wasn't going to work out, but I don't care. I was just so happy to have tried to help—and to empty two pieces of random information from my brain.

Never say good-bye.

I lost a friend today, at too young an age. I will wait for the memorial service, which will help, but in the meantime, what to do? We all shared stories and sorrow on the phone and Facebook today. People talk about her singing with the angels.

But I don't know. I think about going to church and saying a prayer. What I end up doing, because it's a stunning day, and I'm not working, is taking a ferry ride to IKEA, a double treat, though not particularly holy, I guess. I spend some time on the upper deck, thinking about my friend and enjoying being out on the water, in a little more nature than I usually get to enjoy. This seems right. I don't think I would have felt her in a church, but I do here. I think of our times together.

We were fans of each other, in both our work and our play, and that was no secret. I think one often feels there's been too much unsaid at the end of a life, but not this time. Do I wish I had seen her more when she was ill? Of course. Will I try harder to emulate what I admired in her? Absolutely. So maybe the good deed is not finding the right place to say good-bye, but taking up a place on her path.

If you look hard enough, you've always got a little something.

"I don't look forward to the end of this day," a coworker moaned. My ears pricked up. Who says this? We stand up eight hours a day. Just to sit down is enough of a reason for me for a workday to be over.

But I bite. "How come?"

"Well, for one thing, I have a long walk ahead of me." He tells me where he's headed, and it's like five miles away. And it's biting cold out. I think, Who is this kid? This is like Abraham Lincoln walking to school.

So I reach into my pocket. Here in New York, you buy what's called a Metrocard, which gets you all around town, whether you want to travel by bus or subway or both. But the city is clever. Oh, it is clever. The amounts it sells them in are not divisible by the cost of a ride, so it always seems like you have some annoying leftover money on some card somewhere. Like today.

I rummage around in my pocket and give him a leftover card, worth most of one ride. I want to ask him if he's got another dollar on him for the rest of his fare, but I don't want to embarrass him further.

"Thanks." He smiles. "It's just one of those weeks."

We've all been there, my friend, and may be again.

One good turn deserves another.

Over the last several months, as I've been posting some of my deeds on my blog, I've gotten lots of comments—and made some nice e-friends. One, named Barbara, has been very supportive and has chimed in frequently.

Several weeks ago, Barbara asked my opinion on a publishing matter, and we've had a long and not always simple conversation about it via e-mail. Barbara's also a knitter, and as a nice thing, she offered to knit me a hat, and even took my custom order for colors. Today the fab hat arrived, and I am here to tell you that if I had known my opinions would keep me in such finery, well, I'd offer my say more often.

Love love. Hate hate.

I don't even know how to begin here, except to say that today I read a Facebook post by a friend that has had me extremely upset.

I work with this man who's been a friend of mine for more than five years. I'm a middle-aged white woman, and he's a black man in his twenties, but we've been pals for a long time: I've met some of his family, he's hung out in my home, we've shared confidences. It's the kind of closeness that often comes when people work together every day: you gravitate toward who you like.

I got up this morning and turned on my computer, only to find this post from him:

"So, while I was at work, an irate customer who I had not even spoken to compared me to a monkey today."

I can't get this out of my mind. I cannot imagine how long it will stay with him: forever, I would guess. As a homosexual, and an activist, I know a good bit about prejudice and fear. But nothing like this.

I keep thinking of what I would have done had I been there. This is what I hope: that I would have raced to get a manager who would say to this customer, "You cannot treat people like that in this store. Get out and never, ever set foot in here again." I know several of our managers *would* say that—what I hope is that I would have been swift enough and righteous enough to have stepped in and done my part. That I wouldn't be fearful and delay until it was too late. I wasn't there, so now all I can do is repeat this sickening story here, in hopes that it gives us all a running start when something like this happens the next time. Because it will, and it does, every day.

Let's remember, this incident didn't happen in a drunken brawl at a bar, but in a nice store in an affluent neighborhood in Manhattan. Hate and prejudice live everywhere.

I've stopped and started writing this several times today in tears, and as many times as I rewrite it, it's not powerful enough.

There is an ad campaign in New York City right now in the wake of recent antigay violence, but it also stresses that diversity of all kinds is our greatest strength. It has the best advice I could offer today: Love love. Hate hate.

Listen to the quiet.

It's still cold, it's been the snowiest—and seemingly longest— winter in anyone's memory, and I do not feel like leaving the house. In fact, the only thing I would leave the house for would be Miami.

So I've decided that the best deed I could do is stay inside, watch old movies, and not bother anybody at all.

A little something extra never hurts.

Today I dragged some of my wares to a book fair and set up a table to sell them. I shared it with a man who was selling titles from his small press. Almost the minute we sat down, he said, "Ooh, I love these!" and snapped up two little gift books from a trio of titles I had laid out, part of a series I wrote a few years ago. I had a bunch in my apartment, so I thought I'd bring them out and have a bit of a fire sale, offering them at a discount.

This, I thought, was a good omen. I'd barely taken my coat off, and sold two books.

My prediction was a little off. The economy, the window shopping, the crowd—I don't know what it was—but it was a sloooow day. An experiment, mostly, I guess, as it turned out to be not a particularly cost-effective venture. I was asked if I would barter. (No, thanks, I'm trying to make a living here.) I heard a customer ask another author, "Do you have anything for five dollars?" (Nothing like being particular about what you read.) Still, we live and we learn, and what was the harm? I blew a day off, and I made my costs back for the day. Big whoop.

I packed up a little early, and thought, Leave on a positive note. So I reached into my box of books, took out a copy of the title my new next-door friend hadn't bought, and handed it to him. "Thanks for being my first sale," I said, "and a good neighbor. I'm sure we'll meet again." Slightly shocked he was, and thrilled.

MARCH 27

Be hospitable.

I have a pal who's been, as they say, couch-surfing—living in other people's living rooms while between apartments. There's still a couple more weeks to go before she moves into her new pad, and being a guest was getting old, so she decided to go back and bunk with her parents until then. But it's a long commute.

Now, I am one of those people everyone hates in New York. I've been in my apartment a long time, so it's cheap, and it actually has a second bedroom I use as an office. I really need to offer it to her. It's got a real bed, even.

I nearly choke on the words as I say them: "You should come stay with me." And I mean it, I do, but oh, man, how will I ever work, and watch my favorite shows, and clean the whole joint before she moves in, and . . .

"That is the nicest thing," she says. "But I'll just stay where I am until I move for good."

Whew.

Mistakes will happen.

Remember the old cartoon of the Boy Scout trying to help a little old lady across the street who doesn't want to go? That's how I felt today.

I was talking to a woman who had leaned her cane against the counter, only to have it slip and fall over. I bent down to pick it up. "Let me get that," I said—I mean, who wouldn't? "No. That's one thing I *can* do," she said, beating me to it. I would like to say "she snapped," as that would be a better story, but actually, she had sort of an ironic smile. Still, I felt bad, and dumb, like the Boy Scout. Sometimes it's just tough to know what's the right thing to do.

Balance is power.

People ask for crazy stuff all the time in a bookstore. Usually it's nutty (and wrong) titles, or descriptions of books by color (always a blue or green cover). Today was different: the customer was coy, but I unearthed her true mission forthwith.

"Zagat's, please."

"For New York?"

"Yes, but not the restaurants, and not hotels. It's the market one."

After some backing-and-forthing, I figured out that she wanted the shopping edition of Zagat's.

"Actually," she admitted, "I only wanted to look up the address of a store."

Hoo, boy. "OK, how about I just go online and look it up for you?" Splendid.

Turned out to be a little chocolate shop in the neighborhood, and I knew of it. She couldn't remember where it was but feared it was closed. I wondered that, too, having recently peeked in its darkened window one night.

I found the info and went the extra mile. "You know what? Let me call them for you," I said. It rang and rang. No answer, no voice mail, no nuthin'. Not good.

It was a nice thing for me to do. Of course, I did have a hidden agenda, since I wanted to know the fate of the chocolate shop just as much as she did. But now a line was forming behind this lady who wanted to stick around and talk about Chocolates Around the World—a line of people who actually wanted to ask questions about books. You can't win.

Someone just like you needs a pat on the head.

I'm lucky to number several authors among my friends—people who are far more talented and successful than I will ever be (I won't say "than I can ever dream of being," because I still dream big).

I find writing extremely rewarding, if not always terribly profitable (still dreaming!), and I am always shocked when I find other, really famous writers are sitting in their homes, equally nervous and worried that their newest work is going to sink like a stone. So today I said to one of those friends (whose next book I know is going to be a great success), Let's just go for a walk. Take a half hour and forget about what may or may not happen. Let's forget about the *New York Times* bestseller list, and about paying for college educations.

Well, I tried. She was so worried about her *next* project, due any second, I couldn't budge her. I understood, because I'm the same way.

Does it ever end? With any luck, no. Hopefully there's always another big chance right around the corner. Would we have it any other way? What do you think?

Pass on the goodness.

Crap. I missed my train. And it's wicked cold, even though it's going to be April 1 in just a couple of hours.

I've taken a little trip to have dinner with some folks I haven't seen for many, many years, people I used to work with. Consequently, nostalgia reigned, and laughter, too, so that the hours rolled by, and suddenly it was time to get to the station. The train pulled out as I ran up the platform stairs. I had sent the other dinner guest on her way when she dropped me off, so now I was alone, waiting for the next train. It was just me, and Dunkin' Donuts.

Believe me, I was grateful to have it: I had a forty-minute wait, and the station was locked. Inside Dunkin' it was too bright, with just a couple of other loners talking too loud on their cell phones, waiting for the train like me. Oh, and—hand to God—a cop came in for donuts and coffee.

I didn't feel right using Dunkin' as a way station. I figure everybody's got to make a living, so, hard upon my enormous dinner, I bought six donut holes. I ate but one. When I finally got off the train, into a cab, and pulled in front of my apartment almost two hours later, I handed over the fare, a tip, and five donut holes to the cabbie. A double good deed that covered more than fifty miles, and a cabdriver who said he was going to be very happy along about three a.m.

Try, try again.

What's the saying? "Sometimes you can't win for losing." I'm not sure I know what it means, but I think I ran into it today.

I was shopping in an odd-lot discount store and purchased a couple of smallish items that fit into the bag I had with me. I'm always just thrilled with myself when I remember that I already have a bag and don't need another. I'm consolidating! *And* I'm being green!

So I dutifully take the purchases out of the plastic bag the cashier has used and toss them into mine, and I hand the store's bag back to the cashier. Done and done.

Until she, busy already with the next customer, routinely tosses it into the trash.

Watch yourself.

I could not get off this couch today, but I figured I could still do some good.

Who, of all the people I know, I puzzled, would appreciate a nice, long, newsy phone call most?

Actually, I made two. One to an aunt who really never wants to talk long but is thrilled when I just check in and assure her everything's fine. Then a call to a friend who also lives far away; I'd e-mailed several times over the last few months and hadn't heard back from her. Had I slighted her in some way? I wondered. No, I was sure I hadn't, and now I was getting riled thinking about how she had been slighting *me*.

So I dialed her, and she picked up right away. Now, imagine how glad I was that I didn't start right in giving her attitude when I learned she was recovering from a heart attack.

I know, I know: dramatic. But a true story.

Give something a second life.

The other day when I was cleaning (actually, I was looking for something I'd lost), I opened a drawer and there was a little guilt trip, staring me in the face. About fifteen years ago when my friend Leslie left town, she asked me to do something for her that she just couldn't get to before the moving guys came: get rid of several old eyeglasses. "I feel so guilty throwing them away," she said. "Did you know they send them to impoverished people who can't afford glasses?" I didn't know, and I solemnly promised her I'd find the right place for them.

In that drawer were now two pairs of my old glasses, too. As I searched online to find where I could drop them off, I read that a pair of glasses cost as much as a year's salary in some countries. Heartbreaking. I packed them up and brought them to an eyeglass franchise in my neighborhood;

most of these places take them, and Lions Clubs around the country do, too. So I may have just given sight to six people scattered over the globe. I always say that one of the stupidest things in the world is having to look for your glasses. I can't even imagine what it's like to put them on for the first time.

Now, please don't tell Leslie. I did what I promised.

APRIL 4

Open some eyes.

Occasionally friends will include me at their table at an event as a guest. Tonight was one such event, and I was told I could bring a friend, too. I thought long and hard about whom to bring. I didn't want to choose the person who was the most fun or would get the biggest kick out of the celebrities who were performing. The least I could do was turn somebody on to this cause. Find a friend who would say, "Wow, I had no idea these guys existed."

And that's just what I did.

A friend stays by your side.

Am I unfeeling? Today I was going to visit a sick friend, and so I called a mutual pal, thinking she might like to come along. Annnd . . . here came the phrase I deplore.

"I don't do hospitals."

What the hell? What do you mean you don't *do* hospitals? First of all, stop using the verb "to do" when you mean another verb entirely.

But you don't do hospitals. Golly, I'm so sorry! Why, because they're unpleasant and smell funny? Because your dad died in one? Because they give you the creeps?

Step up, sister. Everyone has had a bad hospital experience. Now imagine what it's going to be like when *you're* in the hospital—hopefully it'll be for something tiny, and you just wish you had a bit of company—and people you know say, "Me? Oh, no, I don't do hospitals."

Oh, me? Yeah. Of course I went. I have a sick friend in the hospital.

Stop and say hello.

I was walking up the street to the bank, in no particular hurry, when I passed this shoe box of a store that I will never go into. It sells bespoke draperies, and frankly, I don't know *who* ever goes in. I glanced in the window and saw a nicely dressed woman sitting at a tiny table with a laptop on it, waiting for a customer—any customer. She is probably not allowed to go online or read a newspaper; she has to be at the ready, should someone come in with fifteen thousand dollars for curtains.

So I backtracked and opened the door to the tiny shop.

"Hello." I smiled. "You looked a little bored. I just thought I'd stop by and say hi."

She shot out of her chair, horrified. "Is it that obvious?"

"No, no," I lied. "Not that we haven't all been there."

We both laughed and waved good-bye. I walked away with a huge smile on my face, and I'm betting she went home tonight and said, "The funniest thing happened to me today . . ."

APRIL 7

Comfort a stranger.

My friend Erika has generously agreed to let me share this wonderful story about a good deed sent her way recently. This is the one to turn to when good intentions flag—it's so great to hear from Erika herself what a difference someone's kindness made.

It's not my thing to write a navel-gazer, but I wanted to share this little story because we often lament all the unkindness and selfishness we see around us, and this is a salve to the minor (or not-so-minor) affronts and injustices we experience almost daily.

Last night I did something I've never done in the twenty-plus years I've lived in NYC, and which shocked me. After a terrible day, filthy with sad and depressing realizations smacking me across the face, I got on the subway to meet a friend. To my horror, the minute I sat down I burst into tears. I'm talking burst. Not the discreet single tear running daintily down my cheek, no. This was a full-blown, come-out-of-nowhere torrent. I quickly covered my face with my hand and remained that way until my station. (Why does crying feel so shameful? I felt as if I'd been caught publicly peeing.)

Right before I "lost my sh*t," I noticed a handsome, slightly built, twenty-ish African American kid sitting across from me. I got one of those instinctive flashes: that's a sweet guy. For most of the horrible ride I could feel him across from me and it strangely comforted me. At one of the stops (I don't know which, since I was still burying my now soaked face in my hand), I felt a tap on my arm. Peeking up through my fingers, I saw his outstretched hand, holding a folded piece of paper.

I cried again, later, looking at how he'd poignantly gone over and over the letters with his pen, making sure that I really got it.

The more cynical of us probably think this is trite. But I can't tell you how deeply grateful I was for his gesture—how much it helped me and felt like a gift, delivered by a stranger I'll never see again, who expected nothing in return but the reward of knowing he'd done something small but wonderful.

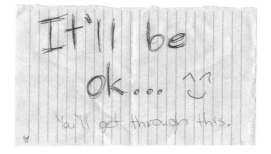

It'll be
ok... ◡◠
You'll get through this.

APRIL 8

Write it down; send it on.

Nobody writes letters anymore. But there was one I'd wanted to write for a while.

I have a friend named Jennifer—she's in her forties now, but I've known her since she was eleven. Her mother, Jane, was my boss at my first publishing job in 1977 and even helped me get my next job, where I was for almost two decades. Jane used to like to tell people that she invented me. She passed away a few years ago. I loved her.

Jennifer has picked up the gauntlet. We have lunch, she comes to my every book signing, buys copies for her friends. Many conversations end in a tear and a "Mom would have loved this." She's right: Jane loved that our deep friendship was already in its second generation.

Ten years ago Jennifer called me from *her* publishing job to say there was a position open, a big job, and she had recommended me. I got that job, and though it was short-lived, it gave me the impetus to go off and start my writing career in earnest at the age of fifty-two. The man Jennifer recommended me to has also moved along, and now he has become my publisher. All because of Jane. All because of Jennifer.

So I sat down and wrote her a letter about it, to thank her for everything she and her mother had ever done for me. I wanted her to know that I knew, and to thank them both for how they changed a life, many, many times over.

Give and Take.

Oh, oh, I love these combo good deeds.

So I call my friend and say, "How about helping me drag these bags of books over to the library sale?" Ever helpful, he agrees, and stops by my apartment so we can make the trek.

But hey, what's this? And this? And he's heard about this one. Next thing you know, he's chosen a few books for his own, which if you ask me, is well-earned compensation for his work.

Everybody wins, and I have one more pile of books off the floor.

Protect and serve.

Tonight the fantastic writer Kaylie Jones and I were walking down the street, gabbing about books and authors and the plot of her next novel. We live in the same neighborhood, and our thing is to go for tea and scones at a little place that I don't think likes us that much because we might laugh too loud. It's fair to say we're not the tearoom type.

So we're heading home, oblivious to almost everything, when a wiry little guy comes up behind us, like a gremlin soothsayer. "Don't stand there!" he cautions. "It's dangerous!"

Kaylie and I glance at each other. Hoo boy, only in New York. But Kaylie's curious. "Why not?"

The gremlin points ominously to the sky. "Pigeon poop!"

And sure enough, we were standing right under the arm of a streetlight, where half a dozen pigeons perched contentedly. He points at the ground. Covered in pigeon poop.

"You're right—thank you, sir!" laughs Kaylie. And obediently we hop two steps into the street and wait for the light. Now another woman comes along, and having observed our shenanigans—pointing, laughing, looking up as if watching for flying saucers—asks what's going on.

"Pigeon poop!" we say in unison, pointing at the birds. "Don't stand there!"

She shuffles up beside us, joining in the snickering.

We manage to cross the street without incident, and all three of us turn back to see our friend, sitting on a wall like a guard in a turret, ready to warn the next group of pedestrians.

APRIL 11

Follow the house rules.

Oh, there was a moment today when I wanted to tell someone to just *Shut up!* But I did not—another Good Deed of Omission. And there's a reason: the "Shut Up" Lesson is one of the most valuable I ever got from my mother.

I was about four, and because I was obedient (ancient history), I had been pestering my mother for permission to say "shut up." No, she tirelessly repeated, it's not polite, and bad manners to boot. But I was equally relentless. One night, as she was giving me a bath, I posed my argument once more, pointing out that all the other kids on the block said it.

"Fine," she said, exhausted, "you can say 'shut up.'" I was thrilled; aside from everything else, I'd won my first parental argument. I began to splash around, flushed with victory. But before long, I had another question to pose, now long forgotten.

"Mum, do you—"

"Shut up!" she shot back.

I burst into tears. And though I now had permission, I've never said "shut up" to anyone, ever since.

A good deed, from my mother to me, to you: "There's no 'shut up' in my house."

Good deeds are like dominoes.

My old college friend Susan, the one who takes me out every single time she's in town, wrote, "Let's have dinner, and can we go to that fab burger place next to your store?" Absolutely, and here comes the start of the good-deed evening: I would pay. And why? Because I had a spanking new gift card that a favorite customer had given me *just for doing my job*. And it wasn't just for five dollars, either. I was giddy to be able to play host this time.

So tonight we trotted over, ordered too much stuff (because gift cards make you do that), and then, during the transaction, there seemed to be a little technical snafu in the world where card meets register. It went on for two or three minutes—a lifetime in a fast-food line such as this one—but Cory, our delightful server, finally made things right. In the meantime, we three had bantered back and forth aimlessly, pleasantly. We weren't in a rush, and I knew it would get straightened out.

We found a spot to sit outside under a heater, and were having a ball, when who should come along but Cory, just to check and see if everything was all right, ask if our food was good, and thank us for being patient.

Let me make this clear: this would be like a server from McDonald's appearing by your side in a tux with a bottle of champagne. We were stunned—and delighted.

So today's lesson is: One Good Deed is working!
To recap:

- merely doing job reaps financial reward

- said financial reward allows me to repay old friend

- kindness and patience at dinner earns points with new friend

- new friend checks on our welfare

- everybody is happy

<hr/>

APRIL 13

Consider the big picture.

I've often wondered about offering a seat on the bus, and when it's age-appropriate. I remember as a kid my mother teaching me to stand up when an older woman enters a room.

"How old?" I asked, already a junior etiquette maven. I was taking mental notes.

"An old lady," she said.

I thought that over. "Well, would it hurt someone's feelings if they thought they were too young for me to be standing up?"

That's the eternal quandary, and one with no real answer. My mother's exasperated catchall was, of course, "Just stand up."

So, just as I was taught, yesterday I offered a seat to an older woman, white-haired, hunched over a bit. My mother would have agreed: an old lady. She was clearly relieved, took my seat, and thanked me. This is a good deed that's easy to do, and that anyone who lives where there's public transportation should always be on the lookout for.

But then, this morning, the inevitable—and the horrifying—happened. That's right, readers: some girl offered me her seat on the bus. I wanted to cry.

So I've revised my thoughts on offering my seat—well, I have to, don't I? If you look exhausted, if you're carrying a mess of packages, if you appear infirm in any way, I'm going to offer you my seat. New rules. But not to kids. I'm standing up eight hours a day, and you're still seven years old. Yeah, maybe you're tired—but not as tired as I am.

APRIL 14

Consider the alternative.

I just came back from dinner with a friend. I set this up at the last minute, because I knew my buddy's heart was in bad shape. Romantic bad shape, not cholesterol bad shape. He has a not-very-good track record at picking partners—some of them repeat offenders.

I knew it would be a night of tears, recriminations, where-did-I-go-wrong, and why-won't-this-work. I also know I'll have this exact same night with him again.

But he's a good friend, and someone I care about deeply. So I listened, and *hmm*ed, tried to dust him off and bolster him up. Because this is what I said to myself as I walked home: It could be you. And it probably will be.

APRIL 15

Step back.

It looks like spring might come again this year, but I'm not betting on it yet. Still, right next door to my apartment building is a nursing home with a wooden bench outside; in today's wan sun, I see a very old lady sitting alone—well, she might as well be alone, since her health aide is on the phone.

As I walk by, though, all I'm thinking about is that it's April 15, Tax Day, every American's most hated and worrisome day of the year. And that's what I'm doing right now, worrying. But something about this lady stops my fretting about money and starts me thinking about her. Her worries are both bigger and smaller than mine: When will my daughter come and visit again? How much longer do I have to live like this?

She's at a point where the world is passing her by. So I stroll over, just for a minute, and we talk about the weather.

The best things can happen
behind your own back.

I brought two people together today, in a most unexpected way....

I was doing a reading and signing of my newest book tonight; an author doesn't always fill a room, and tonight was one of those nights. But there were a couple of nice ladies in the store, and when my event was over they came up to speak with me further. We had fun and naturally started to compare notes. Turned out we had a lot in common: of all things, Mary had grown up in the town next to me—this was almost fifteen hundred miles away from where we stood! I recognized her as Cape Verdean—we have many folks in New Bedford from the islands, as well as from Portugal: they have a long history as fishermen. She had just moved to this town we were in and hardly knew a soul.

Lady number two, named Therese (my aunt's name! I exclaimed), piped up. She said she used to teach a lot of Cape Verdean kids in Boston. Also turned out they both served for many years as social workers. So here were the three of us, far, far away, talking about Cape Cod and Boston and the like. Nice. Homey.

Eventually we kissed good-bye, I bid them farewell, and I went to collect my things. As I headed out the door,

I turned around and spotted them pulling up a couple of chairs at the bookstore's bar, about to sit down and cement a friendship.

Offer up a part of you.

I'm sitting down today to write notes to my high school and town libraries. I'd like to donate some books to them: mine. That is to say, books I wrote. I'm likely to get some yeses and some nos: almost everyone likes to get the free kids' books, but I'd also like them to have my photo essay volume on lesbian heroines in their stacks. I firmly believe young women should have books available that talk about the extraordinary things ordinary people—especially women—do. It's important, and it doesn't really matter that these women are gay. Now, whether my Catholic high school will say yes to that . . . well, we'll see.

My case is pretty unusual, but if you have something to give—a product, an idea, an hour—you'll find it rare that someone says no. It's not like you're cleaning out the junk from your closet—you're giving part of yourself, and people understand that.

Give a little.

Thin Mints.

You all know I have some. But this year I'm already regretting getting only six boxes, and I practically have a lock on the freezer (which any aficionado knows is the best place to keep them).

Unfortunately, I was not able to sneak my treasure into my apartment in the dead of night. Walter noticed.

Walter is the day doorman in my building. Here's him yesterday morning:

"Mmm-mm. You know what's good with a morning cup of coffee, Erin? A Girl Scout cookie."

So, am I just tenderhearted? Or guilt-ridden? Perhaps we'll never know, but I was certain the torture would continue—both from Walter and in my soul.

So this morning, I put three Thin Mints on a napkin and gave them to a joyful Walter on the way out the door.

(Now I gotta go back and do a recount. What if Walter tells the super, who has a key to my apartment?)

Manners matter.

Manners are very important, though you would never know it, because every day people's manners get worse and worse. In fact, they have nearly disappeared.

I consider it a vocation to try to point out people's poor etiquette (in the most polite way, of course). So that this evening, when a woman walking by me made a humongous phlegmy noise and then spit into the street, I think my saying "That's pretty" sotto voce was a tremendous boon to humankind.

Good advice is all around you.

It's six thirty in the morning, and in ErinWorld, it's way too early to have risen, showered, packed, and gotten myself through light-jittery Times Square to the bus station. But here I am, and happy, too, as I'm on my way to my family and an Easter celebration.

My required stop before boarding the bus is Au Bon Pain, and though I'm half asleep I hear a familiar voice.

"Mornin'! . . . Have a great day! . . . How *you* doin'? . . . Hi, good mornin'!"

I start to smile, because I'd forgotten about this lady. She mops the floor here, and for the last few years she has been on duty every time I've come through on my personal early-bird express. She is by no means young, and I can only imagine how far she has to commute to get here. I love her. Somehow, even at this hour, I never find her annoying; she will lift the blackness right out of you.

"Good morning," says me. (Of course I get a fresh "How *you* doin'?")

"You are always so nice to see," I offer. "How is it you stay so happy all the time? I must know your secret!"

She looks at me and grins so hard you would think I was her own daughter. "It's my customers!"

And so, from reaching out to meet a stranger, I have just received the best corporate business advice of the twenty-first century.

APRIL 21

Visit.

One hundred and one.

That's not the temperature, that's how old Aunt Bernie is. Today I went and visited her at the nursing home.

Technically she's not my real aunt, she's Aunt Tessie's aunt, and Tessie is my aunt by marriage.

She sometimes knows you, sometimes not—but certainly she knows she has a visitor, and that must mean something to her.

I think she likes me because she was a librarian and I'm a writer. Every once in a while she comes out of her aged reverie and will say to a grandniece, "When is Erin coming? She's fun!" Meanwhile, those visitors are the people who have cared for her, helped her pay her bills, come in the night when she was scared. Frankly, I'm a fly-by-night, and I know it.

There's a little bit of humor in it, and the others roll their eyes, because once again, when we get there, Bernie is thrilled to see me. We all know it's just because I'm the new toy in the room. But really, ain't it always the way?

Find anew.

Hung out with my cousin Nancy today. When we were little, Nancy was one of the Big Kids. Being five years older than me, she even babysat me at times, and I adored that. I didn't care that she was getting paid to play with me.

As we got older and grew up, Nancy started a family and I moved away. We'd see each other on holidays and the like, but we didn't spend the sort of time together that I tend to do with my gang from the other side of the family.

Then a couple of years ago, Nancy's mother, my aunt Rose, died. Rose was one of my faves, and my dad and I called her Roxy, which totally gives you an idea of exactly how fun loving she was. (Yes, she *was* the one who danced on the table at my parents' wedding.) I started checking in on Nancy; like me, she was an only child, and it just seemed right. I e-mailed her and started seeing her more when I was around town, and then including her in events with the cousins from the other side of the family. She's warm and generous, terrific fun, self-deprecating, and wicked. I love her. We all adore having her around. How lucky I am to have found her again, to share all the old, funny stories one or the other of us had forgotten.

In situations like this, you wonder what you missed all those years; you want to kick yourself. But then you have to brighten and think about all the good times to come.

APRIL 23

Make 'em laugh.

I made a kid laugh today—in fact, I made my whole family laugh—and that's good enough for me.

A friend stopped by the other night and showed me a little bit of Easter techno-magic that had me so in stitches I couldn't wait to share it. Here's how it goes:

1. Go get yourself a box of Peeps. Any color will do, but there's nothing like the original, God-given yellow.

2. Place a single Peep on a small plate in your microwave.

3. Set timer for ten seconds and gather 'round ye olde microwave for the hijinks.

4. Watch your Peep inflate to enormous proportions, then instantly deflate.

5. Laughing, laughing, and more laughing. Insert another and repeep.

Live to tell it.

Dear Ladies,

I know you want to chat with each other and that that's the point of the three of you walking together in the morning. However, I also know that someone taught you when you were about four years old to go single file when you're walking in the road. So this is why I honk and make the international "what gives?" sign. So that the next car that will be plowing around this curve that you could not possibly see (because you are yapping your heads off and walking three abreast) does not knock you over like so many bowling pins.

Oh, sure, feel free to give me your annoyed looks now as I honk. Because you will not be able to say much when you're flattened on the side of the road.

With much love,
Erin

Sometimes you're just the instrument of fate.

You could almost call it springlike, so Meredith and I sat outside at the burger joint, having a bite and a milk shake. Out of the corner of my eye I saw a dad and his son, a kid of about ten years old, sit down at a nearby table. Meredith and I were having a fairly animated conversation of our own, but I saw the dad head back inside, presumably to pick up their food order. And then I saw this kid begin to cry. I mean awash in tears. Big, gulping sobs. Face-in-the-crook-of-his-elbow, up-only-for-air crying. Wipe the tears and snot away and repeat.

What could be wrong? Had his dad refused him an order of French fries? Had he just told his father he was going to stay back in school a year? Did something happen to his mom? I kept up my end of the banter over at my table but finally excused myself: I had to go check on this kid. So I popped over and got down on my haunches next to him. "Hey, buddy," I began. "Is everything OK?" Buddy quickly wiped off his face with his sleeve, gave me a quick look of abject terror, and bolted into the restaurant.

So OK, perhaps I didn't dry the tears of a tiny child—but I like to think I drove him into the arms of a loving father.

What was it all about? Who knows? Eventually they both came back to the table, more crying, the dad made a call and handed his phone over to the kid, residual tear shedding, and then, the silence of hamburger eating. A lot I know about kids.

Talk to someone you think you have nothing in common with.

A garbage truck was backed all the way up onto the sidewalk as I came down the street. I was carrying a bunch of roses that had already been a pay-it-forward gift at breakfast from a friend who was leaving town and didn't want to waste them. I could barely squeeze by, and was sort of annoyed, while this burly sanitation worker was still tossing the "leftovers" that had dropped onto the sidewalk out of various smelly bags into the back of the truck. One soggy mess of half-eaten potato chips whizzed by my right temple.

"Flowers for me again?" he asked.

"They were," I replied, "until you started throwing garbage at me." I said this in the most playful way imaginable, by the way. But just to make sure he knew I was kidding, I added, "Some day, huh? So beautiful outside."

"Every day is beautiful," said the garbageman. "Today is beautiful. Yesterday, when it rained, was beautiful. Tomorrow will be beautiful." All said without the slightest irony or hint of preachiness.

I was thinking to myself, What the heck? When the garbageman is the most optimistic guy I know, with the most finely tuned perception of beauty, who am I to gripe?

What else could be done? I gave a rose to him, received a tip of an imaginary hat, and off we went, already on our way to a better day than we had expected.

<hr>

APRIL 27

Stop counting.

There are two reasons I sometimes get free books: I'm an author, so I have other friends who are authors, too, which is way fun; and I'm a bookseller. This means I'm popular with even more authors for an entirely different reason: I might hand-sell their books in the store.

Tonight an author I have become friendly with (yes, naysayers—via social media again) was doing an event at my store and reading from her new book. She sent me an advance copy of the book months ago, and I loved it. Still, I was going to buy another copy tonight, because every sale counts, and you always want to support your friends.

Here's how the evening went, which unnerved me. The author came into the store, and we spotted each other, hug and kiss, and she picked up my newest book (because I put it in the front of the store) and stated, "I'm buying this." Now I felt bad. That particular title of mine is an expensive one, more than twice the price of her current novel. I was happy but felt guilty. After her wonderful presentation, I bought a copy of her book and had it signed. Then the author's aunt spied my book and said she'd like a copy, too.

Oh, man. My first thought was: people should only be liking my friend's book tonight! But of course folks are interested in more than one thing, and if you're always counting, it isn't much of a good deed.

APRIL 28

It's never too late to say I love you.

There are times when you wonder whether it's appropriate to offer your advice. This was one.

I've been exchanging e-mails lately with someone I've known all my life but have not spent a lot of time with. Her dad is very ill, and she is worried he will not live long. This week she said what countless people have thought: that there are so many things she wishes she had said to him. Perhaps most important, she doesn't remember the last time she told him she loved him.

I didn't hesitate. "I love you" were the last words my father and I said to each other, by phone, shortly before he died; he had been ill with Parkinson's for a long time but passed away rather unexpectedly. I told her it meant the world to me, and since I wasn't there with him at the time, I've carried it with me ever since.

Then I started to worry that I had been too opinionated. That my way didn't have to be her way. But today I got an e-mail—buried in it were these words: "I told him some things." That's when I knew she'd told him she loved him.

Pick up the trash.

Ooh, I learned a good trick today, plus it was really fun.

I'm in Washington, DC, and I went to meet my old friend Craig for lunch in Georgetown. Craig and I met at our first jobs in 1974, at a newspaper in Saratoga Springs, New York, and have stayed in touch since, though with not quite enough visiting, if you ask me. But today we had a great, funny lunch alfresco, followed by an adventure with cupcakes and a walk through his divine neighborhood. But it took me a minute as we walked down the little brick streets to realize he was undoing several people's morning's-worth of work.

All these beautiful town houses have wrought-iron railings on their front stoops, with little curlicues at the bottom. As I looked up and down the street, I realized what Craig was after: each house's railing had several rolled-up pieces of junk mail, flyers, and pamphlets. All unwanted, and Craig was collecting it all and ceremoniously dumping it in the garbage can on the street corner.

"I hate this," he growled. "I do this little cleanup walk every day."

And I happily became his apprentice, trotting right behind him.

Don't doubt yourself.

I never would have thought this would be a good deed, but gee, I guess it was.

What seemed like about forty-seven months ago, my friend Debbie asked if I would appear on a panel with her at a publishing conference. We wouldn't get paid, but I figured the gift bags might be cool. Actually, I was secretly pleased—no one had ever asked me to do something like this before. Also, it was so far in the future that I figured the day would never come. But it did: it was today.

It became apparent a couple of weeks ago when Debbie started sending me and the other panel members talking points and questions that this was actually going to happen. Now I was nervous. The title was "The Table of Contents," a feature that, frankly, few of my books have. But I'm a game girl, so I jumped in.

Today hundreds of writers and hopeful writers were wandering around the hotel, and when it came time for our event, a whole bunch of people actually showed up. It turned out to be lots of fun, and once I realized we were helping these writers with each and every question we answered, it felt amazing. I had been so busy worrying about failing, I hadn't considered the fact that we might actually help.

Pass the buck.

Today, when a man tried to slip me a tip for gift wrapping something for him at the store, I said, "No, no, really, thanks—it's free." Still, he pushed two dollars into my hand. My first thought: lunch.

But I reconsidered. Remember me writing about Thomas, he of the straw hat and rich baritone voice? So when I left work, I crossed the street, waved hello, and pressed that same two dollars into Thomas's palm. As he always says, "So nice to see you! Bless you."

Pass it on.

Sometimes a good deed is just passing something along. Someone sent this to my friend Peter today. He e-mailed it on to me, and now, from me to you:

Do something for yourself today.

Today, speak as kindly to yourself as you do to others.

Allow someone else to help you the way you help other people.

Give yourself the same permission to make mistakes that you give to others.

Do this for yourself today. You deserve it.

Of course, I would add to that, buy yourself some ice cream. But that's just me.

Lend an ear.

A woman in the store was asking about, I don't know, nothing in particular, I guess. It was quiet, and we got to talking, and I asked her what she did for a living. "Well," Tina said— by now we'd introduced ourselves—"I'm about to go back to school."

"That's terrific," I said. "For what?"

"It's a secret," she whispered. "But I can tell you. I want to be a lawyer, but I haven't told my husband yet."

What to say? She was so excited, so eager, and of course I was delighted for her and her undercover feminism. I wished her my best and asked her to come back and let me know how it was going: her studies, her finally telling her husband, everything. Sometimes you can just tell when a person is determined. Tina had a secret, and she just needed someone to say: That's a great plan for you. Do it.

Someone understands.

Many months past, an old acquaintance I knew from business fifteen years ago found me on Facebook; we began having a fun e-relationship. Recently, we even finally got together for drinks and had a blast.

So we kept in touch and planned more fun, and then one day, I got a different and disturbing e-mail from him. In it he said his friends had been pointedly telling him that he was drinking way too much. After a lot of self-reflection, he had to agree. My friend and I had talked a lot when we met up about when and why I stopped drinking, and that evening he had given me kudos for being so strong. So we've traded many heartfelt e-mails over the last week or so, and tonight he wrote, "I'm going to stop. Will you come with me to my first AA meeting?"

I've never been to an AA meeting—and frankly, I've gotten a lot of flack about that from people in the program over the twenty years since I've had a drink. But do I plan to go with my old friend? Yes, I do. And I'm honored to be asked.

Give the gift of life.

I am reminded lately by a friend in need about the importance of being an organ donor. I signed up many, many years ago after the death of my cousin Jeannine. I had no idea she had signed up to be a donor herself until her death. Several months later, her husband, Leo, got a letter outlining how her gift had helped others. The stories were incredible, each and every one, about changing the future of people who felt hopeless about life: her eyes, her heart, her kidneys turned people's futures around. It was the loveliest letter I'd ever seen, telling the stories of people who went back to work again, someone who regained his sight, two teenagers who went to college—something they'd only dreamed of. Six lives were changed because of Jeannine.

I carried a copy of that letter with me for years and showed it to scores of people. I had no idea one person could make such a difference.

Here are some statistics I read today:

- 112,329 people are waiting today for an organ

- 18 people will die each day waiting for an organ

- 1 organ donor can save up to 8 lives

I signed up when I renewed my driver's license. You can also go to www.organdonor.gov.

It may be the greatest thing you ever do with your life.

Carry that weight.

I was late. I was rushing out of the subway when I saw an older woman with a perky new turquoise rolling suitcase, semi-stuck in the turnstile next to me. I stopped for a second and helped her untangle herself, because really, being late to meet people in a bar is not a mortal sin.

She thanked me and then looked morosely at the three flights of stairs ahead.

"Are you strong?" she asked.

"Not at all," I answered truthfully. But then it suddenly dawned on me that this tiny, seventy-something woman was somebody's mom, come to visit for Mother's Day weekend, complete with shiny new suitcase likely packed with home-made cookies and new socks. My own mother suffered from agoraphobia and had never once visited me in New York during her lifetime. This lady was a superstar.

So I gave it a tug. Poor thing: it weighed but a feather. We climbed up into daylight and a beautiful spring evening.

"You are so kind." She smiled.

But I knew better. I knew I'd almost left her stuck in the turnstile for the night.

"Not at all," I replied. "My pleasure."

Grow.

It seems like it's only been about a week since I dragged my Christmas tree over here to the mulcher, but yikes, here it is spring, and on to the next round of Nature.

I've had it on my calendar for weeks to come to my local park's plant sale. This little neighborhood Eden is like a harbinger of the seasons for me; concrete doesn't change much with the weather, and that's certainly most of what you see living in a city.

The money from this plant sale goes back into the park's upkeep and events. There are summer concerts here, a Christmas tree lighting with carols and hot chocolate, and lots more. It's perched on the East River, so to sit on a bench there and watch the watery traffic go by is a delight. Today, there are also volunteers peppered around the park, cleaning up winter's damage. I love it here.

Problem is, everyone else feels the same way, I guess, because when I get here at eleven a.m. to put a dent in my annuals-buying for the season, I look to be about the last in the neighborhood to stop by. The remaining selection is pretty meager. I've been planning on some orange selections this year, and find only one puny plant of indeterminate origin in that range of the spectrum. So now I'll have to do what I didn't want to: buy one plant here, then take a bus to the plant center across town and a cab home. Who am I kidding? I live in a city. Nothing's easy. And I'm lucky to have a garden at all.

MAY 8

Wait for it.

On my walk through the park today, someone called out to me, and I turned to see one of my customers waving me over. Her name is June, and she and I only recently met; so I trotted over, and she introduced me to her husband. She presented me with a great flourish and said, "This is the woman who helps me find good books." But what I heard was: "This is the woman who adds great joy to my life."

I was thrilled, of course. Frankly, I feel like every time I match a customer to a great book, it is a very, very good deed. There are days when I feel like a faceless clerk—but not today.

MAY 9

Let a voice be heard.

I have a friend who turns eighty years old next year, and she is a writer I much admire. I'll tell you right now, Ann Bannon's books may not be for you: she wrote some groundbreaking novels, a series called the Beebo Brinker Chronicles, about a young woman who discovers she is a lesbian in 1950s America, which was when Ann penned this quintet. They are still in print, and she has become quite an icon to gay women, feminists, and girls coming out everywhere.

I knew she was traveling to New York, so I asked her if she would come appear at our bookstore. I got three other stellar names to join us, and I moderated a panel on the history of gay publishing. Tonight at last was the event, and as always, Ann (who later went on to earn a PhD in linguistics and become a college dean) stole the show with her wit, charm, and heartfelt stories.

I worked hard on this, an evening to bring the talent of someone I believe in to a new audience. As I said, you don't have to love what I love: but I might ask you to listen.

MAY 10

If you don't want it, someone does.

This is so tiny it's almost embarrassing to write down here, but I still think that's the way the good deeds add up.

I was eating my soup in the café today, and a woman sat down next to me with a sleeping child wrapped around her neck. I had noticed her earlier: she was young, and this little boy was napping on her when she came in; but she had no stroller or other accompaniments one sees so often with children. Just carrying her kid, who had to be getting heavier by the moment.

I finished lunch and began to clean up and was about to throw my two free packages of saltines away. She had no bag, no food—she didn't seem poor, just tired and unprepared. "Here's a little bite for later," I said, handing her the crackers. Probably all I did was save her from getting up one more time today—but I know that most days, that would be enough for me.

Open up.

I was going to an event tonight and got all dressed up; then the rain started, and between that and rush hour, it was clear I was going to have to take the bus—empty cabs were nonexistent. So I found myself waiting at the bus stop in my raincoat and a baseball cap, when suddenly a blackwatch plaid umbrella appeared over my head, with a gentleman—there's really no other word for him—attached.

"Let me help you out here."

I looked up; he was about twenty-five, handsome as they come, and dressed in a tuxedo. You know how every once in a while you feel like you've been caught in a scene from a movie? This was one of those times.

His name was Justin, and because of the umbrella, we were huddled together, chatting, for some time. Obviously he was off to a black-tie event, and the clock was ticking for both of us. We decided to try another bus since ours didn't seem to be coming, and we splashed off together, running down the street. We managed to catch it, and it went exactly seven blocks in a half hour. By that time, it was raining harder than ever, but we decided to get off and try again for a cab—and believe it or not, after a very wet fifteen minutes, we grabbed one. That leg of the trip took forever, too, and we were both late, but by then we'd become friends.

We could hardly be more different. Justin grew up in the British Virgin Islands, is quite religious, is on the path to becoming a CPA, and was going to a young executives awards dinner. I was off to a gay and lesbian event, and though I suspected he didn't approve on religious grounds, he held his tongue. There's a certain kind of intimacy that comes in the dark, and I swear even more so in the rain. Usually it's romantic, but Justin and I shared it tonight on our adventure. Of course I couldn't say we came to know each other well, and I'll likely never see him again. But it was . . . special—there's no other word for it. For me, it was the best part of my evening. He started with the good deed of sharing his umbrella, but what it became was two strangers taking a chance and making a friend.

A few days later, I got an e-mail from Justin—naturally we had exchanged business cards—saying how nice it was to have met me. Since then, I've seen him on the bus once and received an e-mail or two. This morning, many months later, we are having coffee. Something special indeed.

You can always give something.

I was asked to a fund-raiser for a politician friend and would love to go, but I had to tell the hostess that it just wasn't in the budget right now.

I was disappointed—I'd love to go. But my hostess is a gem and a lady: she e-mailed me back and said, "We'd love to have you. You'll give when you can."

Still, I wished I could do *something*, and I finally came up with an idea. Both the hostess and the politician had been featured in a beautiful photo essay book I had just completed. I called the folks at my very generous publisher and asked if they might consider donating copies for the party guests.

They said yes. I felt like I had done a little something— let's say I contributed to the PR effort of the campaign.

Hostess + my brainstorm + publisher = One Good Deed

When you're wrong, say you're sorry.

I was on Amtrak today, and geez, here it was the Quiet Car and someone just behind me was yapping away— yapping and *laughing*—on his phone, with no hang-up in sight. I turned around and said indignantly (because I'm good at that, indignant), "Sir, you know this is the Quiet Car, right?" Immediately, about a half dozen people piped up and chorused, "No, it's *not!*" which would have been pretty funny, except for my embarrassment.

So I swallowed my mortification and turned around to everyone and said, "I am so sorry! I was mistaken, and I am a jerk." Because if it's one thing I hate, it's someone who doesn't apologize.

MAY 14

Make it easy.

I may be coming to a point in life where I'm mistaking laziness and ease for a good deed.

I'm off to a wedding today that's a couple of hours away; some other people I know are invited, and we've all decided to rent a car together. Now, if you've never rented a car in New York City—and you probably haven't—be prepared to be shocked at the prices. I was thrilled to find a car for today's fete three weeks ago for only $120 for the day—thrilled because last month, when I went through the same rigmarole for another out-of-town jaunt, the company raised the cost to $181 when I changed the parameters the teeniest, tiniest bit.

I e-mailed my buddy Steve with my Great Deal. Nah, said he, he rented a car in New Jersey recently and it was $40 a day. When I pointed out he'd have to leave at dawn to get from where he lives in Brooklyn, through Manhattan, and into an entire other state, he was unmoved. "Knock yourself out then," I said. I'm all for saving a buck, but c'mon, there are four of us sharing the price.

But then when one rider suggested we all meet in Jersey to save the price of the $7.50 bridge tolls coming and going, I was magnanimous: I would happily pay the bridge tolls if we could just meet in the state in which I live.

Good deed? Probably not. An extra hour and a half of sleep? Absolutely.

MAY 15

Give a nudge.

What a happy day.

A couple of years ago I reconnected with an old client and friend of mine. She had become a freelance writer, and we talked about my newish life of writing books. "You should give it a go," said I. "You're so smart; you just need to really concentrate and come up with a concept." I meant it, too. I knew she could do it. I checked in on her every once in a while, and lo, one day many months later I got an e-mail. "I've got it," she said. "I think I have a great idea." And she was right; it was a terrific one, and I even introduced her to an agent I thought would be interested. The agent loved the idea, too, and took Debbie on as a client (which, incidentally, paid back a favor that same agent friend had done for me), and the book was eventually sold.

The whole thing was a much more arduous road than I present here in a couple of paragraphs; but the reason today is such a happy day is because Debbie has posted online that she has finished her manuscript. I am thrilled for her, and so happy that I could pay forward a little of all the help people have given me over the years.

(But there may be a dark underbelly to all this joy. What if her book does better than mine? Will I ever forgive her?)

Turn it around.

Pouring. Pouring, pouring rain. Windy, too. I'm walking to a restaurant to meet a friend, hugging close to storefronts with canopies, because although I was smart enough to wear a raincoat today, I was too stupid to wear a long one.

Suddenly I seem to be involved in a little bit of a traffic jam. The woman inching along in front of me has a tiny, cheap blue umbrella, and *boop!* it has just turned inside out. She stops to try to fix it but is carrying too much stuff in her other hand. She's momentarily stymied, but not me. I pop around in front of her, push the bumbershoot back right side in, and go on my way. And don't you know a few steps later I hear a *splat splat splat* behind me, and I turn to see a blue umbrella, with a huge smile underneath.

"Thanks."

Of course, me, I'm still soaked.

Eventually, good manners are repaid.

A customer asked me if I'd like to try reading a writer he loves, and I said sure. "I'll bring you a couple," said Benny. The very next day (today), he arrived with a twenty-pound bag of books (now there's a good deed right there!), and though I don't live far from work, when I leave I decide to take a cab.

Ah, there's one now. The cab spots me and turns the corner—and just then a woman puts her hand up. When he stops near me, she whips around and gives me the universal "you stole my cab" glare. I've lived in this city a long time, and I'd be lying to you if I said I'd never stolen a cab from anyone. Maybe I've grown. Maybe this One Good Deed thing is really getting to me. But to be clear, this one was mine—the cabbie had seen me first and headed my way.

"That was my cab," the woman growled.

"Actually," I said, "it wasn't. But please, go right ahead." And then I even opened the door for her. "Hop on in."

Oh, she was suspicious, but then she asked where I was going, and it turned out I was only a block from her destination. I agreed to share the taxi.

We chatted, we arrived, and when I got out my money to pay, the impossible happened.

"Never mind," she demurred. "It's on me."

Hear the music.

I've had a lovely dinner with an old friend, and it's a beautiful evening. I'm in no rush and am checking out store windows for nothing in particular.

I think I hear a little music. . . . I do, and as I near the bus shelter, I see him, playing a trumpet, down in the near-dark on the corner. "Someone to Watch Over Me," "You Made Me Love You," "Tenderly." I want to go down and see this guy, but geez, the bus might come, and at this time of night they're sort of scarce. As I'm trying to decide, he starts in on "Moon River," and a woman passes me by, humming along to the tune.

That's the sign I was looking for. So I forget the bus and walk down to the corner, drop a buck in the hornman's case, and thank him. To tell you the truth? He wasn't really very good, but I know at least two women whose night he improved. Besides, I'm a sucker for an old standard, and he just made me feel like I was in a Woody Allen movie.

You can find the time.

"So much has happened. We need to catch up."

My friend lives half the week out of town in East Hampton in an adorable cottage. The days she's in the city, it seems we're both too busy to get together. It's been a while since we spent any time together, and with one thing and another, she's had a lot on her plate. She needs to unload a little.

"When can we get together?"

Well, when we look at our calendars, it seems like the only time in the next couple of weeks is, um, in about an hour. But she's leaving town. No problem. I'm a girl who loves a road trip—I've even written a book about them. So I hop in a cab to our favorite meeting point, which happens to serve a delicious cheesesteak sandwich, and order our usual; when I come out, there she is, idling curbside.

The trip is about three hours, and what with the catching up and intermittent phone calls and gossiping, it goes by in a flash. Naturally, when we get there, we're exhausted. I stay overnight and will take the bus back in the morning.

(And if you think I've never just turned around and done the trip back in the same night, you'd be wrong.)

MAY 20

Give your best.

I've got a big writing project going on, and it comes with a deadline, which is not far away.

Once more, someone I don't know has tracked me down through a friend and wants to ask me a billion questions about how to get published. I'm being helpful, I really am, but I'm trying to concentrate, and every time I write an e-mail back to her, lo, just a few minutes go by, and *ping!* Here comes the next round of queries.

Yes, I realize I should just not even look at these e-mails, explain to the would-be author that I'm busy at the moment and will get back to her, but I just want to get it out of the way. Actually, what I really want to do is write back and say, "I don't know! I don't know! I have never met you and I don't know if you can even write a full sentence! Why are you asking *me*?"

But I don't, and though I can't really help her—I'm not an editor or an agent or even a famous author—now she's talked to someone who knows a little more than she does.

And tomorrow, I'll probably be asking a question of someone who knows a little more than I do.

And that's how the world works.

Mix it up.

The sign in the fancy gourmet store window read:

"Every Coconut Cupcake sale will be donated to City Harvest. Together we can make a difference."

Bought two. Everybody wins.

Rebuild the bridge.

Almost twenty years ago, an old girlfriend made me the god-mother of her newborn son. As often happens in life, even with the best intentions, we were in touch with each other less and less. In the last few years, though, I've made a some-what successful effort to build our relationship again—but I still haven't seen Matt in over a decade.

So I was thrilled when I got an e-mail from Matt's mother, who lives in Washington, DC, asking me about the safety and livability of a New York neighborhood: Matt was coming up for a summer job. There has been a flurry of e-mails and calls, and since neither of them are in town, I've offered to go take a look at a possible apartment and make sure there's not a bedbug convention taking place there.

After all these years, I've made myself useful at last.

Belated is better than not at all.

For days I had the nagging feeling that I'd forgotten some-body's birthday, and today it finally popped into my head. Dang! I did miss it. I'm pretty good at sending my good wishes to friends, if not by card, gift, or phone, then at least by e-mail to say I'm virtually celebrating with them.

Now that I remembered who it was, I sat down to dash off an e-mail. I adore this woman, but we were never super close, and we live just far enough away from each other that we rarely connect. But she's had a sick child for many years, and now a husband who is ill, and, I don't know, I just want her to know I think about her, especially on her birthday. I may remember next year, and I may not. But for this year, it's a few days late. She won't care; everybody likes to know someone's thinking about them.

MAY 24

Be quick.

I was at the ready. Aware. Eyes front and ready to do good. And then I got beaten to the punch.

Here I am on the bus, and the driver puts the special stair thing down so that someone with a walker can board easily. An old, old lady shuffles on and tells him she's just going to sit down and get her card out, and then she'll pay.

Aha! I think. I'm ready to help. But as her lengthy purse search continues, I get distracted. I'm looking in my own bag at the mozzarella I just bought, dreaming of lunch. That's when I hear a voice say, "Can I swipe that for you?"

Curses! I look up, and someone else has taken the old lady's card to pay her fare without her having to get up again. Worse, the nice lady who has taken my do-gooding place is on a cane herself.

Lesson learned: the chance to do a good deed can be like a small town on a road trip—blink and you'll miss it.

MAY 25

Prevent a disaster.

I wandered over to the gourmet food shop in my neighborhood, set on getting some delights; I didn't have anything specific in mind, but I felt like buying good food. I got a shopping cart, looked around, and yet, when I got to the line at the cash register, I had just one item, some odd pasta sauce selection. Hmph. This was disappointing.

I craned my neck to check how the line was progressing and noticed the woman directly in front of me for the first time; she had about fifteen items stacked up and was holding them all with her chin. Disaster was imminent.

"How about you put your stuff in my basket?" I asked her.

"I don't know what happened," she said, dumping everything in. "I came here for one thing."

"Well, I came here for ten but only got this, as you can see. Here, you take the cart. It looks like we ended up reverso-shopping."

Turned out she was having a party.

"I'll be there at six," I said.

"Great." She grinned. "There'll be cupcakes."

"I'm in."

"And lots of two-year-olds."

"I'm out."

We laughed, I wished her a good party, and we were both on our way.

———————
MAY 26

If at first you don't succeed . . .

THE SANDWICH: PART I

My friend and I are gathering up our stuff to go—it is the first beautiful night of spring after a month of rain, and we are finishing up a nice dinner at this great little Italian restaurant with a backyard.

"Hey, take this roast beef sandwich," she says. "I bought it when I thought I was getting on the train tonight instead of having dinner with you." Now there starts a conversation about food only a mother could have.

ME (no children): I won't eat it.

SUSAN (three children): You'll have it for lunch tomorrow.

ME: I have that thing all day. I can't carry around a smelly sandwich. It's going to go bad.

SUSAN: You'll have it for dinner.

ME: I'm going out.

This is going nowhere. Then the lightbulb goes off. "I'll take it," says me, "and give it to someone who looks like they need it on my way home." Simple. Effective. The sandwich will find a customer.

It's a gorgeous night, as I said: so how come no one's in the little park, drinking a beer out of a brown bag? I make a detour: no one's sleeping on the church steps. Where's the lady outside the drugstore who's always panhandling?

You guessed it: I arrive home, and I'm still left holding the bag.

I cannot *give* this sandwich away.

So I put the damn sandwich in the refrigerator, and the bag by the door so I don't forget it in the morning. Because though I have failed in my good deed, I have a plan.

MAY 27

Give with grace.

THE SANDWICH: PART II

I'm off to a conference for the day. With the roast beef sandwich, which barely fits in my tote bag. I need to get to a convention center that is a bus, a subway, and a schlep away. So, onward.

I search the subway. I search Penn Station, for crying out loud. I pass by forty-six beer-bottle-laden scary doorways in a bad neighborhood, and not one person is looking for something to eat. Has the world enjoyed some crazy economic recovery overnight? I reach the convention center at last—only a few short blocks from where the sandwich was born yesterday, by the way—and I still have the roast beef. This means I have no room in the tote bag for gathering things at the convention.

I tell my tale of woe to a friend. That I am now on day two of trying to give away this delicious-looking thing.

"What?" she asks, puzzled. "I'll take that sandwich right now."

So I hand it over to happy Colleen; it means she doesn't have to leave her booth or pay convention floor prices for crummy food. I feel extremely proud. Because not only did I toil over the course of two days to find the sandwich a good home, but I was beginning to realize that it was 11:45 a.m., and that damn sandwich was beginning to look mighty fine indeed, and I *still* gave it away.

MAY 28

Take a breather.

Nuthin'.
>Nuthin'.
>Nuthin'.
>Nuthin'.
>Memorial Day weekend. Everybody's out of town.
>Nuthin'.
>Nuthin'.

Nuthin'.

Nuthin'.

Nuthin'.

I'm a bum.

Nuthin'.

Nuthin'.

Haven't left the house.

Nuthin'.

Nuthin'.

Nuthin'.

And more nuthin'.

Friends don't keep count.

At the bookstore where I work, there is a high-ticket item, a limited amount of which we've been told we can purchase at a discount for family and friends. An old pal asked me recently, half kidding, if I could get one for her at a discount. Yes! I jumped at the chance.

Dilcia has been a friend nearly thirty years, someone I hold dear and just don't see enough; she also inevitably manages to pick up the bill whenever we're out. I was thrilled to be able to help. So we made a date for her to come to the store, did the transaction, and then . . . she insisted on taking me to dinner.

It all comes out in the wash, I guess, but geez, now I want to figure out how I can trick Dilcia into letting me do another favor for her. She sort of brings out the best in me.

MAY 30

Never forget life's wow factor.

I'm going to be selfish today, because I'm going to talk about something that happens only in my little part of the world. Because everywhere else, when you live somewhere not surrounded by skyscrapers, each day brings a chance of a beautiful sunset—but not in the canyons of a city.

Here on my island, Manhattan, there are a very few days per year when I can leave my dark apartment, walk outside, and see the sun come right down my street. Not in the usual way, the way that makes the plants grow and the rain dry up, but right. down. the. street. Smack in the middle. In this borough, today is that kind of day, and it's gotten kind of famous, in a cultish way. It has even been given a name: Manhattan-henge. (At Stonehenge, the sun aligns with its eerie stone structures on the solstices.)

So, islanders, tell your deli guy, remind the dog owner next door, and take your neighbor or your doorman to the street tonight (tomorrow, too). You won't be sorry. I got online and alerted all *my* friends: one's meeting me on the corner.

Consider someone else's future.

I hate asking for money. But for my alma mater, well, that's different.

When I started there as a student, it was still an all-women's college. As an only child, I found the sisterhood of it appealed to me. But more than that, the college, the teachers, the administration believed in women. Sure, my parents thought I could do anything, but that was their job. My college, founded by a woman, also believed girls were up to the task. Any task.

My college gave me the confidence that must have been inside me somewhere. It taught me not to give up. It built a circle of lifetime friends for me, one of whom bought my first piece of writing for twenty-five dollars. My college changed my life and my way of looking at myself. I have not stopped working for it, one way or another, since 1974.

So today I called some classmates and asked them for money, to give back along with me. So that the next group of uncertain, untapped kids can get what I got from Skidmore College.

Good intentions count.

Here are two things I can barely abide:

1. the dentist

2. carrying things (I don't even carry a purse)

Today a friend reminded me she was about to move. A really great friend, who's been good to me. Naturally I offered my services. Enthusiastically, too.

Now I'm just holding my breath to see if she'll accept.

Learn generosity.

I was in the subway this morning when an older man asked me as I passed, "Ma'am, could I have a quarter?" I said sure, and handed it over. I passed through the turnstile and then reviewed the snapshot I had of him in my head. A very polite guy, who seemed to have some sort of senior ID card in his hand. No briefcase, but then again, not carrying his life's possessions, either. Who was he? More to the point, why didn't I just say, "Sir, would you like me to swipe you through?" and buy him his subway ride. As I was pondering this, the train roared up, I stepped on—and cursed myself for the rest of the day.

My mother used to say when I was given an assignment in school that if the teacher asked us to read to page 68, I would stop there, even if the sentence ended on page 69. She was right, and look what it got me: shortsightedness.

Offer your knowledge.

My buddy Joe and I were restless. We'd met for our weekly coffee, but it wasn't enough. It was obvious we were both trying to think of ways to prolong the visit.

"Statue of Liberty?" I offered.

"Too crowded."

"Ferry to IKEA?"

"Mmm, a possibility."

We settled on a lovely spot I'd never been to called Wave Hill, a stunning park and mansion overlooking the Hudson River and New Jersey's Palisades. Joe knew everything and led me around the estate. What a good deed on his part: this was some find! We felt a million miles away from summer in the city.

A major source of Wave Hill's beauty is its gardens and greenhouses, and we wandered around happily. We kept passing by the same few people, with the occasional smile or hello and "Isn't it stunning?" and such. We finally ended up following two older ladies down a path and overheard their conversation. Given that they had on sensible shoes and fanny packs, you'd think they would be talking about rare plant specimens—but no, they were trying to decide on the merits of two rather racy and violent movies currently in theaters. I'd seen both.

I excused myself and intervened, giving them my brief reviews on both pictures, much to their delight. At least they *seemed* delighted and agreed on a pick for that very evening.

And thus, my work as cultural liaison was complete.

Set some rules.

Oh, sure, my good deeds know no bounds. I don't judge; I pay no mind to gender, creed, age, sexual orientation, employment status. But perhaps I should be a teensy bit pickier.

Today I went to spend a delightful day at the beach with some friends. I forgot nothing: lotion, sunglasses, a good book, a delicious lunch. In fact, I was eating a particularly scrumptious sandwich and enjoying a pleasant conversation with my neighbor when along came a seagull out of nowhere and snatched it right out of my hand. Snatched, I tell you!

I like to give, but even a do-gooder has her limits.

Show up.

I was practically supine on the floor in the middle of a big rearranging project when a customer asked me for books about death. I told him that we had a "Death and Grieving" section—did that sound like what he was looking for? "Well, my mother's dying," he said wryly, "so I guess that's for me."

The section was way across the store, and there was somebody there to help him, but I just didn't want to put one more jot of concern on his shoulders. So I took him over, gave him suggestions, searched for some books, sent someone down to Receiving to fetch something that had just come in. Sure, that's my job, but in this case, I really wanted to know that he was well taken care of before he left.

Finally, I told him I had to get back to my post and left him in someone else's capable hands. I touched him on the arm and said, "I'm so sorry for your troubles." That's all. I mean, let's face it: you never know what to say, whether it's a stranger or your best friend. But then he knew I'd been there, too. He looked a little startled and replied, "Thanks. Thank you *so* very much."

It doesn't sound like much of a story here on paper, but you all know what I'm getting at: compassion and just "showing up" comes in the most unusual guises.

Put your two cents in.

Today is the second time I've been asked by a retailer friend for some help on Yelp. If you don't know what Yelp is, it's a site where ordinary people like us can go and review or recommend a restaurant, local service, entertainment, nightlife, and such. The problem is, the thread of comments folks leave is often peppered with people's gripes, pettiness, and high school behavior. For example, if your BFF has a bar in town, you and your friends are going to post fake crappy reviews about the competition on the next street over.

Of course it's not all like that; Yelp is a reputable site and an often extremely helpful way to get the local insider's scoop on what's best. That said, why do people have to go and ruin everything? So when I was asked again today to offset a review from someone with a gripe by writing a good one, I happily agreed. In fact the food there is fantastic. I felt like Internet Robin Hood.

Put people at ease.

I applied for a job recently. There aren't many I'd still like after all these years, but this one seemed a good fit. I think the interview went quite nicely, and I knew the woman who

I interviewed with fairly well. In fact, I went out of my way to say I hoped this wouldn't be an awkward situation for her should she decide on someone else for the position. I told her that whatever happened here, I would understand.

OK, now I didn't get the job. I am half relieved, as I love my writer-cum-bookseller gig—but it would have meant a lot more money. The other half of me thinks, "What?! How dare they miss this rare opportunity!"

The truth is, either outcome would have had its pluses and minuses. And because I am not only a good loser (eventually), but really polite and didn't ever want my interviewer friend to feel she had to cross the street to avoid me, I wrote her another note (naturally I had handwritten one after the original interview). "I understand," I said. "Good luck, and call if you ever need anything." She wrote back and said, "Is it OK if I ask you to lunch one of these days to pick your brain?" Still useful, after all these years.

Good sport, good deed.

Don't push it.

I'm nice to things that crawl into my house. You remember the cricket from last fall? But when I got home tonight, a gigantic daddy longlegs was crawling around on my coffee table.

Shudder.

Still, ever the humanitarian—or maybe it's arachnitarian—I managed to pick him up by one long leg and plop him outside.

Evidently not far enough. When he snuck up on me later this evening again, in the bathroom, well, I think I'll just stop the story right here.

JUNE 9

Be ever-ready for the next round.

A frightful ninety-five degrees here today, and by eleven thirty a.m., I had already been on two subways and three buses. Now I was off to an early dinner to meet my editor, Jennifer, and taking the same damn route I started on early this morning. This was getting to be a not very funny déjà vu.

Then I saw Her Adorableship. She was eighty if she was a day, sitting across from me in the subway in a little navy blue suit, brushing her hair, feet set together in little gray sneakers, wearing matching gray gloves. What a picture. How cute, I thought.

I got to the restaurant, and there was a sign up saying it was closed for a party but that the wine bar was open for dining upstairs. Crap. I turned around and boom! six inches from me was the little lady from the train.

"It's closed tonight," I told her. "Private party."

She was stricken. "But I'm meeting someone here! She's on the bus, and never late. And I don't have her cell phone number."

So I offered my name, found out hers was Sally, and offered to climb up the two flights of stairs in the stifling heat to see if her date was there. I got a full description; I dragged myself up the stairs. No sign of Sally's theater date.

I trudged down and delivered my report. "How could she be late? She's a smart woman, with a PhD!" She frowned for a second. "Is the menu the same upstairs?"

"I didn't check the menu, Sally. I was just looking for your friend."

Sally was shocked at my answer. "You went all the way up there and didn't check the menu? That wasn't very smart." I was beginning to see that no one was smart enough for Sally.

Eventually, I made three trips upstairs to check—did I mention it was two flights?—got the menu particulars, and was practically ready to have dinner with Sally myself by the time Jennifer showed up.

I felt terrible leaving Sally alone. She was gone when we left the restaurant, but I know in my heart that she's going to pop up next to me on the subway again. I haven't seen the end of Sally yet. And she sure as hell hasn't finished with me.

Thank-yous never get old.

I was gazing out into my garden and my eye fell, as it often does, on a sweet statue there, a girl holding a basket of fruit. I've had it for many years, and I love her place there among the flowers. Peg, an old college friend, gave it to me birthdays ago, and it remains one of my favorite possessions.

I rarely see or hear from Peg now, though in my mind she remains one of my closest friends. So I decided to e-mail her and thank her again for such a great present. "Do you recall that statue you bought for me years ago?" I wrote. "Remember, we named her Sophie. She's still out there in the garden. I love her so much, and she always reminds me of you."

Peg wrote right back. "Remember her? I had such a hard time giving her to you that I went and bought one for myself, and she sits out in my garden, too." Now, I had known this and forgotten. I love that writing this little missive brought to mind Parallel Sophie, which I now picture, along with Peg, every time I gaze upon her.

What a nice way to miss someone.

Don't give up.

My friend Tim called recently and I asked if I would cohost his radio show on SiriusXM today. Though he's been doing the show for several years, it would be his first time flying solo: he was a little nervous. I was excited. I love doing radio, and I knew two hours would fly by.

Tim asked me during the show about my writing career, how I started on this path a little later in life than most, and the One Good Deed project. So I began to tell the audience a little bit about it: about how I wanted to inspire other people; how you begin to train yourself to look for opportunities to reach out; and most important, how perhaps I am not, by nature, that nice, which hopefully will make the book kind of fun. I'm Everychick, with an edge. We had a few laughs.

Tim takes calls on the show, and very soon we answered one from a guy named Rick, from South Florida. He was exuberant. "I lived in New York many years ago," he told us. "And I wrote a musical—one that was staged off-Broadway and did pretty well. Then I moved down here, and I have never picked up a pen or written another word."

Tim and I glanced at each other—where was this story going?—but we didn't have to wait long. "That was nearly forty years ago," Rick said. "But today, Erin, you have inspired me to start writing again. I think I thought it was too late, but

I can see I was wrong. I'm your Good Deed for today, Erin, because as of today, I'm starting to write again."

What can I say? This is my wish for this book, and for all of us, in spades.

JUNE 12

Give a kid a book.

Eavesdropping is one of life's great pleasures, and don't pretend you don't agree. I was walking home from work and was only steps from my apartment, when I came up behind a dad and his young son.

"But, Dad," insisted the little boy, who was about six, "videos don't count. Movies count, and TV, but not videos."

"They all count," said Dad. "And if you don't let me read to you, you're on an all-electronic shutdown at seven thirty."

"No!" the kid gasped.

Now you know I couldn't help myself. So I passed them and turned around and said, "Hey, I've written lots of books, and I think your dad's right. Let him read to you a little."

In my head, I was thinking, Do you know how lucky you are to have a dad who wants to take the time to read to you?

In the kid's head, he was thinking, Who are you? Get away from me, Devil Woman—I was just beginning to get somewhere here!

Dad said, "Really? Do you write kids' books or adult?"

Now we were smack in front of my building, where I live on the first floor. "Both," said I. "Can you guys wait here for just a second?" So I popped inside and grabbed a copy of a kids' book of mine called *50 States*. And a pen.

Sure enough, they were still standing right outside. "How about I sign this as a present from me to you, and your dad could read you this?" The book happens to have a states puzzle, a place for state quarters, and a billion illustrations. It is totally up Ben's (now we were friends) alley. "Hey," he said, "I saw that at my school book fair!"

His father, Dan, was really the one over the moon, of course, and offered to pay me, and when I demurred, he promised he'd look for other books from me.

Don't get me wrong—I'll do plenty to get people to buy my books. But to get a kid to read instead of play video games? Then I *will* do anything.

JUNE 13

Ask someone in.

What's one of the best ways ever to repay a kindness, say thanks, show folks that you just love their company?

Ask them to your home for dinner. It's not the same as picking up the tab: once people have entered your space— from mobile home to mansion—you've made them privy to your life. If they've never been to your home, they've got questions about furniture and photos, they get a glimpse of what pleases you. They know you so much better when they leave than when they walked in the door. Old friends, well, they know they're always welcome to the place that means the most to you.

So tonight I had two friends—one who'd been here many times, the other here for her first visit, and we sat outside and grilled steaks and gossiped and I waited on them.

They looked as if they were happy here, as if they were comfortable. As if they'd like to come again. It felt good.

Sign up.

It's early in the morning, glorious June, and I'm thinking about nothing, just looking at the small plots of sidewalk flowers, waiting for the bus to take me to work. It is a nice start to the day. I haven't had to speak to anyone yet: a little Zen time.

"Because I'm not a Communist, that's why!"

Oh, brother.

I look around to see what gives and spot a burly man dressed head to toe in fake camouflage gear, bucket hat decorated with a dozen pins of who knows what nature, storming away. This type of guy confuses me: I would never disrespect a veteran (though I may differ with his political views), but there are also a lot of nuts—not ex-soldiers—who seem to think that a useful way to spend their days is by spewing anger and rhetoric. I have no intention of finding out which type this man is, but I do see the object of his wrath—a very pleasant-looking person with a clipboard.

I've been known to cross the street to avoid someone with a cause, and don't lie, so have you. But now I feel bad for this crusader. Plus, you know how my curiosity gets the better of me. I trot over to Clipboard Guy.

"What was that about?" I ask.

"Oh, I don't know." He smiles graciously.

Turns out all he needs is to get enough signatures to put some judges on the next ballot. I put pen to paper: I would sign it whatever party they are from—because it ain't Communism, sir, it's a democracy.

JUNE 15

Look around.

Once again, Joe and I are to meet for coffee.

This particular venue where we go is right on a city street, with a bunch of tables outside, all full today. I'm standing in the doorway keeping an eye out for Joe. He's not in sight yet, and as I look around I see stuff everywhere, all over the ground. An entire section of a newspaper strewn around the sidewalk and under the tables, page by page. Three empty cups. Stirrers. Napkins galore. Yes, probably soon someone will come outside and pick up a little, but evidently the customers are too busy yapping to look around.

So I pick everything up, and this gets some looks from a few customers. It's as if they think I'm either (a) eavesdropping or (b) interrupting them.

Ah! Here comes Joe. Hugs and kisses all around, and then, as we go inside, he says, "Hey, this door shouldn't be open with the air-conditioning on," and closes it. *Voilà!* We have attended to our part of the world, for a minute anyway, and sit down, have a bunch of laughs, and lay out our next plan. (First stop: Coney Island.)

<hr>

JUNE 16

Be fair.

Oh, I hate the line cutter. It is unforgivable. And no, I do not think it is a New York thing, though certainly it is exacerbated here. There is absolutely no way I am going to risk losing the last window seat because of a sneak. And today I decided I was not going to let it happen to anyone else, either.

I was standing toward the beginning of a long Amtrak line at Union Station in Washington, DC. I was stationed at a turn in the line, which is just what the professional line cutter looks for, like a weak link in the chain. I had already moved a dozen people along; every one of them affected the same shock at having accidentally cut the line and thanked me for pointing out how far down the corridor they actually needed to go. Nabbed. But I noticed one young guy beside me, glued to his BlackBerry, ignoring me. So I poked him.

"The line is waaaay back there, you know," I said firmly.

He stared at me a second, and then pointed to his ear and said, "I'm sorry. I'm deaf."

I was suspicious, so I pointed at the long line and said again, "The line is down there."

So. Maybe he *is* deaf. Maybe not. Maybe I'll be struck down for doubting him. I considered typing on my iPhone, "You are cutting the line. It's way down there," because clearly there's nothing wrong with his sight.

I finally decided to leave him alone, hoping that he'd have a restless night's sleep for cutting. But I was considerably sterner with the line cutter right behind him and moved him with some haste to the end.

JUNE 17

Sing out!

A gorgeous, early summer day. The kind that when you walk outside, it feels like your heart is actually leaping in your chest.

I step outside into my yard here in Manhattan. It's in the back of my building, so in the middle of the block. When I look up, I am in a canyon, enclosed by hundreds of apartments—but I can't help myself. I throw my arms up, all Ethel Mermanish, and sing out:

> *"Oh, what a beautiful morning,*
> *Oh, what a beautiful day!"*

Now, I happen to think that's a nice thing. Over the years out here I've heard Super Bowl huzzahs, domestic quarrels, babies crying, but never a clarion call to a weather alert like mine. Me, I would have been tickled to hear someone sing out like that. But I may be alone in this.

JUNE 18

Never discourage.

I didn't envy these kids: three youngish teens standing on the corner on a hot Saturday—but they had clipboards, so I trundled over to see if I could sign up for anything good.

They were the Wildcats! (exclamation theirs), a basketball team that, I was told, could go to "the next level," whatever that was—but only if they had more equipment and uniforms and stuff. Oh. They wanted money. I had only twenty dollars in my pocket, so I demurred, and off I went.

But there they still were a half hour later as I headed home. I had to hand it to them: they were three African American kids in an impossibly white neighborhood, asking for money. I inquired if they had change for a ten-dollar bill, and my new pal Abraham pointed out that ten dollars was not too much to give at all, if I so desired, and showed me the list of donations. I had to laugh—the kid was a natural salesman.

How could I say no? Kids raising their own money for something cool like playing sports? What kind of witch would pass them by? I loved the Wildcats!—all three of them were funny and competitive. And when I walked away, my guy Abraham called out after me: "Hey, ma'am—thanks for coming back."

Renew a friendship.

Is hunting down and finding an old friend a good deed? Because today I finally found Meg.

Meg and I were very close in college, and we graduated, and I went to her wedding, and she moved out of the area and . . . well, that's it, really. I never saw her again. That was in the late 1970s.

But I've missed her. When I thought about her, I was always sad we were out of touch, and as the years went by, I became more and more certain I wouldn't see her again.

I thought the advent of Google and social media would help, and every year or so I'd do a search: maiden name, married name, anyone with her name that sounded like she might be the same Meg. No dice. But today I wandered around Facebook again, and there was that face I knew so well (just a few years added on) but with a new last name. I made a Friend request. And Meg has already Friended me back; I am overjoyed.

Me, I always think reconnecting is good for the soul and widens—or maybe rewidens—your horizons. And hopefully, two people benefit.

JUNE 20

Spew hate at your own risk.

I was standing in line after work in the park, waiting to get a hamburger at the little hut; it was a popular spot, and I had no doubt it might take a half hour. So I was in a bit of a daze until the twenty-something guy in back of me had to get all Master of the Universe, in the loudest cell phone show-off voice possible.

"Dude. They love me there, are you sh*tting me?" he bragged.

"Dude" evidently made a short comment; it became clear almost instantly that it would be hard to get a word in edgewise with this clown.

"Nah, I bought a ton of that sh*t. It's going to be huge."

From his chatter, I learned that my linemate had something to do with trading and the financial industry.

"Bro, you gotta get on board."

(Brief reply from "Bro.")

"Whaddya mean? What, you gotta get *permission*? What are you, a f***ing homo?"

How I would have loved to have turned around and decked him right then and there. But I waited until he finally got off the phone, which was an eternity, and then I turned around.

"You know, calling somebody a f***ing homo because you want to belittle him is not only ignorant but completely offensive to anyone gay, and that would include me. I'm going to ask you to never do that again."

I think that's what I said, or something like it. I was so upset, it's hard to say. He looked at me, stunned, and at last was completely speechless. "Uh, oh, sorry," he finally muttered. I didn't hear another peep out of him.

Here's what I hope: that he never spouts that ignorant hate again. But since that's unlikely, I hope he gets a new homosexual boss, for whom he has to show some respect.

JUNE 21

Just connect.

Here's what the economy is like, or at least what it seems like these days. People are losing their jobs all the time. And most of the time it's not about performance, it's about money: Can we do without this job? Can we get somebody younger, cheaper, to do it? Can people we already employ do this job on top of the one they're already doing? What it means is that as time goes on, more and more of my friends are out of work.

Of course it's financially debilitating, and once you hit about fifty, you worry that you won't be able to get back into the workforce at all. But I've found—because it's happened to me, too—that one of the worst side effects is the paralysis that can set in. It's hard to call your friends; you're sad or embarrassed, and they're busy . . . at work. It's hard to look for a new job, because you might be rejected. And it's harder for some than it is for others.

I've been on both sides, and I know this: a lot of times if you're out of work you don't want to do anything, and yet you're pretty much always happy once you drag yourself out of your house and your relentless rut. So today I called a friend who is out of work, making sure we have a date on the calendar, because I know that time goes by much, much slower when you're home waiting for the phone to ring.

JUNE 22

Don't keep it to yourself.

It was the end of a long day—but a really good day. Summer is finally here, and I had been to an enlightening event and spent the evening listening to lots of smart people. You know how sometimes your brain heats up and you feel like there are still a lot of great ideas out there to have? That was how I felt tonight when I started home: buoyant.

I found a cab, and it was a continuation of my New York state of mind: we curled under the lights of the Brooklyn Bridge and up the FDR Drive, my favorite view of the city, with skyscrapers on your left and the river rolling on your right. I don't know, I felt . . . hopeful somehow.

I rolled down my window to breathe in the summer and said to the cabdriver, "Look at this. Is this the most stunning thing you've ever seen?"

"It's so beautiful," he instantly agreed; it was as if he had been thinking the same thing. "What a night," he breathed.

We continued our lazy conversation the rest of the trip—what our favorite routes were in the city, how we had a whole uncharted summer in front of us, where we were from, how lucky we were to have met up to enjoy this ride.

"I'm so glad I hopped into your cab tonight," I said as he dropped me at my corner. "You were the perfect person to share that ride with—it might have been my best ride ever."

"I feel the same way," the driver said. "So nice to meet you."

And off we went, likely never to cross paths again. But I was so glad I had decided to chat up someone I might usually ignore. Turned out he was the cherry on the cake of my day.

Ask for help.

My opinion may not be the same as yours, but then, that's what opinions are—what one believes to be true. Over the last few years in New York State, and this week especially, gay rights advocates and much of the state legislature have been trying to pass a marriage equality law, which would allow same-sex marriage in this state. We are very close—just one vote shy of making this a reality. Now all over Facebook and Twitter and wherever else the community and its friends could hear a shout-out, people were urging others to call a senator who was on the fence.

I was checking my Facebook feed on the street on my way to an early-morning meeting today and decided I had to call right then and there. I left my message, urging the senator to vote our way, and when I hung up, I started to cry. Right on the street. And then I couldn't stop. All of a sudden, the fight seemed so interminably long. I guess I just suddenly ran out of gas (for the moment anyway, because I came home and made several more calls and sent out several more posts to folks, asking them to follow suit).

And now we wait some more. But I've shared my opinion, and I've asked for help. And I've stopped crying, at least for now.

JUNE 24

Love is blind.

This is less about me than it is about community and open-mindedness.

There was a groundbreaking vote in New York State today; a gay marriage bill was passed. For those of us who have worked on this over the years, and for everywhere, this was as important and exciting a day as LGBT people and their friends and supporters will see in our lifetime. And I wasn't going to spend it alone.

Once we learned that the vote would take place, I started to think about where I'd like to be when it happened. On a Friday night in the summer, lots of people would be out of town, but I had an idea. I had interviewed a wonderful rabbi whose flock is the largest gay congregation in the world, and I became an instant fan (if rabbis are allowed fans). A friend asked if I'd like to go along with her to tonight's services, and I happily accepted. It was packed, and the air was electric with . . . I guess I'd call it imminent joy. The lone Catholic girl was embraced by all, including Rabbi Kleinbaum, who, oddly, did not seem the least bit surprised to see me.

All I want to say, I guess, is that after all the years full of dissension and hate this issue has caused, it was wonderful to feel so welcomed by all these people who were like me, but then again, not.

Timing is everything.

I was headed to meet a friend at the movies, running about five minutes late. Suddenly, passing on my left, came a beautiful dog—maybe a young Doberman, but it happened so quickly it was hard to tell. Also, there was the double take: in my head, I still live in a 1960s world where dogs run free, they can bite the postman, and there are no leash laws. It took me a couple of seconds to remember that that hadn't been the case for decades, plus, this was New York City. It was just plain dangerous.

The dog had no leash or collar, and though he didn't seem scared, he was certainly traveling at a considerable clip. He turned the corner a block ahead, and by the time I got there, he was out of sight.

I was worried when I reached my movie pal, and then got caught up, as always, in the thrill of the popcorn. But I woke up worrying about the dog today. And maybe today's too late. I searched all over the web where to report a runaway dog in this town, with no luck. So I posted it on Twitter and asked people to retweet it and send out the message.

I'm sorry, pup. I should have done that yesterday. Hope you and your owner are reunited.

JUNE 26

Kindness begets kindness.

This sounds like some little kids' Bible lesson. But in truth, it's exactly the way we wish the world would work, day in, day out.

I was talking to a lady about e-readers, and also some of the fantastic-looking covers that are available for them. She had one in her hand, in fact. One that I had tossed in my wastebasket the night before, because I had upgraded to a newer model. My job is to sell her the one she had in her hand, of course—but she was so nice. "Shelley," I said, because by now I knew her name and a bunch of other stuff about her I needn't repeat here, "if you come back tomorrow, I'll happily give you that same cover. I just threw mine away last night, and it's like new." Imagine her delight.

And lo, before the end of the day, along came Nina, whom I had helped just a couple of days ago. Nothing out of the ordinary. Just my job. When we had chatted before, she was so grateful that she offered to buy me a cup of coffee or a treat from the café. I told her that, sadly, we weren't allowed to have food on the sales floor—and that's why, this afternoon, she stopped in with a ten-dollar Starbucks gift card for me.

See how the world works? At least now and again?

JUNE 27

Show respect where it's due.

I was riding crosstown on the bus this afternoon, when three people came on: a mom and two kids, a boy about nine and his little sister. Mom allowed them to sit alone, though she was close by, pretending not to keep a watchful eye. The first tip-off that it was a special school day was the clothes: pressed khakis, short-sleeved white shirt, and tie. Clean baseball cap. The pants were a little short, maybe hand-me-downs.

But the clincher was the trophy.

What I wouldn't have given to win a prize like that as a kid! Wow. It stood over a foot high, and this boy was squirming around so much he could barely stay in his seat, though he remained well behaved and quiet. At my stop, I detoured and went over: clearly it had been field day at school, and this kid was a big winner.

"Hi," says me. "That's some huge trophy. Did you win it at school?"

The kid barely glances at me, then down, squirms a little more, and nods.

"What's it for?" I ask, like I can't see the gigantic gold-colored baseball player perched atop the prize.

"Baseball," he whispers.

"That's incredible," I say with awe. "You must be the best in the entire school."

And with that I stick out my hand, not for a high five or a fist bump, but for a truly grown-up handshake. He looks up at me and sticks out his hand. "Congratulations," I say.

Now, I don't know if he was headed home for a gigantic party, or whether the trophy got stowed on a shelf and was never talked about again. But I do know how it feels when someone, especially a grown-up, praises you.

JUNE 28

Stand up for community.

Yup, I was at it again, just a few weeks ago. I dragged a couple of bags of books over to the little used bookstore at my local library branch, and there was a clipboard by the door. You know that was like a magnet for me.

It was a petition, asking city residents to speak up by signing it and help "Save the Libraries." It might sound drastic—and it was, sort of. Branch hours had been cut, and I'm sure that means jobs have been cut, too. There are currently ninety locations here in New York City with over forty-four million items in their collections. With the advent of the Internet—and, yes, I also blame the parents who come into a bookstore and say, "Give me all your Civil War books," only to return them all the next day when their kid's report is done—there's less and less call to study and research at the libraries. In Manhattan, only the main branch is open on Sundays.

So I was thrilled to see in the newspapers and on the library's site today that $36.7 million of the $40 million earmarked to be cut was restored. When the website says, "We want to thank the people of New York for making their voices heard"? Yeah, that's right, they're talking to me.

I'm Erin McHugh, library cardholder—in one city or another—since 1958.

Occasionally, there is a free ride.

I think people have found, in general, that the thing about New Yorkers being rude is generally a myth. We love to point out things in our city—we give advice, recommend a good place for a hamburger, the best route to the Statue of

Liberty, offer to buy someone on the next bar stool a beer. We're proud of our city!

On the other hand, New Yorkers are impatient. The city is fastfastfast, and you'd better get out of the way if you can't keep up.

But, evidently, today I was in a giving mood. Here came a couple, obviously excited to be in New York, knowing not so much English, apparently shocked to find that the bus cost actual money. They didn't have it. For once I wasn't in too much of a hurry—in fact, I was heading off on vacation. So I handed them my Metrocard, explained that it had three rides on it and *was not good for forever and needed to be refilled*, and made their (and everyone else on the bus's) day.

They felt good—I felt better. Maybe it was just the vacation.

JUNE 30

Nagging kills.

Driving to the beach today, I see a teenage girl on the side of the road, on her cell phone, with her bike in the grass on its side. Naturally I figure she's got some mechanical trouble. So I go up the road, double back, and pull over across from her to see if she needs me to load her in and take her somewhere.

"Hey, do you need some help?" Nothing.

"Hellooooo, are you OK?" She doesn't even look up. I shout a third time, and still she doesn't acknowledge me. Is anyone this rude? So I honk, and she finally settles her gaze on me. That's when I realize she's got her iPod plugged in. She deigns to take one earplug out.

"Are you OK there?" I ask, for the fourth time.

She looks at me like I've ruined her day and says simply, "Yeah."

So if you're thinking my good deed is stopping to help a rider in trouble, which I already wrote about some months ago, you'd be wrong. My good deed is biting my tongue and not saying this to her:

"'*Yeah?*' I'm guessing what you mean to say is, 'Oh, gee, no, thank you, I'm just fine, but it's awful nice of you to have stopped.'"

Or this:

"Are you *kidding* me? You're going to bike down this road with your iPod plugged in? Are you *trying* to kill yourself?"

Of course, you may say the best thing to do would be to absolutely say both of these things, and more.

But nay, because today's lesson is: don't become your mother.

JULY 1

Be kind to strangers.

The beach here in my hometown is lovely. It's quiet water, usually, because it's on the bay, in a cove. It's for town residents, but you have to pay an annual fee to get through the gate. Some people don't want to pay, some are teenagers, without cars. They're allowed to walk in, down a lovely, winding, sun-dappled road.

Then there's walking up the road, at the end of the day. Now you see it for what it is: almost a half mile long, uphill all the way, and suddenly you find that you're sticky and sandy. All the joy of your day at the beach is but a memory. It is hell-hot walking back to your car.

Or at least, it sure looks that way. That's why I often stop—and I'm not the only one—and pick up strangers, with all their gear, and pile their sweaty bodies into my car, to take them to the gate.

What's a day at the beach, if it's not a day at the beach?

Make someone feel welcome.

She is my cousin's wife's mother (got that?) and she came into my life less than ten years ago, but I adore her. She is a pip, for sure. She grew up in Hawaii and was rather well off; her dad had something to do with the Dole plant, so her kids have always called her "the Pineapple Queen." Life was grand until it wasn't: she had four wonderful girls, and then suddenly, in his early forties, her husband died. Now here's one of the things I love about her most: he's been gone now at least forty years, but when she talks about him, she always refers to him as "my Donald," as if he's gone away on a short business trip.

She has an array (as I do) of holiday gear. I covet the Thanksgiving turkey feather felt headband, but her favorite day is July Fourth, and I swear there's a closet somewhere containing only her red, white, and blue hats, necklaces, and sweaters.

But now she's failing some and, though happy to be included in festivities, will also often opt for her soaps and a day in bed. She's upstairs doing just that today, so I brought a bunch of flowers and headed up for a visit before I started the day's activities with her family. I hopped into bed with her; she checked in on me and how things are in her beloved New York and thanked me for the flowers.

Every time I step into a room to see her, she always says the same thing: "Oh, dear girl . . ." There's just something about the warmth in the way she says it; each time it makes me feel like I've come back from afar and have arrived safe at last. We are always happy to see each other, and frankly, how many people can you say that about?

JULY 3

Include.

A few years ago, right before the Fourth of July, I found an article called "Hot Dogs from Around the World." My heart soared. I love a hot dog, and the possibility of finding out about others from all over the planet who share my love? A dream come true. The recipes were strange and divine, and so I decided to share my discovery with my family in the form of the First Annual International Hot Dog Festival.

I grilled a gigantic pile of dogs and buns and prepared eight stations, each with an international recipe and the attendant array of condiments. It was an immediate melee. There were the stubborn types who held fast to their mustard-only ways, but in the main, there was delight, experimentation, and seconds and thirds.

The IHDF has been a summer staple for several years now—there is even talk of a recipe contest for next season. And yes, though originally the group was small, stories of the fest's success have become legion, and others have been asked to join in; Cousin Nancy, from the other side of the family, made her second appearance this year (complete with a pupu platter, which added an even more international feel), and friend Gay graced us with her debut. Out of sheer demand, I have had to host smaller, pop-up festivals here in my Manhattan backyard.

P.S. My favorite recipe? From Chile: an unusual and tantalizing delight of a dog dressed with diced tomatoes, avocado slices, and mayo. Trust me on this one.

Freedom for all.

I did nothing. Beach, lie around, have a hot dog. Have some laughs. Watch fireworks.

Did I spread some Independence Day love among my family and friends? Yes, I did.

Did I toast my country and its democratic, wayward, complex, nutty ways? I did indeed.

Did I thank whoever is out there for what I have and the many freedoms I enjoy?

Today, of all days, you bet I did.

And if that's not enough, well, it's a federal holiday.

Send a card. Any card.

It was a dumb card.

But my friend was very sick, and far away, too. There are lots of times when there aren't any cards that say what you want. Things like "There is no way I can help you, is there?" or "Please don't be sick—I need you."

But you want to let them know you're thinking about them. This card said something about getting well enough to monkey around, with, yes, of course, a stupid monkey on the front. I think I made it a little less dumb by writing on it,

"Geez. What a dumb card." I hope so. I hope he gets better, and I hope we all get to laugh about the dumb card, another day.

Don't overdo: just enough is just enough.

I was wandering up and down the mayonnaise aisle when I heard a little peep behind me.

"Excuse me, dear," was what the peep sounded like.

I looked around, and finally spotted a tiny old lady down near the salad dressings. She was pointing.

"Could you please help me and reach that olive oil?" she asked nervously.

Of course I could, and I did so. "Anything else?" I said, handing her the bottle.

"How much is that marinade?" she wanted to know, so we checked that out, decided no, it was not for her.

"What else?" I ventured. "Need sugar, toilet paper, bacon? How about a little extra cash?" I was smiling, kidding her, and trying to put her at ease, but she faltered a little, confused.

I'd gone too far; I could see it on her face. Now she would just like me to go away. It's easy to cross the line, intrude, forget about somebody else's feelings—even when you're trying to do something nice. It's not like I did anything horrible, but today, I forgot that.

Help Nature on its course.

I'm sitting around the house because I'm waiting for the cable guy to come. The first shift is eleven a.m. to two p.m. Why? What's wrong with eight a.m., the time the rest of the world gears up? When is the second shift—the disco shift, midnight to three a.m.?

Anyway, we had a huge storm last night, and I've been outside all morning, gathering up twigs, and at last here's the cable truck, and only half the day gone. A little twist of a wire here, a little banging around, and my new pal Ryan says he's got to go out to the truck. Would I like to join him? Um, what? No! Then he explains: he's got a praying mantis he wants to show me.

And it's true, he does. It is so gigantic I have to give an "Eek!" I mean, scary big, like eight inches. Ryan says he found him on one of the busiest streets in town, trying to avoid the traffic. Out of its element after the storm, we guess. We admire the bug in his bucket for a few moments, then, suddenly very serious, Ryan asks if we might give him a new home at my place.

So this huge lug of a guy and I wander around my back-yard until he finds the *exact* tree and the *particular* branch to relocate the bug. Ryan is thrilled and I am charmed—but also pretty sure this monster bug is going to come smother me in the night.

Insist.

I don't even want to call this a good deed. I mean, it was nice of me, but who wouldn't do it? Yet I log it in here, just as a reminder to listen.

There's a fun engagement party for Cousin Mimi's son Nate this weekend, and the plans have been hatching for months. Tent, food, beer, guests, all is in place except the weather, always the we'll-see part of the equation. Earlier this week I asked Mimi what was up for Friday night. The bride-to-be's family was arriving. What was everybody doing?

"Ohhh, I can't decide," said Mimi. Well, that's nutty, I told her. Everyone should just come to my house. No question. It was settled, the visitors contacted, the food and wine bought, and bing, bang, boom, we had a terrific time, two families getting to know each other a little better tonight. I believe there was even a little dancing.

I guess all I'm saying is, sometimes you have to listen for what no one is asking for.

Use everything.

OK, now this *is* nice. I took the leftovers of all last night's food and made sandwiches for everybody for the beach today. The upside is that my fridge is almost empty—less to clean out when I return to New York tomorrow.

This reminds me of a funny story. I lived with some girls in a beach house one summer, and a bunch of them were chefs. I woke up early one Sunday morning because there was a lot of slamming around in the kitchen; I stumbled out of my bedroom and was informed that breakfast was about to be served. We had a deck with a gorgeous bay view, and everybody sat down to a huge feast: scrambled eggs, bacon, a vegetable omelet, a tasty frittata, Bloody Marys, and a pie.

"Wow," I marveled, "you guys have outdone yourselves. What's all this?"

"We were cleaning out the refrigerator," said Roxanne. "Everywhere we looked there were eggs, so we decided we'd cook 'em all." We ate like soldiers on leave, until no one could take another bite. Everyone leaned back, stuffed and satisfied, until one of the cooks broke the silence.

"Problem is," she observed, "now we need eggs."

<hr />

JULY 10

Divide the spoils.

It's always the same. The family gets together to celebrate something, and there's food left over. I usually have to leave town soon, so I'm trying to offload stuff from my house. The conversation never changes.

"Mimi, take the rest of the cheese," I'll say.

"No!" she insists. "You'll eat it on the bus."

"No, I won't."

"You'll have it on Monday at home."

"I'm going out Monday."

"You'll have it Tues—"

"Please. Please! I won't have it Tuesday. You have to take it."

"Are you sure?" she asks, hesitantly, and finally stows it guiltily in her pile.

So it takes twenty minutes to get rid of the food, because *every single item* has to go through this torturous exchange. But the good news is that no food is wasted, and everybody helps out everybody else. This morning, there was a complex redistribution.

I had half a flank steak left over. I carted it to Aunt Tessie's house at breakfast time. "I love free food!" she is often heard to say, so I knew I was at the right starting line. Cousin Suzy arrived, and the dividing of the spoils began. I actually even had the tinfoil left over from various dishes for packaging.

Tessie got steak. I got steak. I packed up steak and brought it to Aunt Peg. Suzy finished carving up the rest and divided it between herself and Mimi.

I decided to take a sandwich on the bus. Tessie gave me two slices of bread, so I wouldn't have to waste a loaf. I traveled over to Suzy's because she had all the leftover grilled vegetables. She doled out a generous portion.

Et voilà, I had my bus sandwich, and seven people were fed for a second day. So if you previously have been suspicious about the loaves and fishes parable, believe.

Make it yourself.

My plants in my little city garden don't seem to be doing so well (including that damn orangey plant from the park plant fair—see May 7), but for some reason the herbs are going gangbusters. So I'm going to put up some bottles of herb oil. You can do it, too, even if you cheat and get your herbs from the grocery store. Who am I going to tell?

I get smallish glass bottles from a housewares store, the kind that come with little corks or Mason jar–like stoppers. Crush three or four peppercorns if you have them, and toss that in the bottom of the bottles. Then get two or three small bunches of your favorite herbs: I'm doing combos of rosemary and thyme and sage and thyme. Wash them, pat them dry, bruise them gently by rubbing them between your fingers, then pop them in.

Fill with the best olive oil you can afford. Put the stoppers in. Place the bottles in a cool, dark place for two weeks, then take them out and refrigerate them until use.

This will totally impress your friends—each little bottle is a perfect thank-you or dinner-party gift.

(Oh, one thing: make sure every single bit of the herbs is covered by the oil. If, while it's in that dark place, even a tip of an herb peeks out above the oil, it'll get all blue and penicillinish, and then your friends won't be your friends because they'll be dead. Throw it out, clean the bottle, and start over.)

JULY 12

Let it be?

So yet again I was on the bus (and if you think that seems perpetual to you, imagine what it feels like from over here), and there in front of me were a young man and woman; from their body language I assumed they were on their first date. Their conversation was sort of background chatter to me, until I heard the guy start telling the girl all sorts of misinformation about Central Park and New York history. What a clown, I thought. There are few things that irk me more than people blabbing on with a superior air who have their facts wrong. I was about to butt in and correct him, which is my usual M.O., and then I thought: Will I ruin what could become a beautiful relationship? A sweet courtship? Marriage and children? Wealth and a life of international excitement?

I leaned back, shut my mouth—with great effort—and plugged in my headphones. It was another Good Deed of Omission—but was letting her find out about the blowhard for herself the right decision on my part? Or do we all have an inherent human duty to stop horrible dating mistakes?

Treat someone.

I got down to the café today after work, and the line was long. That's hot weather for you—everyone's inside and needs something cold to drink. I was chatting up a coworker who was in line in front of me. He had done me a solid when I was extra busy earlier in the day. When his coffee came, I told the server it was on me. It wasn't a big deal; it was just a nice thing to do. Everyone likes to be treated once in a while.

There are lots of ways to run a race.

Here's what I would like: if I could hire someone to go to the gym for me.

But that's not going to happen, is it?

So I was happy when the next best thing came along. My good friend Martha announced that she will be running in the New York City Marathon this year, and as if that weren't cool enough, she is raising money for a nonprofit sports foundation here in New York. Not only will the money she raises help out the environment on the tiny island the sports facilities are on, but it'll sponsor kids who want to play sports, too.

I didn't give much. And yet I get to feel doubly good—I can cheer my buddy on and hopefully help some kids have a place to play. Kids who hopefully won't grow up wishing they could hire someone to go to the gym for them.

Love is all around.

Of course there are days when I try to do something nice for people and I'm absolutely thrilled when they say no. Today on the subway it was pretty hot, and the man next to me rolled a little stroller with his son in it onto the platform and bent down to pick it up and climb the stairs. I asked if he needed a hand. What had come over me? This guy was twenty years younger than me if a day. "Nah," he said, "thanks anyway, but carting this little guy around is the only exercise I get." Thank God—maybe he knew what I didn't: it turned out to be five flights up.

One thing the One Good Deed project has taught me is to keep my eyes open a little more in a way I hadn't before. And as I went through the day today, I saw other folks doing nice things: a young guy popping off his high stool at Starbucks to help a tiny older woman with packages climb up next to him. Watching a girl help an old man get on the bus, while he yelled at her the whole time. The subway conductor coming out of his locked compartment—twice—to help someone with directions.

For some reason it all reminded me of that old song Sinatra sings, "Chicago." There's a line in it that goes, "I saw a man who danced with his wife," as if that were an impossible sight. And that's what this day was like. I found myself thinking, Shame on you: why are you so surprised?

Be aware.

I just finished a big writing project, and I am elated. It means I can move forward onto the next big writing project. That is the good news/bad news: I'm exhausted—but what if there were no next project at all?

"You look happy," says a work friend. "What's up?"

I tell her what I just told you, and she looks around and whispers, "I'm happy, too."

"How come?" I whisper back.

"I've just finished my cancer treatment." She grins. I hadn't even known.

Big, big hugs all around. Now *that* is thrilling. And it reminds me to stop thinking about myself so much.

Saving costs money.

I'm sorry. I just couldn't ignore it a day longer.

For years, I've been melting at the sight of scientists or environmentalists or whoever they are saving those tiny, oily ducks found in polluted places and washing them off in Dawn dish detergent. And since the Gulf oil spill of 2010, I've found the pictures of these poor birds even more heart-breaking.

I checked out Dawn's website and found that although it had originally promised to donate one dollar for every bottle sold up to fifty thousand dollars, that match had been surpassed, and the company was still honoring and matching those dollars. The site told me simply to enter the number from the back panel of the detergent bottle, and my dollar would be "activated."

So yes, I actually made a special trip to the grocery store; I had a whole bottle of detergent left. But I couldn't let another duck suffer! I scanned the shelf prices, hoping I was wrong; but yup, Dawn was more than sixty cents costlier than all the others. OK, so maybe I'm "activating" 60 percent of the dollar, and they're tossing in 40 percent. And maybe that 40 percent is made up on their end by somehow selling my e-mail, which I'm sure they can suss out, even though they didn't ask me for it. And maybe they . . .

Ah, hell, what do I care? I guess if I want to live in a *Make Way for Ducklings* kind of world where I save ducks, I have to pay for it.

Do unto others.

I work with a young woman who is chomping at the bit to get an entry-level job in publishing. She's eager, with a great education, and excited about literature, and of course, she reminds me of myself all those years ago. I've been trying to help her and today I gave her another hot tip about an open position I knew of. I know what's a good job, and I know who's a great person to work for. It's a small industry, and when we're not eating our young, we help each other out. (Just kidding.) (Not really.)

Passing along your knowledge and giving a leg up to the next round of kids who are as wide-eyed as you were—or if you're as unbearably optimistic as I am, still are—is not only a great kindness but a wonderful way to protect the future of something you love. When I came to New York, I contacted a friend from college who was two years older than I was and had already begun to make her mark. She sat down and wrote me a list of people to talk to and said I could use her name. It was three pages, both sides, in green fountain pen ink, and I was so impressed and touched by her generosity that I still have that list. I didn't get a job from those names, but I got go-sees and interviews, and it did a lot to help me understand both the process and the business.

My mentor, by the way, went on to write books, become the publisher at a major house, and start one of the most successful online venues for women ever.

And yes, we remain friends to this day.

Keep on truckin'.

I let someone in line in front of me, even though I was in a hurry. I dragged another baby carriage up the stairs. I bit my tongue when someone elbowed me and didn't even turn around. I was pleasant to someone I don't much care for.

Some days it's just "rinse and repeat." And there's nuthin' wrong with that.

Share the bounty.

This morning, early, I went out back with my little clippers so I could share that fresh sage, rosemary, basil, and thyme with some coworkers.

May not seem like a big deal to those of you who don't live in a city, but today I am very popular with three friends.

Pass the book.

First item of interest: I still have a milk box.

And I only remembered today that I hid something in it.

The milk box hasn't been used for milk delivery in some time (though more recently than you might think), but it's always the place I put something for someone to pick up later. I know, I know, but it's a small town, and we also sometimes still leave the door open.

But what I'd forgotten was that two weeks ago, I left an advance copy of a hot upcoming novel there for Daphne. The very first day of my vacation—now more than three weeks ago—I brought some books to the beach. "Ooooh, what's that?" all the girls I sat down with said. I told them I had just started reading it, and though I intended it to be my Big Summer Read, I had a feeling I wouldn't get to finish it before week's end. "This looks good," Daphne said, leafing through the pages. "I would read this." So I promised her when I finished it, she'd be next on the list.

The vacation came and went too fast, as vacations do, and as I got into the car, racing as usual to make the last bus back, I saw the book on the top of my bag, about eighty-seven pages read. I hopped out and threw it into the milk box—and only remembered it today.

So then I had to get Daphne's e-mail from the cousins and notify her of the Secret of the Old Milk Box. I know she'll be thrilled—what a fun surprise.

Now I guess there are folks who may think me giving this advance copy to Daphne takes away from a sale or two, but me, I think it only helps spread the word. Daphne may pass it along to two other people, and eventually they'll tell eleven folks. And some of them will indeed buy more books.

JULY 22

Check in.

A couple of months ago my e-mail evidently got hacked and everyone I ever knew got some crazy link purportedly from me that I so obviously would never have sent. In fact, seventy-nine people e-mailed me to tell me this. Yes, people, I *know*. Thanks.

One of them was someone whom I don't see very often but have known socially for a long time. We've only ever been in big groups together, but I've always liked and respected her. "I'm having some health issues and lying low for the moment," she wrote. I wrote back and wished her better health.

Today I was thinking about her, so I e-mailed her to check in. "Don't know if you're up and around, or if you're still lying low and could use some company. If so, I can come over and trade gossip."

You know, you just never know what someone will need, when. It could be she's bored stiff, and a friendly face without too much history would be the very thing. Or not—who knows? I really believe one of the great lessons you learn in life is Who Shows Up. And if you're doing your job right, there are going to be some times you'll be surprised to find it's you.

Persist, if you dare.

Today I went crazy on a guy.

My pal and I had just had dinner and were standing around outside the restaurant when I spotted an employee from the joint next door come outside to have a smoke. As he was lighting up, he tossed a piece of paper from his pocket to the ground. Just for the hell of it.

Oh, yeah, I stepped up. "I can't believe you just threw that piece of paper on the ground."

Guy totally ignored me.

"You're just going to leave it there? You should pick it up."

I got a sideways glance. Now I was mad. It had to be the heat, because I turned to my buddy and said, "Can you believe this guy, just throwing his crap on the ground?"

With that, he flicked his cigarette and hurried back inside. But I couldn't stop myself. What the hell was wrong with me? I walked right up to the plate-glass window of the restaurant; the perp was standing just inside.

"I cannot believe you," I yelled, so he could easily hear me. "You're just going to throw your sh*t wherever you want?"

And yes, ladies and gentlemen, yes, he did. He walked out of the restaurant, picked up his litter, and retreated back inside, without a glance or a word.

So today, I am my own hero. A crazy-ass one, but I am proud. And miraculously, uninjured.

JULY 24

Take what you need; leave the rest.

Have you even noticed those plastic recycling bins in stores? I know you're going to say yes, who hasn't? but they are only ever-so-slightly on my radar. I'm talking about the sort of opaque plastic square bins that say "Recycle Your Bags Here." They're usually pretty full, too.

A lady stopped me in the store a couple of weeks ago and asked me where she could recycle her plastic bags. I looked at her blankly for a minute, and then brought her over by the cash registers, pointed, and said, "You mean this?"

"Oh, great," said she, and she took a big wad of plastic bags from her purse and stuffed them in. That's right: she'd collected them, made a whole trip of it, and recycled her old bags.

I was impressed. Then I forgot about it.

Until today, when a lady cut me off going into the drugstore in order to make a quick detour to the bin there. Slam-dunk, she went. I already had two plastic bags from my purchases just in the last three blocks; so I stopped, consolidated, and deposited one in the bin.

I have no idea what they do with them—or who "they" are—but I was happy to be in on doing the right thing. It took me another half block to realize I'd had my credit card in my hand at the time and dumped that plastic in the bin, too, but I went back and recovered it without a hitch.

So I need a little practice. Sue me.

Pay what you owe.

Some days doing a nice thing is as easy as it can be. In fact, it does itself, even if by accident. And, like my very favorite kind of good deed, it doubles back on itself.

I was eating lunch in the store break room when I heard one of my coworkers at the soda machine. She uttered a four-letter word, not a particularly bad one, but enough for me to look up out of curiosity. "This isn't what I meant to get," she said. "You drink Diet Coke? You can have it."

"Yeah, thanks, I do," I said. Which is true. I didn't particularly want one at the moment but would put it in my locker and save it. For a nanosecond, I reveled in my score. But that wasn't right, and I knew it.

"Let me give you the money," I offered. "I was just going to buy one anyway."

Everyone needs encouragement.

Being a writer means you're alone a lot. There's a host of other writers out there, but they're home alone, too, so what good is that? So when one of them reports on Facebook or Twitter that he's finished his book or she's gotten the first copy off press or sold a new work, we all jump in with virtual horn-tooting and congratulations.

This seems to me an improvement over the garret.

This morning I was happy to join in with a legion of friends when someone reported that yes, she had finally typed

"THE END."

Back up.

It was nothing. It was less than nothing.

I was walking home in the dark from a really fun birthday dinner, and I had almost passed by a little soup shop when I saw the door start to open, and then close again. Don't know why, but I backed up and saw a woman in one of those electric Jazzy chairs, trying to kick the door open with her foot enough so that she could then try to plow through. I turned and stepped aside and opened the door for her. She couldn't have been more cheerful. "Thank you *so* much!" She beamed at me. And "My pleasure," I returned.

Nothing, absolutely nothing on my part. And she does this forty-three times a day, I'll bet. How many times does she get any help?

Love is everything.

Three hundred sixty-four days ago, I told you I was my parents' first anniversary present.

Well, not technically; I was born the day after, but my mother refused to have me put a crimp in their celebration, so they took the top layer of the wedding cake, which had been in the freezer, and a saved bottle of champagne, and went to a restaurant. During the entrée my mother snuck off to the pay phone and called the doctor to say she'd meet him at the hospital in about an hour.

"Where are you?" said the doctor, probably hearing a rumba in the background.

"Bert's Grille," said Mom.

"You're out to dinner? You're not ready to have this baby," he sniffed.

"Get the room ready, Art," she said. "But I'm going to have fun first if it kills me."

This story was told every year, and a few times in between. It was about the beginning of our family. And every year on my birthday, my mother would be the first to call, very early in the morning, just like it was on the day I was born. "Ohhh," she'd say annually. "I feel *so* much better now." Tradition.

I think one of the very good deeds my parents did in bringing me up was to teach me to celebrate everything. A half-birthday; visiting Plimoth Plantation each Thanksgiving season ("The coldest place on earth," my mother groused); green carnations every St. Patrick's Day; my dad and I singing torch songs together every night before bed when other children were reading Dr. Seuss; church and the funny papers every Sunday. You know, family stuff.

This doesn't mean we didn't have problems, or that we each didn't have our failings. Of course we did. But they were my parents, and I love them. Now I tend their grave and think about the kind of person they made me: a person who grew up and wanted to write a book about doing a good deed every day.

Teach your children.

Everything is everything.

It's been a year.

Don't know about you, but I can't believe it: I've been working on my One Good Deed project since my last birthday on July 29. I've been reading some entries today, and looking at my calendar, laughing some here and shedding a tear there. But you know me by now: I cry at everything.

Last year at this time I felt off track. I wanted to be a better citizen of this world—I'd taken a break, and it had gone on too long. I was looking not only to help others out, but to find a more comfortable skin for myself. And I hoped to inspire my readers to look outward, too. What was my biggest discovery? I found lots of my deeds came from sharing ideas, help, and advice and just plain cheerleading for other readers and writers. It sort of became my "thing."

One Good Deed has been about reconnecting with myself, but also meeting and talking to all of you on the blog that preceded this book. My favorite comments there have been when someone would read about one of my adventures (or misadventures) and say, "What a good idea: I'm going to do that next time myself." Has it all become second nature to me? No, I still have to concentrate some days, tell myself to think of others. On the other hand, I took a nap today (birthday reward) and dreamed I tried to help a woman keep her marriage together. So perhaps I am getting somewhere after all.

If the idea of One Good Deed interests you at all, my advice is this: search for one thing that moves you, and for the rest of the time, try not to always look at the sidewalk, as I tend to do. Try hard to train yourself to keep eyes front and see what's happening around you. And don't worry about making headlines: Little is fine. Little and constant is life-changing.

ACKNOWLEDGMENTS

I think the first thank-you has to be to all the folks who appear in the pages of *One Good Deed*: as sidekicks, good and bad influences, unwitting accomplices, kind souls, jerks, people I wanted to kiss, others whom I wanted to strangle. Lots of the people herein are friends, but most of the people I ran across in my 366 days I'll never see again; I hope I made a difference in their day for even a moment, as they did in mine. I often wonder if any of them will pick up this book and recognize themselves.

I want to thank my family at Abrams Books: Michael Jacobs, who supported me long before I became an Abrams author; Mary Wowk, stalwart friend and cohort from many publishing lifetimes ago; Leslie Stoker, who believed in *One Good Deed* the minute I broached the idea; David Cashion, the perfect editor and friend, who talks me up or down as the situation warrants; Marisa Dobson, my once and future publicity maven; Chris Blank, my go-to techno guy; Jennifer Levesque, my other great Abrams editor, always lurking (in a good way) in the shadows; managing editor Jen Graham, my secret weapon behind the scenes; and all the other terrific people there who welcome me like an old friend when I walk in the door, and spend their days putting their hearts into making beautiful books.

A special salaam goes to my friend and agent, Chris Tomasino—everyone needs someone in their life who believes in them so, and works tirelessly to make the rest of the world get on board.

To my incredible friends who supported me in every way possible: you know who you are, and you know how you helped. Thank you.

And, of course, my huge, wonderful, hilarious, fete-crazy family, who seem to love me no matter what. Every day I depend on that love to get me through.

Erin McHugh is a former publishing executive and the author of more than twenty books.

She lives in New York City and South Dartmouth, Massachusetts.